Haidar

SPEECH COMMUNICATION MADE SIMPLE

2

PAULETTE DALE, PH.D., PROFESSOR EMERITUS

JAMES C. WOLF, M.A., PROFESSOR

MIAMI DADE COLLEGE

Speech Communication Made Simple 2

Pearson Education, 10 Bank Street, White Plains, NY 10606

Staff credits: The people who made up the *Speech Communication Made Simple* team—representing editorial, production, design, marketing, and manufacturing services—are Tracey Cataldo, Dave Dickey, Nancy Flaggman, Amy McCormick, Lise Minovitz, Liza Pleva, and Jane Townsend.

Development: Lida Baker
Cover design: Mary Ann Smith
Text composition: S4Carlisle Publishing Services
Illustrations: Roger Penwill
Text font: 11/13 pt Minion Pro
Cover Photos: (top) Ljupco Smokovski/Shutterstock, (center) Tatiana Popova/Shutterstock, (bottom) Winston Link/Shutterstock.
Photo Credits: Page 4 (left) Peter Hermes Furian/Fotolia, (middle left) Joshua Haviv/Fotolia, (middle right) David Touchtone/Fotolia, (right) Beboy/Fotolia; p. 5 top row: (left) Dimitri Surkov/Fotolia, (middle left) Pavel Losevsky/Fotolia, (middle right) Kathy Gold/Fotolia, (right) erwinova/Fotolia, middle row: (left) Digital Image © The Museum of Modern Art/Licensed by SCALA/Art Resource, NY, (middle left) krzysztof siekielski/Fotolia, (middle right) Elnur/Fotolia, (right) auremar/Shutterstock, bottom row: (left) Jeffrey Blackler/Alamy, (middle left) discpicture/Shutterstock, (middle right) paul/Fotolia, (right) auremar/Shutterstock; p. 6 (left) crisod/Fotolia, (middle) Lars Christensen/Fotolia, (right) sonya etchison/Shutterstock; p. 12 (top) inarik/Fotolia, (middle top) pzAxe/Shutterstock, (middle bottom) Dani Simmonds/Fotolia, (bottom) Sergej Razvodovskij/Fotolia; p. 19 (left) rgbspace/Fotolia, (middle) Robert Kneschke/Shutterstock, (right) 101imges/Shutterstock; p. 21 (top left) Samuel Borges/Shutterstock, (top right) gosphotodesign/Shutterstock, (bottom left) ostill/Shutterstock, (bottom right) Rido/Shutterstock; p. 27 (top) Angelina Dimitrova/Shutterstock, (bottom) DAVID J JACKSON KRT/Newscom; p. 28 Steve Cukrov/Shutterstock; p. 50 David Grossman/Alamy; p. 63 Lisa F. Young/Shutterstock; p. 70 (top left) Beboy/Fotolia, (top middle) Kmaeda/Fotolia, (top right) Andy Dean/Fotolia, (bottom left) ABBYDOG/Shutterstock, (bottom middle) dodecaedro/Fotolia, (bottom right) imabase/Fotolia; p. 74 (top) Kenneth Man/Fotolia, (middle) Janina Dierks/Fotolia, (bottom) onepony/Fotolia; p. 75 (top) Picture-Factory/Fotolia, (bottom) arieliona/Fotolia; p. 76 (top) alexsalcedo/Shutterstock, (bottom) Radius Images/Alamy; p. 77 keller/Fotolia; p. 81 (left & right) Courtesy of the authors; p. 89 Accent/Fotolia; p. 103 www.lightningsafety.noaa.gov; p. 114 smirno/Fotolia; p. 169 moodboard/Alamy; p. 171 Elena Schweitzer/Fotolia; p. 187 Onkelchen/Fotolia; p. 191 Jenner/Fotolia; p. 193 F.Schmidt/Fotolia; p. 194 nenovbrothers/Fotolia.

Library of Congress Cataloging-in-Publication Data

Dale, Paulette.
   Speech communication made simple. 1 / Paulette Dale.—1st ed.
     p. cm.
  ISBN: 0-13-286168-2
  ISBN: 0-13-286169-0
    1. Public speaking—Problems, exercises, etc.   2. Oral communication—Problems, exercises, etc.
  3. English language—Textbooks for foreign speakers.   I. Title.

PN4121.D327 2012
302.2'242—dc23

                           2012024143

ISBN 10: 0-13-286169-0
ISBN 13: 978-0-13-286169-4

PEARSON ELT ON THE WEB

PearsonELT.com offers a wide range of classroom resources and professional development materials. Access course-specific websites, product information, and Pearson offices around the world.

Visit us at **www.pearsonELT.com**.

CONTENTS

SCOPE AND SEQUENCE

Chapter	Title	Speech Genre	Pronunciation Practice	
1	DEVELOPING SELF-CONFIDENCE	Autobiography	Final Consonants	
2	DELIVERING YOUR MESSAGE	Exceptional Experience	-ed as [t] [d] and [əd]	
3	PUTTING YOUR SPEECH TOGETHER	Point of View	Contractions	
4	POWERFUL PRESENTATION AIDS	Poster Presentation/Slide Presentation	-s as [s], [z] and New Syllable [əz]	
5	SPEAKING TO INFORM	Informative	Phrasing and Pausing	
6	UNDERSTANDING INTERPERSONAL COMMUNICATION	Job-Interview Role-Play	Intonation	
7	LISTEN TO LEARN	Impromptu Speech	Linking	
8	PROBLEM-SOLVING GROUP DISCUSSIONS	Discussion Involving Research	Stress within the Word	
9	SPEAKING TO PERSUADE	Persuasive Speech	Stress within the Sentence	
10	DARE TO DEBATE	Debate	[l] and [r]	

Playing with Sayings	Useful Language
Put the cart before the horse; Strike while the iron is hot; Cry over spilled milk; Bit by bit; My mind went blank.	Beginning Your Speech; Summarizing Your Speech; Inviting Audience Questions; Introducing Your "Old Bag"; Thanking Your Listeners
Look before you leap; A penny saved is a penny earned; Keep your fingers crossed; Leave no stone unturned; Keep me posted.	Closing Your Speech
(It's) six of one, half dozen of another; You can't fight city hall; Can't believe one's ears (eyes); Don't count your chickens before they hatch; That's the way the ball bounces.	Expressing an Opinion
Actions speak louder than words; Go from rags to riches; Hit the books; A leopard can't (doesn't) change its spots; A picture paints a thousand words.	Inviting Questions Acknowledging Questions
What will be, will be; All that glitters is not gold; It's better to be safe than sorry; Where there's a will, there's a way; An ounce of prevention is worth a pound of cure.	Citing Sources
What goes around, comes around; When the cat's away, the mice will play; When it rains, it pours; When in Rome, do as the Romans do; A stitch in time saves nine.	Responding to an Interviewer's Invitation for Questions
You can't teach an old dog new tricks; A drop in the bucket; Give (him) an inch and he'll take a mile; Land on one's feet; Bark up the wrong tree.	Preview Statements for Impromptu Speaking
Necessity is the mother of invention; All that glitters is not gold; The handwriting is on the wall; Birds of a feather flock together; Leave well enough alone.	Encouraging Participation Feedback and Reinforcement
Kill two birds with one stone; Haste makes waste; Half a loaf is better than none; His bark is worse than his bite; You catch more flies with honey than vinegar.	Building on Areas of Agreement Transitions
Let sleeping dogs lie; Rob Peter to pay Paul; Have the last laugh; Rub (someone) the wrong way; Last but not least.	Disagreeing with Your Opponents

PREFACE: TO THE TEACHER

Speech Communication Made Simple 2 is a practical, user-friendly presentation-skills course for advanced ESL students. Now in its fourth edition, the program features rich academic content, varied activities, and a step-by-step approach to building students' confidence as speakers.

Chapter Organization

Each chapter contains sections designed to help students improve their speech communication abilities and express themselves effectively in front of others. Exercises and assignments prepare students for the ultimate chapter goal: the preparation and delivery of a presentation to the class.

The **Chapter Challenge** serves as an introduction to the chapter topic. It provides an overview of the objectives of the chapter.

The **Presentation Preview** provides an engaging introduction to the speech assignment. It helps students consider the topic of the presentation and relate it to their own experiences. It includes a sample presentation (a speech, interview, or discussion, debate) that follows the organization and contains the content required in the chapter assignment.

The **Pronunciation Practice** section is designed to teach a variety of American English pronunciation patterns. The pronunciation points selected are those that are difficult for most non-native speakers of English. Students are encouraged to practice the pronunciation skills presented in each chapter when preparing and delivering their speeches.

The **Playing with Sayings** section presents idiomatic sayings in popular use. The related activities help students to understand the sayings and to use them for enhancing their spoken communication. Students are encouraged to use one or more of these sayings in their presentations.

The **Presentation Project** provides specific guidelines and useful language for students to follow in order to prepare, practice, and deliver their own presentations on the assigned topic. Step-by-step instructions are given for choosing and researching a topic, citing sources, using transitions, and outlining information. Instructions vary by chapter and directly relate to the nature and complexity of the assignment.

Book Contents

The chapters in *Speech Communication Made Simple 2* are as follows:

Chapter 1: Developing Self-Confidence is designed to help students overcome stage fright and succeed at public speaking.

Chapter 2: Delivering Your Message has numerous activities to help students improve their use of eye contact, posture, gestures, and voice so that they can speak more effectively.

Chapter 3: Putting Your Speech Together teaches students how to organize and outline information for their speeches.

Chapter 4: Powerful Presentation Aids gives general guidelines for the effective use of speech aids (both audio and visual) including presentation software such as PowerPoint®.

Chapter 5: Speaking to Inform gives step-by-step procedures for preparing a speech that presents new information in a comprehensible and memorable way.

Chapter 6: Interpersonal Communication helps students avoid misunderstandings while enabling them to interact more effectively.

Chapter 7: Listen to Learn includes both suggestions and activities to improve a wide variety of listening skills.

Chapter 8: Problem-Solving Group Discussions teaches students how to identify a problem as well as its causes, probable effects, and possible solutions, in order to contribute responsibly to a problem-solving group discussion.

Chapter 9: Speaking to Persuade gives step-by-step procedures for preparing a speech that persuades others to change their beliefs, opinions, or behaviors.

Chapter 10: Dare to Debate teaches the basic techniques of effective debate, including choosing and researching a proposition, organizing compelling constructive and rebuttal speeches, and formulating and responding to cross-examination questions.

Approach

Speech Communication Made Simple 2 incorporates a scaffolded approach to the development of students' public speaking skills. At the beginning of each chapter, students participate in a directed discussion of a model presentation as a prelude to preparing and delivering their own speeches. The next series of steps focuses on skill building. Students select an appropriate topic and learn the language needed to speak about it. They complete outlines to help them organize information and prepare note cards to consult during their speeches. In the practice phase of the lesson, students rehearse their presentations and complete a speech checklist to confirm that all required presentation elements are included.

Components

In addition to its interactive activities and extensive speaking assignments, *Speech Communication Made Simple* 2 offers an array of components to facilitate ease of teaching and learning. These components include:

- Evaluation forms in the Appendix that provide suggested evaluation criteria for each presentation
- A CD-ROM in the back of the book that contains MP3 audio for all the sample speeches, pronunciation, and listening activities
- An online Teacher's Manual that includes chapter-by-chapter teaching suggestions, quizzes, answer keys, and the audioscripts for the listening exercises in the student book

ABOUT THE AUTHORS

Paulette Dale, Ph.D., Professor Emeritus and Endowed Teaching Chair at Miami Dade College, has taught speech communication, public speaking, and pronunciation classes for international students for more than 35 years. She has authored a variety of textbooks and series for Pearson Education including *English Pronunciation Made Simple* and *Speech Communication Made Simple*. She has been the featured speaker at international conferences including MexTESOL, BrazTESOL, VenTESOL, PanamaTESOL, ELT Horizons in Peru, ABLA in Guatemala, and SHARE in Argentina. Dr. Dale is currently an English-language specialist for the U.S. State Department and travels around the world conducting workshops for English-language teachers. Her areas of expertise include English pronunciation, speaking, listening, and teaching young learners.

James C. Wolf, M.A., Professor of Speech Communication at Miami Dade College, has taught classes in speech communication, interpersonal communication, fundamentals of group discussion, and argumentation and debate for 43 years. He has directed highly successful, national-level forensics and debate programs at Miami Dade College and the University of Miami. He has presented papers at national conferences, including those of the National Communication Association, the League for Innovation in the Community College, and the World Future Society. Professor Wolf also coordinates the Poster Speaking Festival, which he founded.

Acknowledgments

The authors wish to express their sincere gratitude and indebtedness to the many people who assisted in developing this book:

Professor Marie Knepper of Miami Dade College, Academic Directors Leo Mercado and Anthony Acevedo of the Instituto Cultural Peruano Norteamericano, Melody Chaykin, and other colleagues who recommended valuable improvements;

Our editors, Amy McCormick, Lise Minovitz, and Lida Baker, who were extremely helpful, understanding, and patient, and who helped transform the manuscript into this wonderful new book;

The following reviewers, who read the material and provided valuable feedback and suggestions for improvement: Brigitte Barshay, English Language Institute UCSD, La Jolla, California; Christina Hankwitz, St. Norbet College, De Pere, Wisconsin; Lisa Kovacs-Morgan, English Language Institute UCSD, La Jolla, California; Alice Lee, Richland College, Dallas, Texas; Sarah Saxer, Howard Community College, Columbia, Maryland; and Floria Volynskaya, Howard Community College, Columbia, Maryland;

Our students, for encouraging us and for giving us many practical suggestions to help us meet their needs better;

Our family and friends, for their support and encouragement throughout the project.

INTRODUCTION: TO THE STUDENT

At some point in your life, you will probably have to make a speech in front of an audience. You might want to convince people to change their opinion about a topic or demonstrate how to make or do something. You might need to teach an audience new information about a subject or share a personal experience with them. Maybe you will be asked to participate in a group discussion at school, work, your place of worship, or a club. In any of these cases, you will need to be able to organize your thoughts and express them so that others can easily understand and remember them. As you can see, the ability to make a presentation before an audience is an important skill to have in life.

If the ability to make a presentation is important in your life, then *Speech Communication Made Simple 2* is for you! Among many other skills, this book teaches you how to:

- choose a topic that will interest your listeners and decide what to say about it;
- organize your thoughts and information so that listeners can follow your ideas easily;
- get your audience's attention, develop the body of your presentation, and conclude your speech in a memorable way;
- use your voice, natural gestures, good posture, and eye contact to "wow" your audience.

Most important of all, *Speech Communication Made Simple 2* will help you overcome your fears about speaking before a group and give you the self-confidence to take advantage of opportunities to speak in public.

As you work through this book, you will have many chances to speak in class. The assignments will give you confidence and help you to improve future speeches. With the help of this book and your teacher, you will learn how to select topics, make them interesting to your audience, get over problem spots, and improve your ability to speak in front of a group—large or small.

The more effort you put into studying and practicing the skills *Speech Communication Made Simple 2* teaches you, the more you will benefit. Though you may be nervous about the idea of standing before an audience and making a speech, your fears will fade as you progress through this book. By the time you have finished, you will be very proud of yourself and of your progress.

We hope you enjoy all the fun activities in *Speech Communication Made Simple 2*. Let's begin!

CHAPTER 1

DEVELOPING SELF-CONFIDENCE

It is the beginning of the semester, and this speech class has just begun. Perhaps you are nervous about speaking in front of people you've never met before. Relax! Soon your new classmates will start to feel like friends instead of strangers. Moreover, you will soon learn that the anxiety ("stage fright") you are experiencing is natural and can be controlled.

CHAPTER CHALLENGE This chapter has many activities to help you develop confidence when speaking in front of an audience. When you complete this chapter, you will know how to:

- use a variety of techniques to control your presentation anxiety
- plan, prepare, and present an autobiographical speech

I. How to Control Presentation Anxiety

Feeling anxious at the thought of public speaking is perfectly normal. You respond the same way you would to any stressful situation: Your body produces extra adrenaline. This is what makes your heart beat faster, your hands shake, and your knees feel weak!

The good news is that you can learn to control your nervousness and make it work for you instead of against you.

A. Controlling Negative Thoughts

Many speakers have negative thoughts before speaking in front of an audience. They tell themselves things like "I know the audience won't like me" or "I know I am going to look silly." With practice, you can learn to control your negative thoughts so they don't control you!

ACTIVITY 1 Talk Yourself Out of Negative Thoughts

1 Think of five fears that cause you to have presentation anxiety or stage fright.

EXAMPLES:

I'll forget what I want to say.
I'm afraid no one will be interested in my topic.
My English isn't very good.

2 Rank your fears from 1 to 5. Assign the number 1 to the fear that causes you the most anxiety.

Rank	Fear
1.	
2.	
3.	
4.	
5.	

3 Substitute at least two positive thoughts for each fear you identified. Record your positive beliefs in the chart.

Fear	Positive Thoughts
EXAMPLE: The audience is too large.	The size of the group doesn't matter. People are listening one at a time.
1.	
2.	
3.	
4.	
5.	

4 In small groups, share the positive thoughts you substituted for each negative one.

5 Compare and discuss your positive thoughts with the entire class.

ADDITIONAL STRATEGIES FOR CONTROLLING PRESENTATION ANXIETY

Take Advantage of Small Occasions to Speak Up

Speak up in fun or nonthreatening situations. Try one or more of the following:

- Make yourself give the toast at a birthday party.
- Order food in a restaurant.
- Ask a question in class.
- Ask a question after another speaker's presentation.

Plan and Prepare

Being fully prepared will help you feel confident that you know your subject and have just the right amount of information for the allotted time.

Use Audio and Visual Aids

Audio and visual aids create a lot of interest. They can help you feel less self-conscious as the audience will focus some of their attention on these speech aids instead of on you.

Practice

Rehearse your speech in front of family or friends. Ask them for feedback. Practice on your own in front of a mirror at home. This will help you to feel more comfortable when you face an audience.

B. Breathing Correctly

Breathing exercises are one of society's oldest techniques for relieving stress. When we exhale, we release carbon dioxide. This increases the oxygen in our brains, which helps us to relax. If you learn to breathe properly, you will find you are calmer and more focused before your next speech.[1]

ACTIVITY 2 Learn to Breathe Correctly

1 Place both hands on your lower stomach. Breathe in and out slowly. Feel your stomach push forward as you inhale and pull in as you exhale. (If you feel your stomach pull in as you inhale, your breathing is incorrect!)

2 Keep practicing until you feel your stomach push out when you inhale and pull in when you exhale.

ACTIVITY 3 Time Yourself while Breathing

1 Sit in a comfortable chair with your feet flat on the floor. Breathe normally. Use a watch with a second hand and count your breaths for a full minute. How many breaths did you take? Record that number here _____. (Strive to take between six and ten breaths a minute.)

2 Place both hands on your lower stomach again. This time:

a. Inhale slowly for five seconds and exhale slowly.

b. Make your exhalation last for ten seconds. If you are out of air before ten seconds, you have exhaled too quickly.

c. Try it again. Slow your exhalation and make it last for ten seconds.

3 Count for thirty seconds while exhaling.

a. Keep your hands on your lower stomach. Inhale slowly for five seconds.

b. As you begin to exhale, count aloud softly. Feel your stomach slowly pulling in as you count.

c. You should be able to count for approximately thirty seconds before you run out of breath.

---

[1]Adapted from Dr. Jon Eisenson, *Voice and Diction: A Program for Improvement* (Massachusetts: Allyn and Bacon, 1997).

4 Now time yourself again as you breathe for one minute. Remember, your goal is to take between six and ten breaths in a minute. How many breaths did you take this time? Record that number here _____.

Remember: Nervousness is normal. To control it, talk yourself out of negative thoughts, and breathe slowly and deeply!

C. Being a Supportive Listener

You can help other speakers control their presentation anxiety by being a supportive listener. Follow these suggestions:

- Show speakers you are interested in them and in what they are saying.
- Give them encouragement by listening attentively.
- Look at the speaker, smile reassuringly, and nod your head from time to time.
- If a speaker invites questions from the audience after the speech, please participate! Asking questions shows speakers that you are interested in their topics and would like to know more. It is very discouraging when a presenter asks, "Does anyone have any questions?" and no one responds.

II. Presentation Preview

You will overcome your speech fears more quickly if you have an opportunity to speak about a very familiar topic—yourself. This is a wonderful way for your classmates to get to know you. Your first assignment will be to give a speech about yourself.

ACTIVITY 1   **Listen to a Model Presentation**

🎧 Listen to Juan's model presentation. Pay attention to his use of visual aids.

Juan's Presentation: About Myself

INTRODUCTION Good morning! My name is Juan Manuel, but you can call me Juan. I'd like everyone to get to know me, so I am going to tell you some interesting things about myself.

First I will tell you a little about my background by explaining my first set of pictures.

BODY [Juan shows his first set of pictures.]

I'm originally from Bogota, Colombia, where I lived until I was 5. Then my family moved to the United States. We lived in New York City for one year, and then my father was offered a job in Miami. So we decided to *strike while the iron is hot*, and we packed up and moved to Florida.

Now I'll tell you about my family.

* Take advantage of an opportunity before it's gone

[Juan shows his second set of pictures.]

I live with my family in an apartment near the campus. My sister, Juana, is 15 years old. She loves to dance ballet. My mother, Marta, is a stay-at-home mom. My father, who is also Juan, is a chef in a seafood restaurant in downtown Miami. That's my family. Of course I also have lots of aunts and uncles and cousins in Bogota, but that's a different story!

Next I will describe what my schedule is like. I currently go to school full time and have a part-time job on the weekends.

[Juan shows his third set of pictures.]

My major is art, and this semester I'm taking classes in art history, photography, math, and English. On Saturday and Sunday, I work as a waiter in the same restaurant as my father. *Bit by bit* I'm saving to buy a waterproof camera.

* *Little by little*

In my free time, I have a few hobbies. I'd really like to tell you about those.

[Juan shows his fourth set of pictures.]

(continued)

(continued)

I like to read murder mysteries. Also, I play the drums with my friends, and I like to go sailing and fishing with my dad. We usually go to Key Largo to fish for grouper and snapper.

Now that you know about my hobbies and special interests, let me tell you about my future goals and dreams.

[Juan shows his last set of pictures.]

My dream is to become a famous underwater photographer and travel around the world photographing sea life. I also want to have three sons and a golden retriever and marry my girlfriend. OOPS, *I put the cart before the horse*! I meant to say that I would like to marry my girlfriend and have three boys *after* we are established in our careers.

* *Put things in the wrong order*

CONCLUSION   Now you know a little about my background, my family, my daily life, my hobbies, and my future goals.

Thank you for listening to my speech about myself.

Does anyone have any questions?

ACTIVITY 2   **Discuss the Model Presentation**

Discuss these questions in small groups.

1. How was Juan's presentation organized?
2. How many sections did Juan have in the body of his speech? What were they?
3. How did you know when Juan was about to begin a new section of his speech?
4. How did Juan conclude his speech?
5. What other final remarks could Juan have used to end his speech?
6. Were Juan's pictures effective? Why or why not?

III. Pronunciation Practice: Final Consonants

Most English words end in consonant sounds. If you are not used to pronouncing final consonants in your native language, you might omit them at the ends of words in English. For example, you might pronounce both *cat* and *can* as [kæ]! This can confuse your listeners.

> Although **e** may be the last letter in a word, it is usually silent; the last SOUND is actually a consonant.
>
> Examples:
> ma**d**e   pho**n**e   bi**t**e   ha**v**e

ACTIVITY 1 Practice Words

The words in each of the following rows sound the same if their final consonant sounds are left off. Listen and repeat them aloud. Exaggerate your pronunciation of the final consonant in each word.

1. cat	cap	cab	can	calf
2. rack	rat	rap	rag	ran
3. soup	soon	suit	sued	Sue's
4. week	weep	wheat	weed	weave
5. robe	rode	wrote	rope	roll

ACTIVITY 2 Practice Sentences

Repeat the following sentences aloud. Be sure to exaggerate your pronunciation of the final consonant in each boldfaced word.

1. **Have** you **had ham**?
2. I **like** bright **light**.
3. The **coal** is very **cold**.
4. **Can't** Amy **catch** a **cab?**
5. **Doug** ate a well-**done duck**.
6. We **paid** for the **pane** of glass.
7. **Ben** couldn't **bend** his knees.
8. She **sighed** at the beautiful **sight**.
9. He carried a black **bag** on his **back**.
10. The **sign** is to the **side** of the **site**.

ACTIVITY 3 Practice the Model Speech

1 Reread Juan's model speech on pages 4–6. Circle the words with final consonant sounds.

2 With a partner, take turns reading Juan's speech aloud. Be sure to pronounce the final consonants clearly.

IV. Playing with Sayings: Saying with Final Consonant

ACTIVITY 1 Learn the Meanings

Read the following sayings. Check √ the ones you heard in the model speech on pages 4–6. Refer back to the speech if necessary.

_____ 1. **Put the cart before the horse:** Do things in the wrong sequence.

Yousef bought a motorcycle before learning how to ride one. He *put the cart before the horse*!

_____ 2. **Strike while the iron is hot:** Take advantage of an opportunity before it is gone.
You'd better ask the boss for a raise while he is in a good mood. *Strike while the iron is hot*!

_____ 3. **Cry over spilled milk:** Complain about something that has already happened.
I failed my exam, but it's useless to *cry over spilled milk*. I'll study harder next time.

_____ 4. **Bit by bit:** A little at a time; little by little.
If you practice, your English will improve *bit by bit*!

_____ 5. **My mind went blank:** I forgot everything I was going to say or do.
I was so nervous that *my mind went blank*.

ACTIVITY 2 **Use the Sayings**

1 Work in small groups. Think of a situation that relates to each saying and write notes about it on the lines.

1. put the cart before the horse

   _____

2. strike while the iron is hot

   _____

3. cry over spilled milk

   _____

4. bit by bit

   _____

5. my mind went blank

   _____

2 Take turns sharing your situations with the entire class. Be sure to pronounce final consonant sounds clearly.

EXAMPLE:

Don't put the cart before the horse.

I bought a wedding present for a friend before she was even engaged. Then she and her boyfriend broke up, and I was stuck with a present I couldn't return. I put the cart before the horse!

V. Presentation Project: A Speech about Yourself

Your first project is to present a speech about yourself. You will not write your speech out word for word. Instead, you will use one of the two methods described in this section to plan and prepare your speech.

Method A: Picture Story

Your goal is to prepare a speech using one set of pictures for each of five areas of your life.

STEP 1 | Plan Your Speech

A Review Juan Manuel's model presentation on pages 4–6 as a guide.

B Read the guidelines for organizing your speech.

Introduction
1. Greet the audience.
2. Introduce yourself by name.
3. Tell the audience the topic of your speech.

Body
1. Include information about these topics:
   - Your background
   - Family
   - Present activities
   - Hobbies and special interests
   - Future goals and dreams
2. Show the pictures that accompany each topic.

Conclusion
1. Summarize the five topic areas of your speech.
2. Thank the audience for listening.
3. Invite audience questions.

C Read the Useful Language you can use to begin your speech, summarize, and invite audience questions. Place a check (✓) next to the expressions you like best.

USEFUL LANGUAGE: BEGINNING YOUR SPEECH

_____ Good morning everyone! *or* Hello everybody!

_____ Today [this morning], I am going to tell you about myself.

_____ I'd like you to get to know a little bit about me.

_____ I'd like to introduce myself to you.

_____ My name is _____ [but my friends all call me _____].

USEFUL LANGUAGE: SUMMARIZING YOUR SPEECH

_____ Now you know a little about my background, my family, my daily activities, my hobbies, and my future goals.

_____ I hope you liked learning about my childhood, my family, my present activities, all my special interests, and my plans for the future.

_____ I really enjoyed telling you about myself. I described my background, my family members, my current involvements, my hobbies, and my dreams.

D Include a saying from pages 7–8 in your speech. Write it here: _____.

STEP 2 | Prepare Your Pictures

A Decide where you will find your pictures. Check √ the possibilities you like best.

_____ Computer clip art (cartoons or pictures)

_____ Photographs from your albums at home

_____ Pictures cut out from magazines or newspapers

_____ Pictures you draw yourself. (You don't have to be an artist! Simple stick figures work great as long as they represent what you want to say.)

B Prepare five sets of pictures corresponding to the five areas of your life in the body of your speech. Each set of pictures should be on a poster or construction paper (minimum size 8½ by 11 inches.)

STEP 3 | Practice Your Speech

A Practice your speech using your sets of pictures. Record it and listen to it at least once. Make sure it is between two and three minutes.

B Complete the Speech Checklist on the next page. Is there anything you want to change or improve before you present it in class?

Speech Checklist	YES	NO
1. I included an opening greeting.	☐	☐
2. I introduced myself by name and included the topic of my speech.	☐	☐
3. I included five areas of my life to speak about.	☐	☐
4. I have at least one set of pictures for each topic area.	☐	☐
5. I included a summary and thanked my listeners.	☐	☐
6. I invited audience questions.	☐	☐
7. I included a saying from the chapter.	☐	☐
8. I included Useful Language expressions.	☐	☐
9. My pronunciation of final consonant sounds is distinct.	☐	☐
10. My speech is between two and three minutes.	☐	☐

C Practice one or two more times with your pictures.

D Your teacher and/or your classmates may evaluate your speech. Study the form on page 229 so you know how you will be evaluated. You may use the items on the form to make final changes to your speech.

STEP 4 | Present Your Speech

A Relax, take a deep breath, and present your speech.

B Listen to your audience's applause!

Method B: The "Old Bag" Speech

Your goal is to prepare your speech using a "bag" and three objects. The objects will be your "notes"; they will help you remember what to say.

STEP 1 | Choose Your Objects

A Choose a "bag" that is meaningful to you for some reason. It could be a briefcase, a backpack, a handbag, a shopping bag, a duffle bag, and so on.

B Hide three objects in your bag. The objects should represent something about your childhood, your present activities, and your future goals.

A Study these segments from four model presentations. Notice the speakers' use of objects and the details they include about them.

Leo's Old Bag

This old, beat-up, mildewed suitcase has a lot of meaning for me. I used it to hold everything I owned when my family and I escaped from Cuba on a raft fifteen years ago.

Inska's Item Symbolizing the Past

This communion dress reminds me of my childhood in Munich, Germany. My family was very religious and my parents, brothers, and I went to mass in a beautiful old cathedral in the main square every Sunday. I grew up in a small town about an hour from Munich.

Tony's Item Symbolizing the Present

This hat is part of my uniform. I work part time as a security guard at a bank to help pay for my books and school expenses. I am majoring in accounting. I am currently taking classes in micro- and macroeconomics.

Ivana's Item Symbolizing the Future

This blood-pressure cuff represents my dream for the future. I would like to become a nurse in a children's hospital in my country, Russia. After I learn to speak English very well, I want to go to nursing school here. Then I want to return to Russia to help sick children.

B Read the guidelines for organizing your speech.

Introduction
1. Greet the audience.
2. Introduce yourself by name.
3. State the topic of your speech.

Body
1. Hold up your "bag." Explain why it is important to you.
2. Take out your first item. Explain how it represents your childhood.
3. Take out your second item. Explain how it symbolizes your present life.
4. Take out your third item. Explain how it symbolizes your future plans.

Conclusion
1. Summarize the areas you spoke about.
2. Thank the audience for listening.

C Read the Useful Language you can use to introduce your "old bag" and thank your listeners. Place a check (✓) next to the expressions you like best.

> **USEFUL LANGUAGE: INTRODUCING YOUR "OLD BAG"**
>
> _____ This is my "old bag." I chose it because . . .
>
> _____ I bet you're wondering what I have in my bag. First let me tell you about the bag itself!
>
> _____ Before I show my three items, let me explain why I chose this (old suitcase) as my "bag."

> **USEFUL LANGUAGE: THANKING YOUR LISTENERS**
>
> _____ Thank you all so much for listening to my speech.
>
> _____ Thank you for your interest in learning more about me.
>
> _____ Thank you for allowing me to share my "old bag" with you!

D Include a saying from pages 7–8 in your speech. Write it here: _____.

STEP 3 | Practice Your Speech

A Practice your speech with your objects. Record it and listen to it at least once.

B Complete the speech checklist. Is there anything you want to change or improve before you present it in class?

Speech Checklist	YES	NO
1. I included an opening greeting.	❑	❑
2. I introduced myself and included the topic of my speech.	❑	❑
3. I explained why the "bag" is meaningful to me.	❑	❑
4. I explained how an item symbolizes my past.	❑	❑
5. I explained how an item symbolizes my present.	❑	❑
6. I explained how an item symbolizes my future.	❑	❑
7. I included a summary and thanked my listeners.	❑	❑
8. I included a saying from the chapter.	❑	❑
9. I included Useful Language expressions.	❑	❑
10. My pronunciation of final consonant sounds is distinct.	❑	❑
11. My speech is between 2 and 3 minutes.	❑	❑
12. I invited audience questions.	❑	❑

C Practice one or two more times with your objects.

D Your teacher and/or your classmates may evaluate your speech. Study the form on page 230 so you know how you will be evaluated. You may use the items on the form to make final changes to your speech.

STEP 4 | Present Your Speech

A Relax, take a deep breath, and present your speech.

B Listen to your audience's applause!

CHAPTER 2
DELIVERING YOUR MESSAGE

William Shakespeare wrote that all speakers give two speeches at the same time: the one that is heard and the one that is seen. Believe it or not, most people are frequently influenced more by what they see than by what they hear. A professor at UCLA found that only 7 percent of our credibility with listeners comes from the actual words we speak, while 93 percent of it comes from our vocal qualities and visual characteristics. Your listeners will pay more attention to you and your message if you have effective body language and speech patterns.

CHAPTER CHALLENGE This chapter will challenge you to develop natural and confident body language and vocal qualities. When you complete this chapter, you will be able to:

- use appropriate body language
- use effective vocal characteristics
- understand different modes of speech delivery
- use notes effectively
- plan, prepare, and present a speech about a memorable personal experience

I.   Using Body Language

Body language means posture, eye contact, facial expressions, and gestures. Your body language, as well as your speech patterns, reflects how you feel about yourself. It also affects how others react to you. It can help you project an aura of confidence, or it can make you appear uncertain before you even open your mouth.

A. Posture

Your posture says a lot about you. It can say, "I'm timid. Don't listen to me; just ignore me." Or it can say, "Listen to me. I know what I am talking about." Certain postures give the impression that you are ashamed and insecure. These include:

- looking down or dropping your chin
- tilting your head to one side
- rounding your shoulders
- wrapping your arms around your body
- clasping your hands tightly in front of you

ACTIVITY   **Analyze Posture**

1 **Look at the body language of the following people. Who looks the most confident?**

DIANE   CARL   CHERYL   SIMON

If you said Cheryl, you're right!

2 **Discuss the following questions in small groups.**

a. What is it about Cheryl that causes her to project courage and confidence?

b. What could Diane do to look more confident?

c. What is wrong with Carl's posture and appearance?

d. What is wrong with Simon's body language?

3 Study the tips for confident posture when standing or sitting.

TIPS FOR CONFIDENT POSTURE

Tips While Standing and Presenting a Speech to an Audience

- Keep your head erect.
- Keep both feet flat on the floor and slightly apart.
- Keep your back straight and your shoulders back.
- If you are using a lectern, stand up straight and gently rest your hands on the sides of the lectern. (Be careful not to bend over it or lean on it!)

Tips While Sitting and Listening to One Person

- Sit straight while leaning forward slightly to show interest in the speaker.
- Rest your hands lightly in your lap or on the arms of your chair.
- Keep your legs together with your feet flat on the floor or crossed at the ankles.

B. Walking

A famous Spanish matador, Manolo Martin-Vazquez, once said, "The most important lesson in courage is physical, not mental. I was taught to walk in a way that produces courage. The mental part comes later." If you want to appear and feel confident when you walk to the front of the room, walk the "walk of the matador"!

ACTIVITY Walk Like a Matador

1 Come to class prepared with a favorite saying or a quote from a parent, grandparent, or relative.

EXAMPLES:

- Do unto others as you would have them do unto you.
- Don't put off until tomorrow what you can do today.
- Blood is thicker than water.

2 Practice the walk of the matador. Take turns.

    a. Walk to the front of the room with your head up, spine straight, and shoulders back.

    b. Stand at the lectern and look directly at your audience. Then smile, say "Good morning" or "Good Afternoon," and state your saying or quote.

    c. After the applause stops, say "Thank you."

    d. Walk back to your seat with your head up, spine straight, and shoulders back.

C. Eye Contact

Eye contact customs vary from culture to culture. In some cultures, it's customary for people to lower their eyes when speaking with authority figures such as parents, bosses, or government officials. However, the reverse is true in the United States. In this culture, making eye contact is an essential part of effective communication. Good eye contact does the following:

- Shows you are sincere and honest (Looking away often conveys insincerity or embarrassment.)
- Indicates you have confidence in yourself and what you are saying
- Encourages listeners to pay attention to you and to respect you
- Allows you to see your listeners' reactions to your speech (Their nods, gestures, and smiles tell you they understand and are interested in your message.)

Note that effective eye contact does not mean staring at a person! It means shifting your focus to and from a person's eyes.

ACTIVITY 1 **Look Your Partner in the Eyes**

Work with a partner. Take turns talking for one to two minutes about any topic (e.g., your weekend, your summer vacation, a pet, a movie). Follow the steps below.

1. Focus on your partner's entire face for four seconds.
2. Shift your focus to your partner's right eye for four seconds.
3. Look at your partner's left eye for four seconds.
4. Glance at your partner's nose, chin, and forehead for three to four seconds each.
5. Repeat steps 1–4.

Look the Audience in the Eye

Select any topic and practice speaking while making eye contact. Follow these steps.

1. Walk the walk of the matador to the front of the room and greet the audience.
2. Speak about your topic for one minute. As you speak, move your eyes from one section of the audience to another. Look at one person for four or five seconds, then another person for four or five seconds, and so on until you have surveyed the room.
3. Thank your audience.
4. Walk the walk of the matador back to your seat.

ACTIVITY 3 **Group Discussion**

Discuss the following questions in small groups.

1. As a child, what were you taught about eye contact?
2. How did you feel about Activity 1 as the speaker? As a listener?
3. How did you feel about Activity 2 as the speaker? As a listener?
4. What were your listeners' reactions to your efforts to maintain eye contact with them?

D. Facial Expressions

Facial expressions vary greatly from culture to culture. In the United States, for example, a smile shows listeners that you are confident and looking forward to speaking to them. Raised eyebrows show that you are surprised. These same facial expressions may have different meanings in other cultures.

ACTIVITY **Practice Facial Expressions**

1 **At home, make the following facial expressions while looking in a mirror. (It may help you to think of a time when you felt these emotions.) This exercise will help you become aware of how you appear to others while speaking.**

happy	interested
unhappy	excited
worried	fearful
neutral	frustrated
impatient	angry
surprised	doubtful

2 Practice with a partner. Take turns making facial expressions from the list and guessing the meaning of your partner's expressions.

3 In class, go to the front of the room and make one of the facial expressions you practiced. Your classmates should guess the meaning.

E. Movement

Posture, walking, and facial expressions can be used to enhance or emphasize what you are saying. In contrast, many speakers unconsciously move their bodies in ways that are distracting to listeners. For example, some speakers nervously fiddle with their hair, their eyeglasses, items of jewelry, or buttons on shirts. Others hide their hands in their pockets and jingle their keys or loose change. These are movements that you should definitely avoid!

ACTIVITY   Become Aware of Distracting Movements

Make the following movements at home while looking at yourself in a full-length mirror. Try to avoid these movements while speaking before an audience.

- Covering your mouth with your hand while speaking
- Swaying back and forth on your feet
- Crossing your arms in front of you
- Wrapping your arms around your body
- Tilting your head
- Twirling a strand of hair around your finger
- Playing with a button or item of jewelry
- Looking down at your feet

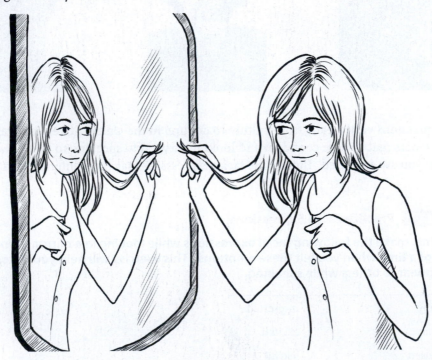

F. Gestures

You can emphasize important points in your speech by using gestures—finger, hand, and arm movements. Gestures are used to illustrate a wide range of concepts. Study the examples.

Meaning	Example
Size	Show the width or height of an object by using your hands.
Location	Point your index finger to show a location on a map or use your arm in a sweeping motion to show a wider area.
Number	Hold up three fingers when you say "There are three causes of this problem."
Symbolic action	Wave your hand in greeting to show how you felt when you saw a childhood friend.
Enthusiasm	Punch the air with your fist to show your support for a new policy or decision.

Remember that a gesture can have different meanings in different cultures. For example, the popular hand gesture for "OK" in the United States (a circle made with the thumb and forefinger), when slightly rotated, is an obscene gesture in Brazil!

ACTIVITY 1   Analyze These Gestures

Work in groups. Study the gestures in the photos. Then discuss the questions.

1. How do you interpret the gestures in each of the photos?
2. Did you and your classmates interpret them the same way?
3. Have you seen people in North America use these gestures?

1 Read the list of messages. Imagine the gestures you would make to illustrate them.

I don't know.	Great job!	You're crazy.
Wait a moment.	Absolutely not!	See you later.
I'm not interested.	You're late.	Don't do that.
You're right.	That's enough.	That's OK.
Go away.	Take it easy.	It's getting late.
Oh no!	Stop!	Come here.

2 Practice with a partner. Make a gesture from Step 1 and have your partner guess the message. Then switch roles.

3 Go to the front of the room and act out a gesture in front of the entire class. Call on a classmate to guess the message.

4 Work with the class. Demonstrate the gestures you think North Americans use to convey these meanings.

II. Using Your Voice Effectively

It is important to use your voice effectively when you are speaking before an audience. Careful control of your volume, rate of speech, phrasing and pausing, and pronunciation will help your audience understand your message and stay involved in your speech.

A. Volume

Volume refers to how loud or soft your voice is. There are two common problems with volume. Some speakers never vary their volume, causing them to sound monotonous. Other speakers speak too softly, so it is difficult to hear them. Aim to vary your volume to keep your listeners' attention and to speak loudly enough so that everyone in the room can hear you.

ACTIVITY 1 Vary Your Volume

1 Listen to the following sentences. Notice the increase in volume from Level 1 to Level 4.

Level 1: I am speaking softly.

Level 2: I am speaking at a normal volume.

Level 3: I am speaking loudly.

Level 4: I AM SPEAKING VERY LOUDLY.

2 With a partner, practice the sentences in Step 1. Increase your volume from level to level.

3 Work with a partner. Practice reading the following sets of sentences aloud. Vary your volume to match the size of the words.

a. (1) Sorry, I can't hear you.

(2) I'm sorry. I can't hear you.

(3) Can you speak up? I can't hear you.

(4) SPEAK UP! I CAN'T HEAR YOU!

b. (1) I want you to come home now.

(2) I want you to come home now.

(3) You need to come home now.

(4) You need to come home RIGHT NOW!

ACTIVITY 2 **Project Your Voice**

1 Think of five casual questions to ask a classmate. For example: What are your favorite restaurants? Where do you get your hair cut? What was the last movie you saw?

2 Stand in a corner of the classroom while a classmate stands in the corner farthest from you. The class observes silently.

3 Ask your questions with sufficient volume that your partner can easily hear you and respond.

4 Repeat your partner's responses to demonstrate that you heard them clearly.

B. Rate

Rate refers to how quickly or slowly you speak. A common problem is speaking so fast that your listeners can't understand you. Your goal should be to speak at a rate of approximately 150 words per minute.

ACTIVITY **Speak 150 Words per Minute**

Work in pairs. Take turns reading the following 150-word paragraph aloud. Use a watch to time each other's reading. If it takes less than one minute, your rate is too fast. If it takes over one minute and fifteen seconds, your rate is too slow.

Your rate of speech will be perfect if it is slow enough for your listeners to understand yet fast enough to keep their interest. An ideal rate of speech is approximately one hundred fifty words per minute. There is an easy way to learn and practice how to speak at this rate. Choose a simple passage from a book, magazine, or newspaper that is one hundred fifty words. Count them to be sure. Read the passage while you time yourself in seconds. If the reading took you sixty to seventy-five seconds, your rate of speech is great. If you finished reading in less than a minute, slow down your rate of speech. Read the passage again. Strive to take at least one minute to finish reading. After several practice sessions, you will learn how it feels to speak at the ideal rate of one hundred fifty words per minute.

C. Phrasing and Pausing

Phrasing means dividing the words in a sentence into logical groups. In written English, phrases are usually separated by commas or periods. Consider the following sentence: *My younger sister, the tallest girl in the class, is also the smartest.* How many phrases does it have? If you said three, you are correct!

Pausing refers to separating phrases with a tiny moment of silence. A short pause between comments provides a moment for you to think about your next words, remember your next point, look at your notes, or take a breath. A short silence also enables your listeners to consider what you've just said. Think of pauses as oral punctuation marks, just as commas and periods are written punctuation marks.

ACTIVITY Practice Phrasing and Pausing

1 Work in small groups. Take turns reading the pairs of sentences below. Be sure to pause at the commas. Your partners should guess which sentence you are saying.

   a. (1) He doesn't know Steve.   (2) He doesn't know, Steve.

   b. (1) If you're overweight, don't eat fast. (2) If you're overweight, don't eat, fast!

   c. (1) Can you see Sue?   (2) Can you see, Sue?

   d. (1) Dave Johnson isn't here.   (2) Dave, Johnson isn't here.

   e. (1) It is there for the third time.   (2) It is, therefore, the third time.

2 Discuss the sentence pairs in small groups. How are sentences (1) and (2) different in meaning?

D. Vocal Fillers

Vocal fillers are noises, words, and phrases that speakers use when deciding what to say next. (Examples are *um, uh, er, you know*?) While fillers are a natural part of spontaneous conversation, they can be distracting in a speech. They can cause the speaker to appear nervous or lacking in confidence. Instead of fillers, confident speakers pause silently to consider their next words.

ACTIVITY 1 Listen to Yourself in Conversation

1 Record yourself while having a conversation outside of class.

2 Transcribe one minute of the conversation. Write down exactly what you said, including fillers.

3 Circle all the fillers.

4 Read the transcript out loud, leaving out all vocal fillers.

5 Be prepared to discuss your observations in class.

ACTIVITY 2 Play a Classroom Game

1 Walk the walk of the matador to the front of the room. Your teacher will call out a simple topic to you. For example:

apples	pens	dogs	chairs	computers
rocks	rain	eyes	teeth	cell phones
belts	paper	trees	trees	socks
shoes	windows	games	jewelry	sports

2 Speak about the topic for about one minute. Try not to use any vocal fillers. Say whatever comes to your mind about the topic. Organization of ideas is not important.

3 Your teacher will time you. The first time you use a vocal filler, your teacher will clap and ask you to sit down.

4 Walk the walk of the matador proudly back to your seat.

5 The student who speaks the longest without using a vocal filler will be the winner!

III. Different Modes of Speech Delivery

There are four general methods of speech delivery.

   1. Manuscript delivery

     • The speech is written out word for word.

     • The speaker reads the speech to the audience.

2. Memorized delivery
   - The speech is written out word for word.
   - The speaker learns it word for word and recites it from memory.
   - The speaker does not use any notes during the delivery.
3. Impromptu delivery
   - The speaker receives no advance notice of the speech.
   - The speaker has no time to prepare notes.
   - The speaker must gather his or her thoughts on the spur of the moment.
4. Extemporaneous delivery
   - The speech is not written out word for word. It is delivered from notes or an outline with main ideas, key words, and phrases.
   - The speech is delivered naturally and conversationally.

ACTIVITY **Discuss with Classmates**

Discuss the following questions in small groups.

1. What are the advantages and disadvantages of each mode of speech delivery?
2. Which methods have you tried in the past? What was the situation? What did you talk about?
3. Which method do you like best? Why?
4. Which method do you like least? Why?

IV. Effective Use of Notes

In Chapter 1, you practiced extemporaneous speaking using two unusual techniques—the Picture Story and the "Old Bag"—for remembering your information. A more traditional memory aid is to write your main points and brief notes on index cards. Use the guidelines below to make note cards for your speech.

1. Buy a packet of 5- by 7- or 4- by 6-inch index cards.
2. When preparing a speech, write only key words or short phrases on the cards to help you remember your points.
3. Use one card for each part of your speech.
4. Write on only one side of each card.
5. Number the cards. If you accidentally drop them, you will quickly be able to put them in the correct order.
6. Write your notes in large letters. It should be easy to glance at the notes quickly without losing your place.
7. To emphasize key words, use underlining, capital letters, or other marks.

Sample Note Cards for a Speech about Identity Theft

INTRO: ATTENTION GETTER   1

    1. The FBI calls it the FASTEST GROWING crime
        in the U.S.!!
    2. A MILLION people will be victims this year!
    3. What is it? It is IDENTITY THEFT.

INTRO: PREVIEW   2

Today, I will present four important points about
identity theft:
    1. How it happens
    2. How thieves use your information
    3. How to prevent identity theft
    4. What to do if you are a victim

TRANSITION   3

First, I will explain how identity thieves steal your
personal information.

HOW IDENTITY THEFT OCCURS   4

A. According to www.ftc.gov:
     (Federal Trade Commission)
    1. Stolen wallets/purses
    2. Dumpster diving
    3. Mail/phone/e-mail scams

V. Presentation Preview

You are going to give a speech describing an exceptional personal experience. Your challenge is to make the audience relive the experience with you. For example, if you had a happy experience, try to make your listeners feel happy. If you had a sad experience, try to make them feel sad. If you had a scary experience, try to make them feel afraid. If you had a funny experience, try to make them laugh.

Strive to speak naturally and maintain eye contact with your listeners. As in Chapter 1, you will not write out the speech and read it. Instead you will write your main ideas on cards and consult them as you speak.

ACTIVITY 1 Listen to Model Presentations

🎧 **1** Listen to Francisco's model presentation. Pay attention to his organization and vocal characteristics.

Francisco's Presentation: My Journey to Freedom

INTRODUCTION Do you think it's possible to have an experience that is dangerous, happy, sad, uncomfortable, and very scary at the same time? I had one, and I'll remember it for the rest of my life.

BODY Three years ago, when I was 18, I escaped from Cuba with my 14-year-old brother, Jose. My father wanted us to live in a free country, get a good education, and have many opportunities. In Cuba, there was no hope for a good future. My father took me and Jose to the beach in the middle of the night and put us on a raft. Before we pushed off, he photographed the raft and said, "*I will keep my fingers crossed* that you will arrive safely."

* Wish for good luck

Our father told us it would take three days to reach a city in Florida called Key West. For three days Jose and I were all alone in the ocean without food or water. Sharks were swimming all around us. The waves were very high and splashed over us. I thought we were going to starve, drown, or be eaten by the sharks. I comforted my brother by telling him how much better our lives would be when we finally got to Florida. I made myself feel better by thinking that one day I would go to heaven and meet my parents there. Finally, by some miracle, someone contacted the U.S. Coast Guard about us. The water was too rough for them to reach us in a boat so they rescued us in a helicopter.

Relatives of ours in Miami were notified by the immigration authorities. Our aunt and uncle picked us up in Key West, and we went to live with them in Miami. After two years, our parents finally escaped from Cuba also and we saw them again. That was a very happy day for me.

CONCLUSION Now that you know my experience, I think you can understand why it was scary, sad, dangerous, uncomfortable, and finally, happy all at the same time. Even though our journey was risky, I'm glad we decided to do it. If we hadn't, I wouldn't be here today in this free and wonderful country talking to all of you. Thank you for listening.

2 Discuss these questions in small groups.

    a. How did you feel when you heard Francisco's presentation? What made you feel this way?

    b. What are some gestures that Francisco might have used during his presentation?

    c. Were Francisco's vocal qualities effective? Why or why not?

3 Listen to Leila's model presentation.

Leila's Presentation: A Stinging Experience

INTRODUCTION   In my hands I have a jar of honey.

If you look closely, you can see part of the beehive in the jar. You are probably wondering why I brought a jar of honey to show you today. Every time I see honey I am reminded of a "stinging" experience I had when I was in the sixth grade.

BODY   As a child I grew up on a farm not far from Kuala Lumpur, Malaysia. One warm summer day, my friend and I were walking home from school. We happened to see a beehive in a tree.

We had just studied in school about bee colonies and how bees make honey. This was my big chance to show off to my mother and father what I had learned in school. It looked easy. I searched for a stick and found one about two meters long. I handed it to my friend and told her to sneak up to the tree and hit the hive with the stick.

I said I would wait until the bees came out and then I would grab the hive and run away with it. I soon learned a very important lesson. I learned that things don't always work out the way you planned them. My friend pushed the hive down from the tree and then hurried off at full speed. The bees did not go after her. However, they were all over me instantly. They stung my arms; they flew down my blouse and stung me. They flew up my skirt and stung me; they got in my hair and stung me.

My parents carried me to the hospital. I stayed there for two days until my fever was gone. Oh, I wish I had *looked before I leaped*!

CONCLUSION That was the first and last beehive I ever touched. I have never approached a beehive again and never will. I'm sure you can see how this jar of honey I brought to show you reminds me of a very "stinging" experience! *Keep your fingers crossed* that you never get stung by a bee.

* *Analyze a situation before you take action*

* *Wish for good luck*

4 **Discuss these questions in small groups.**
   1. How did you feel when you heard Leila's presentation? What made you feel this way?
   2. What gestures might Leila have used to enhance her presentation?
   3. Were Leila's vocal qualities effective? Why or why not?

ACTIVITY 1 **Complete a Model Speech Preparation Worksheet**

1 **Study the Speech Preparation Worksheet for Francisco's speech.**

Francisco's Speech Preparation Worksheet

1. What type of experience was it?	dangerous, happy, sad, uncomfortable, scary—all at the same time
2. Where were you?	beach in Cuba
3. When were you there?	middle of the night, three years ago; I was 17 years old
4. Who was with you?	brother Jose—14 years old
5. What were you doing?	Father put us on raft
6. Why were you there?	escaping Cuba to freedom
7. What was your goal?	arrive in Key West; freedom, better life
8. How were you feeling?	alone, scared, uncomfortable, helpless
9. Why did you feel that way?	no food or water; afraid of starving, drowning, being eaten by sharks
10. How did you react?	comforted my brother; thought about better life ahead
11. How did the story end?	U.S. Coast Guard rescued us
12. Why will you never forget this experience?	I'm here today!

2 Now complete the Speech Preparation Worksheet for Leila's speech.

Leila's Speech Preparation Worksheet

1. What type of experience was it?	dingars, scary
2. Where were you?	
3. When were you there?	
4. Who was with you?	
5. What were you doing?	
6. Why were you there?	
7. What was your goal?	
8. How were you feeling?	
9. Why did you feel that way?	
10. How did you react?	
11. How did the story end?	
12. Why will you never forget this experience?	

VI. Pronunciation Practice: -ed Endings

In written English, the ending -ed forms the past tense of regular verbs and past participles used as adjectives. In spoken English, the -ed ending can have three different pronunciations. It can sound like [t] (as in *stopped*), [d] (as in *lived*), or [əd] as in *loaded*). Study the pronunciation guidelines in the chart.

Pronounce -ed ending as	After	Examples
[t]	voiceless consonants [p], [k], [f], [s], [ʃ] (as in *wash*), and [tʃ] (as in *watch*)	talked, crossed, laughed
[d]	• all vowels • voiced consonants [b], [g], [v], [z], [m], [n], [l], [r], [ð] (as in brea**the**), and [dʒ] (as in ple**dge**)	lived, turned, played
[əd]	[t] and [d]	wanted, rested, ended

ACTIVITY 1 Pronounce -ed as [t]

Listen and repeat the following words and sentences. Be sure to pronounce the -ed ending like [t].

1. looked
2. missed
3. stopped
4. worked
5. picked
6. wished
7. Mom baked a pie.
8. He finished early.
9. Tara stopped singing.
10. The children danced to the music.

ACTIVITY 2 Pronounce -ed as [d]

Listen and repeat the following words and sentences. Be sure to pronounce the -ed ending like [d].

1. loved
2. stayed
3. filled
4. burned
5. fibbed
6. cried
7. We played a game.
8. He moved again.
9. I mailed a letter.
10. They followed the leader.

ACTIVITY 3 Pronounce -ed as [əd]

Listen and repeat the following words and sentences. Be sure to pronounce the -ed ending like [əd].

1. ended
2. added
3. hunted
4. wanted
5. needed
6. painted
7. I rested at home.
8. The car started.
9. He avoided his boss.
10. We painted our house.

ACTIVITY 4 Identify Words with *-ed* Endings

1 **Circle all the *-ed* forms in Francisco and Leila's model speeches on pages 27 and 28. Write them in the chart below. (The first two are filled in as examples.)**

Francisco's Speech

[t] (6 words)	[d] (2 words)	[əd] (4 words)
escaped		*wanted*

Leila's Speech

[t] (8 words)	[d] (7 words)	[əd] (2 words)

2 **Work with a partner. Practice pronouncing the words in the charts.**

ACTIVITY 5 Practice the Speeches

Take turns reading the sample speeches aloud with a partner. Be sure to pronounce the *-ed* endings correctly.

VII. Playing with Sayings: Sayings with *-ed* Endings

ACTIVITY 1 Learn the Meanings

Read the following sayings. Check √ the ones you heard in the model speeches on pages 27 and 28. Refer back to the speeches if necessary.

_____ 1. **Look before you leap:** Analyze a situation carefully before you take action.
Martin moved to New York City. He immediately hated it. It was too cold and he couldn't find a cheap place to live. He should have *looked before he leaped!*

_____ 2. **A penny saved is a penny earned:** It's better to save money than to waste it.
Mary works hard to save money; she knows that *a penny saved is a penny earned.*

_____ 3. **Keep your fingers crossed:** Wish for good luck; hope for a positive outcome.
The runner said, "Please *keep your fingers crossed* that I win the race."

_____ 4. **Leave no stone unturned:** Look everywhere to find something; do everything possible to solve a problem.
Leave no stone unturned in your efforts to find a new job.

_____ 5. **Keep me posted:** Keep me informed; keep me updated on the progress of a situation.
Keep me posted about your plans to visit next month.

ACTIVITY 2 Using the Sayings

Complete the statements with the correct saying. Use each saying once.

1. My family wanted to know when they could come visit me. I told them I would let them know after I found out my final exam schedule. They asked me to _____.

2. My friends wanted me to go to a restaurant for dinner. I was trying to save money to pay for my plane ticket home for the holidays. I knew that if I spent the money to go out to eat, it would take me longer to save up for the ticket. After all, _____.

3. I lost my wallet while jogging on campus. I retraced my steps, called the "lost and found," organized friends to help me search, and put up flyers offering a reward for my wallet. I was determined to _____ in my efforts to find it.

4. I almost accepted the first job I was offered. After asking lots of questions, I realized that I wouldn't like the work, and the salary was very low. I'm glad I didn't accept the job. It's a good thing I _____.

5. I want to go to the beach this weekend to relax. I hope it will be sunny and warm. I am _____ that it doesn't rain.

VIII. Presentation Project: An Exceptional Experience

Your project is to prepare and present a two- to three-minute speech about a memorable experience you have had as an adult or as a child. The experience you choose may be one of the following:

dangerous	exciting	happy	surprising
educational	frightening	interesting	uncomfortable
embarrassing	funny	sad	unique

Your goal is to use body language and vocal variety to make your speech more effective.

STEP 1 | Choose a Topic

A Think of memorable experiences you have had in your lifetime and list them in the chart. Include an adjective to describe the experience. Follow the examples.

Experience	Adjective
The day I ran away from home	lonely
Getting braces on my teeth.	painful

B Choose one of the topics for your speech.

STEP 2 | Plan Your Speech

A Review the Speech Preparation Worksheet for Francisco's speech on page 27.

B Read the Useful Language for closing your speech. Place a checkmark √ next to the expressions you like best.

USEFUL LANGUAGE: CLOSING YOUR SPEECH

_____ Now you know why I am afraid of (noun) _____.

_____ Now I'm sure you can understand why this was an unforgettable experience.

_____ I'm sure you'll agree that my experience was (adjective) _____.

_____ I hope that you, too, will be able to (verb) _____ one day!

_____ I hope that what happened to me will never happen to any of you!

C Complete the Speech Preparation Worksheet for your speech. You may change or add questions as needed.

Speech Preparation Worksheet: Memorable Experience

1. What type of experience was it?
_____

2. Where were you?
_____

3. When were you there?
_____

4. Who was with you?
_____

5. What were you doing?
_____

6. Why were you there?
_____

7. What was your goal?
_____

8. How were you feeling?
_____

9. Why did you feel that way?
_____

10. How did you react?
_____

11. How did the story end?
_____

12. Why will you never forget this experience?
_____

D Include at least one saying from Playing with Sayings, page 33, in your speech. Write it here:
_____.

E Choose at least one visual aid to show your audience during your speech.

STEP 3 | Add Body Language and Vocal Characteristics

A Write down gestures and facial expressions to enhance specific places in your speech. Practice this body language in the mirror when you rehearse so that it looks natural.

Place in Speech	Gestures/Facial Expressions
EXAMPLE: (from Leila's speech) Introduction	Hold up jar of honey. Point to piece of beehive.
Leila said the bees stung her.	Painful expression

B Write down ways you might use your voice to enhance specific places in your speech.

Place in Speech	Vocal Characteristic
EXAMPLE: (from Francisco's speech) Introduction	Say "rest of my life" very slowly, with emphasis.

STEP 4 | Prepare Note Cards

A Write the notes from your Speech Preparation Worksheet on index cards. Use one card for your introduction, one for the conclusion, and as many cards as you need for the body.

B Include the saying you selected and the Useful Language. Also include reminders about the gestures and facial expressions you selected in Step 3.

C Write on one side of the card only. Number the cards.

STEP 5 | Practice Your Speech

A Practice your speech at least three times. Use the following tips to help you.

REHEARSAL TIPS

- Begin practicing several days before your presentation. Don't wait until the last moment!

- Practice in a location that is private and distraction-free.

- Rehearse your speech with your note cards. Become so familiar with the information that you only need to glance at the cards briefly to remember your ideas.

- Time yourself with a stopwatch or a clock with a second hand.

- Practice your speech in front of a mirror. Pay attention to your eye contact and body language.

- Record yourself while rehearsing. View or listen to the recording. Check for errors in content and delivery. Try to correct any problems during your next rehearsal.

- Practice your speech in front of friends or family. After your speech, ask them to comment on your delivery.

B Complete the following Speech Checklist. Is there anything you want to improve before you present the speech in class?

Speech Checklist	YES	NO
1. My speech is about a memorable experience.	☐	☐
2. I prepared an introduction.	☐	☐
3. I used enough details to describe my experience fully.	☐	☐
4. I used an expression from the Useful Language box in my conclusion.	☐	☐
5. I included a saying.	☐	☐
6. I used effective eye contact, facial expressions, movement, and gestures.	☐	☐
7. I used my voice effectively.	☐	☐
8. My speech is between two and three minutes.	☐	☐
9. I chose at least one visual aid to show my audience.	☐	☐
10. My pronunciation of words with -*ed* endings is clear.	☐	☐

C Your teacher and/or your classmates may evaluate your speech. Study the evaluation form on page 231 so you know how you will be evaluated. You may use the checklist to make final changes to your speech.

STEP 6 | Present Your Speech

A Relax, take a deep breath, and present your speech.

B Listen to your audience's applause.

PUTTING YOUR SPEECH TOGETHER

"Where do I begin?" This is a question students often ask when faced with the task of writing a speech. The answer is that you must begin with a speech topic and a clear purpose for speaking. Once you have selected those, you can start gathering and organizing information for your speech. As you will soon learn, writing a speech is like following a recipe or using step-by-step instructions to put something together after you take it out of the box.

CHAPTER CHALLENGE This chapter will help you organize and outline your thoughts and information so that you can deliver a logical, clear speech. When you complete this chapter, you will be able to:

- prepare the introduction, body, and conclusion of a speech
- use an outline to plan and deliver a speech
- plan, prepare, and present a personal opinion speech

I. Preparing the Speech

Every speech has three parts: the introduction, the body, and the conclusion. Which part of a speech do you think you should prepare first? Write the numbers 1, 2, and 3 to indicate the correct order.

_____ Introduction

_____ Body

_____ Conclusion

The correct answers may surprise you. They are 3, 1, 2. First you prepare the body of your speech. Then you prepare the conclusion. Finally you prepare the introduction.

Prepare the Body

The body of a speech contains any number of sections to develop the topic. It includes major ideas as well as details that support and clarify those ideas.

To prepare the body, first list subtopics that you might include in your speech. Write them as you think of them. Some ideas will be important, and some will not. At this stage you should just concentrate on writing all the ideas you can think of that relate to the topic of your speech. Study the example from a student speech entitled "Land the Job of Your Dreams."

EXAMPLES:

- Dress appropriately.
- Behave appropriately during the personal interview.
- Submit a resume.
- Find the desired position.
- Schedule appointments.
- Get a flexible work schedule.
- Learn new skills.
- Choose accessories.
- Don't chew gum or smoke.

Second, narrow your list of subtopics. Review your list and select the three or four subtopics that will best develop your speech in the time allowed. These subtopics will become the main headings of your speech.

EXAMPLES:

- Behave appropriately during the personal interview.
- Submit a résumé.
- Find the desired position.
- Schedule interviews.
- ~~Get a flexible work schedule.~~
- ~~Learn new skills.~~
- ~~Choose accessories.~~
- ~~Don't chew gum or smoke.~~

Next, order your subtopics logically so that one leads naturally into the next one.

EXAMPLES:

I. Find the desired position.

II. Submit a résumé.

III. Schedule interviews.

IV. Behave appropriately during the personal interview.

Finally, develop your subtopics with factual information, logical proof, and presentation aids. If your subtopics are supported and well organized, they will be interesting and your listeners will understand and remember your speech better.

Prepare the Conclusion

A good conclusion includes two parts:

- A summary of the main points in the speech
- Memorable final remarks

A good summary briefly reviews your topic and repeats or restates the main ideas. Effective final remarks are delivered after the summary and leave your audience thinking about what you've said long after your speech has ended.

EXAMPLE:

"Land the Job of Your Dreams"

Summary

Now you know four important steps to follow when applying for a job.

- A. First, find a job you would like.
- B. Second, submit a résumé.
- C. Third, schedule interviews.
- D. Fourth, act professionally during the interview.

Final Remarks

Be sure to follow the steps I explained and you'll be on your way to landing the job of your dreams!

Prepare the Introduction

A good introduction includes an attention-getting opener that captures your listeners' attention immediately. The introduction also contains a preview of the main points in the body of the speech.

Some methods for opening your speech and getting listeners' attention include:

- telling a brief story;
- asking your listeners a question to arouse their curiosity;
- shocking your audience with a startling fact or quotation.

An effective preview:

- tells listeners the main ideas in the body of the speech;
- helps listeners to follow information easily as you progress through the speech.

EXAMPLE:

"Land the Job of Your Dreams"

Opener

What I'm about to tell you could change your life. If you listen carefully to what I have to say, you'll be able to land the job of your dreams.

Preview

I'm going to discuss four important aspects to consider when applying for a job:

- A. Finding the desired position
- B. Submitting a successful résumé
- C. Scheduling interviews
- D. Behaving appropriately during the personal interview

ACTIVITY 1   **Label the Parts of a Speech**

Work with a partner. Below is a list of the parts in a typical speech. On the line to the left of each exercise item, write the letter of the corresponding speech part from the list.

a. attention-getting opener
b. preview
c. body subtopic
d. summary statement
e. final remark(s)

_____   1. My presentation will cover three aspects of electronic spying in the computer industry.

_____   2. In my hand I have a tiny microphone that can hear the sound of a fly walking on a pane of glass a block away! Sounds incredible, doesn't it! But it's true!

_____   3. Advantages of using electronic espionage

_____   4. Types of devices used in electronic spying

_____   5. So, if you have a business, beware! You never know if a competitor is looking over your shoulder or listening to your conversations from a mile away!

_____   6. Disadvantages of using electronic espionage

_____   7. My investigation of electronic spying in the computer industry is complete. You are now aware of three issues related to this topic.

ACTIVITY 2   **Complete the Outline**

Still working with your partner, fill in the lines below with items 1–7 from Activity 1. Note that each body subtopic will be used three times.

Electronic Espionage in Business and Industry

Introduction

  I. _____
     _____
 II. _____
     A. _____
     B. _____
     C. _____

Body

  I. _Types of devices used in electronic spying_
 II. _____
III. _____

Conclusion

  I. _____
     A. _____
     B. _____
     C. _____
 II. _____
     _____

II. Purpose of Outlines

With a good outline, you'll never have to worry about forgetting what you want to say. Outlines do the following:

- Make it easy for you to deliver your speech
- Assure that you have organized your ideas
- Help you remember all your information

Even when you're not giving a speech, an outline can make your life easier. It can help you to accomplish tasks in a logical order, saving you time and even money. An outline also helps you to remember all that you need to do. For example, if you have several errands to do after class, you could organize them as follows:

EXAMPLE:

I. Post office

II. Grocery store

III. Gas station

IV. Bank

When one item doesn't depend on another, any random order of organization is fine. However, suppose your car is almost out of gas and you don't have any cash. You would need to go to a bank first! So you would change the order of the errands. Your new outline would look like this:

I. Bank

II. Gas station

III. Grocery store

IV. Post office

But wait! You are going to buy ice cream at the grocery store. You don't want it to melt while you go to the post office, do you? You decide to stop at the grocery store just before heading home. Now your outline looks like this:

I. Bank

II. Gas station

III. Post office

IV. Grocery store

You may have a lot on your mind. As a result, you may forget what you want to do at each of the places you need to go to. No problem! Add specific details to each point of your outline.

EXAMPLE:

I. Bank

   A. Cash check from Uncle Mario

   B. Deposit paycheck into savings account

   C. Pay fine for bouncing check

II. Gas station

   A. Fill up tank

   B. Check water in battery

   C. Check oil level

   D. Put air in tires

III. Post office

   A. Buy stamps

   B. Send package to Venezuela

IV. Grocery Store
   A. Ice cream
   B. Cottage cheese
   C. Skim milk

As you can see, the key to outlining is to identify subtopics and add specific details. With such an outline, you will never arrive home having forgotten something you had to do. Do this for your speeches and you will never again worry, "What if I forget what I am going to say?"

III. Outlining Supporting Points

Once you have gathered enough information to prepare the introduction, body, and conclusion of your speech, you will need to organize and outline it. A good outline meets four basic requirements.

1. Each Supporting Point Relates to a Main Point

All the supporting points under each main point in the body of your speech must directly support that section of the body. In the example below, which supporting idea does not support the main point?

Alcoholism is an international problem.

   A. Russia has a high alcoholism rate.
   B. France has the highest alcoholism rate in Europe.
   C. Alcoholics have more car accidents than nondrinkers.
   D. Japan has a severe juvenile alcoholism problem.

If you said C, you're right! Although it is an interesting fact, it does not directly relate to the main point: Alcoholism is an international problem.

2. Each Supporting Point Contains Only One Idea

Supporting points under each main point should not contain more than one idea.

Study the example. Which supporting idea contains more than one idea?

Small cars are better than large cars.

   A. They are less expensive and easier to park.
   B. They get better gas mileage.

If you said A, you're correct! Point A contains two separate supporting ideas. The example should be outlined like this:

Small cars are better than large cars.

   A. They are less expensive.
   B. They are easier to park.
   C. They get better gas mileage.

3. Supporting Points Are Not Repeated or Restated

Supporting ideas under each main point should not repeat the same information in different words. Each supporting point needs to express a different idea. Which supporting ideas in the example below contain the same information?

Students dislike the school cafeteria.

   A. There is very little food to choose from.
   B. The food is too expensive.
   C. The menu is extremely limited.

If you said A and C, you are correct again! These two points use different words to state the same idea.

4. Supporting Points Have an Equal Level of Importance

All the supporting ideas under each main point must be equally important. They must belong to the same category or be parallel to each other.

Which supporting point in the example below belongs to a different category than the others?

Sales in South America have fallen drastically.

A. Colombia

B. Lima

C. Ecuador

If you said B, you are right! A and C are countries. B is a city. The supporting points should be all cities or all countries.

ACTIVITY 1 Recognize What Makes a Good Outline

Work in small groups. Choose the best description for each example outline.

a. Incorrect: At least one supporting point does not relate to the main point.

b. Incorrect: At least one supporting point contains more than one idea.

c. Incorrect: Supporting points are repeated or restated.

d. Incorrect: Parallel supporting points do not have an equal level of importance.

✓ Correct

EXAMPLE:

___b___ Polyester is better than cotton.

    a. It is less expensive and easier to wash.

    b. It lasts longer.

    c. It requires less ironing.

1. _____ Tourists buy many products in the United States.

    a. They buy camera equipment.

    b. They buy toasters.

    c. They purchase kitchen appliances.

    d. They purchase designer clothing.

2. _____ There are many advantages to freeze-drying food.

    a. Foods keep their nutritional value almost indefinitely.

    b. Freeze-dried foods don't require refrigeration.

    c. It's a relatively new technology.

    d. Freeze-dried foods maintain their flavor longer than regular frozen foods.

3. _____ There are many ways to invest your money.

    a. Stocks

    b. Mutual funds

    c. Real estate

    d. Corporate bonds

4. _____ The bank offers a variety of accounts.
    a. Traditional savings accounts
    b. Checking and money-market savings accounts
    c. Retirement accounts

5. _____ Attending college is very expensive.
    a. Tuition fees are quite high.
    b. Prices for books are prohibitive.
    c. Textbooks are extremely expensive.

6. _____ Juvenile delinquency is a nationwide problem.
    a. The Northeast
    b. New York
    c. The Southwest
    d. The Midwest

7. _____ Cats make wonderful pets.
    a. They are easy to care for.
    b. They were worshipped in ancient Egypt.
    c. Cats provide excellent companionship.

8. _____ Reasons for students' parking problems on campus
    a. There are too many students with cars.
    b. Many outsiders illegally park in the lots.
    c. Students could take the bus to campus.

9. _____ Gambling takes many forms.
    a. Casino gambling
    b. Horse racing
    c. Lotteries

10. _____ Ways to fight inflation
    a. Buy things on sale.
    b. Comparison-shop for the best prices.
    c. The annual inflation rate is approximately five percent.

ACTIVITY 2   **Add Supporting Points to a Main Point**

1 **Work in pairs. Fill in appropriate supporting points for each of the main topics.**

  a. I. Safety tips for traveling with pets
    a. _____
    b. _____
    c. _____

  b. I. Countries receiving U.S. exports
    a. In Asia
      1. _____
      2. _____
      3. _____

b. _____

    1. Germany

    2. _____

    3. _____

c. _____

    1. Brazil

    2. _____

    3. _____

c. I. Reasons why dogs should be allowed in restaurants

    a. _____

    b. _____

    c. _____

2 Switch papers with another pair of students. Check each other's outlines to be sure they meet the four basic requirements described on pages 44 and 45. Return the outline you checked and discuss suggestions for improvement with the writers.

ACTIVITY 3 Complete the Outline

1 Work in small groups. Complete the speech outline on pages 48–49 with the missing headings and supporting ideas from the list. Some items have been filled in as examples.

Casino open twenty-four hours a day	Every cabin has a balcony
Olympic-size swimming pool	Guided tours of each port
King-size beds in every cabin	Cartagena, Colombia
Widescreen TV in every cabin	Three elegant restaurants
Shipboard activities	Visits to four exotic places
Water sports	Sailing
Nightly entertainment in ship's nightclub	Ping-pong tournaments
Puerto Plata, Dominican Republic	Costume party
Poolside shuffleboard tournaments	Hiking
Georgetown, Grand Cayman	Passenger talent show
Horseback riding	Guest accommodations
Fishing	

A Fabulous Fantasia Cruise

Introduction

I. Are you wondering what to do for your next vacation? I have the perfect suggestion for all of you. Why not take a cruise?

II. I'm going to tell you about five highlights you can expect on a Fabulous Fantasia Cruise.
   A. Luxurious cabins
   B. Excellent shipboard facilities
   C. Exotic ports of call
   D. Interesting shore-visit activities
   E. Fun shipboard activities

Body

I. _____
   A. Fully air-conditioned cabins
   B. _____
   C. _____
   D. _____

II. Ship's facilities
   A. _____
   B. Swinging disco open all night
   C. _____
   D. _____

III. _____
   A. _____
   B. _____
   C. _____
   D. Cozumel, Mexico

IV. Shore-visit activities
   A. _____
   B. Activities for sports lovers
      1. _____
         a. Waterskiing
         b. _____
         c. _____
      2. Land sports
         a. _____
         b. _____

V. _____

    A. Bingo in captain's lounge

    B. _____

    C. Competitive games

       1. _____

       2. _____

    D. _____

    E. _____

Conclusion

I. I'm sure you will now agree that a Fantasia Cruise would be the perfect vacation.

    A. The passenger cabins are fabulous.

    B. The ship has wonderful facilities for you to enjoy.

    C. You'll visit four unforgettable places.

    D. There are many shore-visit activities.

    E. There are many things to do while aboard the ship.

II. Your dream vacation awaits you. Make your reservation soon and cruise to paradise with Fantasia!

2 Work in small groups. Take turns delivering the parts of the outlined speech to your group members.

IV. Presentation Preview

Your goal is to present a speech about a strong point of view or personal opinion.

ACTIVITY 1 **Listen to a Model Speech**

 Listen to Fatimah's Model Speech. Pay attention to her organization.

Fatimah's Presentation: A Point of View

INTRODUCTION

Attention Getter

I never go out to lunch with friends. I don't go to movies. During the holidays, I can't go home to Egypt to be with my family. Why? I have no money! After paying for my tuition, books, rent, and transportation every month, I have almost no money left. When I applied for my student visa to come to the United States, I *couldn't believe my ears** when I found out I wouldn't be allowed to work full time and go to school at the same time.

* *To be very surprised by what one hears*

Statement of opinion

In my opinion, it isn't fair that most international students aren't allowed to work full time while they're studying in the United States.

Preview

So today, I'd like to present three good reasons why I believe foreign students should be allowed to work as much as they'd like.

First, working would help us pay our many different expenses.

(continued)

(continued)

Second, being in a workplace with Americans would help us improve our proficiency in English.

Third, working would help us learn American customs.

BODY   My first point is that we should be allowed to work as much as we need to in order to help us pay our bills.

Before I came to the United States, I knew it would be expensive to live here, but I didn't realize *how* expensive. The reality is, I don't have enough money to pay for my tuition and living expenses and buy all my textbooks, too. To save money I try to borrow books from friends, but sometimes they can't lend me their books and I can't do my homework. A couple of times I even had to borrow money so I could buy groceries. I felt like this beggar.

[Fatimah shows audience this picture].

Also, I have to share an apartment with four other students. They like to play loud music and I can't study. It stresses me out when they won't be quiet. If I could make more money, I could get an apartment with just one roommate. Then I could have some peace and quiet and get my studying done! Also, during the holidays, I would be able to afford a plane ticket back to Egypt.

OK, my second reason for wanting a full-time job is that it would help me improve my English. I would have the opportunity and the need to practice speaking English more. I would also have more chances to practice listening to different English speakers. So you see, being allowed to have a full-time job would help me learn English faster, and then I would do better in school, too.

My last reason for wanting to work full time is that it would help me learn more about American customs. Depending upon where I worked, I'd see how Americans conduct business and act in different places like offices, restaurants, stores, or sporting events. For example, my friend is a volunteer at a sports stadium. She learned that everyone stands up to show respect when the American national anthem is played at football and basketball games. Learning about customs like these would help me understand Americans better and make friends with them more easily.

CONCLUSION   As you can see, I have some good reasons for my opinion that international students should be allowed to work as much as they want to.

Summary   First, being able to have a full-time job would help us pay our bills.
Second, it would help us improve our English.
Third, it would help us learn more about American customs.

Final Remarks   Before I arrived in the United States, I was sure I'd be able to buy a car and live in a nice apartment. I was positive I'd have enough money to go out to eat and see a movie once in a while. But as they say, *"That's the way the ball bounces!"* If I want to study in the United States, I have to accept the law.

* *You can't control everything that happens*

ACTIVITY 2   **Discuss the Model Presentation**

Discuss these questions in small groups.

1. How did Fatimah get the audience's attention?
2. What did Fatimah say in her preview?
3. How did you know that she was about to state her opinion?
4. How many reasons did Fatimah give to support her opinion? What were they?
5. Did Fatimah's presentation aid make the speech more interesting? How?
6. How did you know when Fatimah was finished explaining her first reason?
7. How did you know when she was about to explain her third reason?
8. Were Fatimah's final remarks effective? Why or why not?

V.   Pronunciation Practice: Contractions

A contraction is the short form of a word or words. Contractions are frequently used in spoken English and are grammatically correct. Use contractions when you speak. They will help your speech sound smooth and natural.

ACTIVITY 1   **Write Contractions**

Listen and repeat the following two-word expressions and their contractions. Write the contractions in the blank spaces.

EXAMPLE: it is <u>it's</u>

1. does not _____
2. I am _____
3. should not _____
4. will not _____
5. he is _____

6. I will _____
7. cannot _____
8. we have _____
9. you are _____
10. is not _____

ACTIVITY 2 **Practice the Sentences**

Listen and repeat the pairs of sentences. The sentences with contractions should sound smooth, natural, and informal compared to those without contractions.

1. a. Omar does not know.
   b. Omar doesn't know.
2. a. I do not think she cares.
   b. I don't think she cares.
3. a. You are coming, are you not?
   b. You're coming, aren't you?
4. a. She is very tall.
   b. She's very tall.
5. a. We are not going.
   b. We're not going.

6. a. It is not funny.
   b. It's not funny.
7. a. Antonio is not a good cook.
   b. Antonio isn't a good cook.
8. a. Leo will not eat cake.
   b. Leo won't eat cake.
9. a. How is the new baby?
   b. How's the new baby?
10. a. They cannot leave now.
    b. They can't leave now.

ACTIVITY 3 **Identify the Contractions**

Read Fatimah's Model Speech on page 49 again. Circle thirteen different contractions and write them in the chart below. Next to each contraction write the full form it represents. The first one is done as an example.

Contraction	Full Form
1. don't	do not
2.	
3.	
4.	
5.	
6.	
7.	
8.	
9.	
10.	
11.	
12.	
13.	

ACTIVITY 4 **Practice the Speech**

Work with a partner. Take turns reading Fatimah's speech aloud. Be sure to pronounce the contractions correctly.

VI. Playing with Sayings: Sayings with Contractions

ACTIVITY 1 Learn the Meaning

Read the following sayings. Check ✓ the ones you heard in Fatimah's Model Speech on page 49. Refer back to the speech if necessary.

_____ 1. **(It's) six of one, half a dozen of another:** Either of two options or choices is equal or acceptable.
My friend asked if I wanted a Pepsi or a Coke. I told him, *"It's six of one, half a dozen of another."*

_____ 2. **You can't fight city hall:** It's useless to fight against a government or large organization.
I gave up trying to convince the tax office they made a mistake on my tax bill. *You can't fight city hall.*

_____ 3. **Can't believe one's ears (eyes):** To be very surprised by what one hears (sees).
I *couldn't believe my eyes* when I saw photos of the earthquake damage.

_____ 4. **Don't count your chickens before they hatch:** Don't rely on an event you expect to happen until it actually occurs.
I thought I was going to get a promotion, so I had a party to celebrate. I didn't get the promotion. Next time, I won't *count my chickens before they hatch.*

_____ 5. **That's the way the ball bounces:** You can't control everything that happens; sometimes you should accept that bad things occur.
I was very upset that the airline lost my luggage and delivered it to my hotel three days late. My sister told me, *"That's the way the ball bounces."*

ACTIVITY 2 Use the Sayings

1 **Work in small groups. Read the following situations. Write the saying from Activity 1 that best applies to each situation.**

a. Sam was sure he was going to win the lottery, so he went out and ordered an expensive car.
_____

b. Aziz was sick during his entire vacation. There was nothing he could do about it.
_____

c. Five thousand people wrote letters to state lawmakers to fight for more money for education. Their efforts didn't do any good. _____

d. My mom asked what color dress I wanted for my birthday. I told her that color wasn't important, that I liked them all equally. _____

e. I was absolutely amazed when I heard the news. I never expected it.
_____

2 **In small groups, tell about a personal experience that matches one of the sayings. Your classmates should guess which saying it matches. Be sure to pronounce contractions clearly.**

EXAMPLE:
Celia: I couldn't decide if I would have more fun going to Disney World or Miami Beach for my birthday. I finally decided that either option would be the same amount of fun.
Classmates: *It was six of one, half a dozen of another.*

VII. Presentation Project: A Point of View

Your project is to prepare and present a two- to three-minutes speech about a strong opinion you have. It could be about an issue, a policy, a situation, an attitude, or someone's behavior.

STEP 1 | Choose a Topic

People have strong feelings about many topics. You can choose one of the following topics or select your own.

a problem in your country	learning a second language	world peace
corruption	punishing criminals	child rearing
lying	gay marriage	a problem in your city
dishonesty	required classes	politicians
gun control	abortion	diets
capital punishment	alcohol	discrimination
an unfair rule	impolite people	cruelty to animals
adopting children	immigration laws	classroom policies

STEP 2 | Plan Your Speech

A Review Fatimah's model speech on page 49.

B Read the following guidelines for organizing your speech.

Introduction
1. Get listeners' attention.
2. State your opinion.
3. Preview the reasons for your opinion.

Body (support with examples and presentation aids)
1. Explain first reason for opinion.
2. Explain second reason for opinion.
3. Explain third reason for opinion.

Conclusion
1. Summarize the reasons for your opinion.
2. Make memorable final remarks.

C Read the Useful Language you can use to express your opinion. Place a check mark ✓ next to the expressions you like best.

USEFUL LANGUAGE: EXPRESSING AN OPINION

_____ In my opinion . . .

_____ It is my firm belief that . . .

_____ I strongly feel that . . .

_____ My point of view is . . .

D Complete the following outline with notes for your speech.

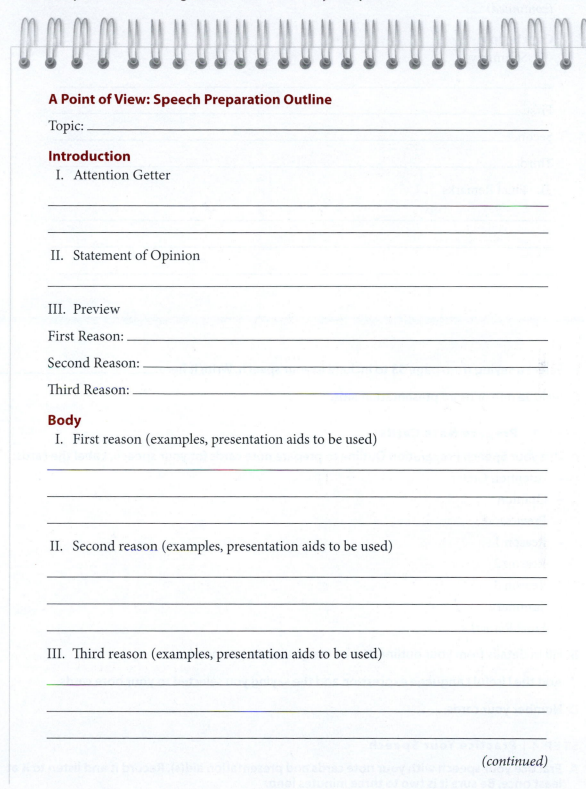

A Point of View: Speech Preparation Outline

Topic: _____

Introduction

I. Attention Getter

_____

_____

II. Statement of Opinion

_____

III. Preview

First Reason: _____

Second Reason: _____

Third Reason: _____

Body

I. First reason (examples, presentation aids to be used)

_____

_____

_____

II. Second reason (examples, presentation aids to be used)

_____

_____

_____

III. Third reason (examples, presentation aids to be used)

_____

_____

_____

(continued)

(continued)

Conclusion

   I. Summary

_____

First: _____

Second: _____

Third: _____

  II. Final Remarks

_____

_____

_____

E Select a saying from page 53 to include in your speech. Write it here: _____

F Include one or more presentation aids.

STEP 3 | Prepare Note Cards

A Use your Speech Preparation Outline to prepare note cards for your speech. Label the cards:
- Attention Getter
- Opinion
- Preview
- Reason 1
- Reason 2
- Reason 3
- Summary
- Final Remarks

B Fill in details from your outline. Use as many cards as you need.

C Add the Useful Language expression and the saying you selected to your note cards.

D Number your cards.

STEP 4 | Practice Your Speech

A Practice your speech with your note cards and presentation aid(s). Record it and listen to it at least once. Be sure it is two to three minutes long.

B Complete the speech checklist. Is there anything you want to change or improve before you present the speech in class?

Speech Checklist

	YES	NO
1. I prepared an attention getter and stated my opinion.	☐	☐
2. I included a preview.	☐	☐
3. I included three reasons for my opinion.	☐	☐
4. I included a summary.	☐	☐
5. I included final remarks.	☐	☐
6. I included a saying from the chapter.	☐	☐
7. I included a presentation aid.	☐	☐
8. I included a Useful Language expression.	☐	☐
9. My pronunciation of contractions is clear.	☐	☐
10. My speech is two to three minutes long.	☐	☐

C Your teacher and/or your classmates may evaluate your speech. Study the evaluation form on page 232 so you know how you will be evaluated. You may use the items on the form to make final changes to your speech.

STEP 5 | Present Your Speech

A Relax, take a deep breath, and present your speech.

B Listen to your audience's applause.

CHAPTER 4

POWERFUL PRESENTATION AIDS

It is an established principle of psychology that people learn far more when information is presented through more than one sense. Tell listeners something and they will remember some of it; tell and *show* listeners and they will remember much more! Audiences enjoy eye-catching, colorful visual aids and interesting, "ear-catching" audio aids. Audio and visual aids enhance a presentation by helping the audience understand and remember your information more easily.

CHAPTER CHALLENGE Speakers use many different types of presentation aids to enhance a speech. When you complete this chapter, you will be able to:

- identify the many different types of presentation aids
- use presentation aids effectively
- plan, create, and present a speech accompanied by a poster display or presentation aids

I. Guidelines for Using Presentation Aids

The following are some general guidelines to observe when giving a speech using presentation aids.

1. Visual and audio aids should have a specific purpose.

They should explain, clarify, illustrate or summarize information from your speech. It should be clear to both you and your audience, why you are using a particular speech aid at a particular place in your presentation.

2. Visual aids should be LARGE enough for everyone to see.

Confirm the visibility of your visual aids by viewing them from the back of the room. If you see them clearly, so will your audience.

3. Audio aids should be loud and distinct enough for everyone to hear.

Listeners should not have to strain to hear recordings or sound effects, nor should they feel compelled to cover their ears due to an uncomfortably loud audio aid.

4. Keep charts, maps, and graphs very simple and uncluttered.

Don't try to show too many details in one visual aid. Less is more!

5. Be sure to look at your audience, not at your aids.

The trick is to maintain eye contact with your listeners while explaining and displaying your visuals. Remember: Do not talk to your aid. Talk to the listeners!

6. Cover all visual aids you are not using, and put them away after you have finished showing them.

For example, if you are starting to speak about the Temple of Heaven in Beijing, don't leave up a picture of the Great Wall of China from an earlier section of your speech.

7. Never pass out objects, photos, or papers during your speech.

If your audience is looking at objects or reading papers, they will not be listening to you.

8. Practice your presentation while using your presentation aids BEFORE you deliver the speech.

Become familiar with your aids by practicing when, where, and how you will use them.

9. Ask an assistant to handle your presentation aids so that you can concentrate on your audience while you are speaking.

Be sure to arrange this with a classmate before the day of your speech.

ACTIVITY Discuss Lectures You Have Attended

1 Work in small groups. Discuss the questions.

   a. Think of your favorite class in high school or university. Did your teachers use many audio or visual aids?

   b. Did the audio or visual aids help you understand and remember the information better? How?

   c. What other presentation aids might have helped improve the class?

   d. Outside of school, have you ever attended a lecture or talk where audio or visual aids were used? How did you the speaker use them?

2 Discuss your answers with the class.

II. Types of Presentation Aids

It is helpful to think of presentation aids in three categories:

- No-tech aids
- Low-tech aids
- Hi-tech aids

A. No-Tech Presentation Aids

No-tech presentation aids do not depend on computer-based technology or machines. Examples are posters, flip charts, black or white boards, and physical objects.

1. Flip charts, posters, black or white boards

These can be used to display a variety of images, including diagrams, graphs, charts, maps, and photographs.

a. Diagrams

Diagrams are simple illustrations that make concepts or descriptions clearer and more vivid.

b. Graphs

- Bar graph

  Use a bar graph to compare rankings. In this graph, the North ranked highest in the first quarter, while the East ranked lowest for the same period.

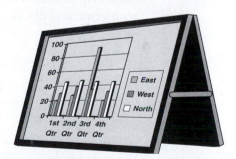

- Pie graph

  Use a pie graph to compare percentages.

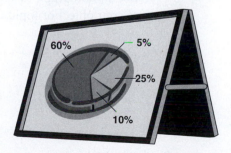

- Line graph

  Use a line graph to show how a trend has changed over time.

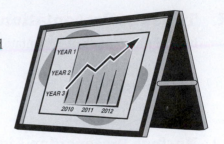

c. **Charts**

- Flow chart

  Use a flow chart to explain the sequence of steps in a process.

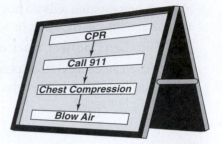

- Bullet chart

  Use a bullet chart to list key points.

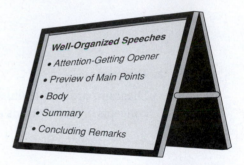

d. **Maps**

Use a map to show location or physical arrangement of places.

e. **Photographs**

Use a photograph to show authentic details of your object or topic.

2. **Physical Objects**

Various types of objects can be used to clarify explanations and help maintain listener interest.

a. **Objects**

Examples could be as various as a scuba mask, paintball equipment, cooking utensils, rocks, large dolls, or even an actual person!

b. Animals

Some students bring in pet parrots, hamsters, snakes, and so forth in their cages as visual aids for speeches.

c. Models of objects

Use a model if an object is too large to display, like an airplane; impossible to display, like the human brain; or too small to display, like a molecule.

HOW TO EXPLAIN YOUR NO-TECH VISUAL AID

1. Tell your listeners what kind of visual aid you are displaying.

   EXAMPLE:
   This is a picture of a victim receiving CPR.

2. Explain what the visual aid is designed to do or show.

   EXAMPLE:
   It shows the correct techniques for administering CPR.

3. Emphasize what listeners should focus on.

   EXAMPLE:
   First, notice how the victim's head is tilted back. Second, notice the placement of the rescuer's hands while doing chest compressions on the victim.

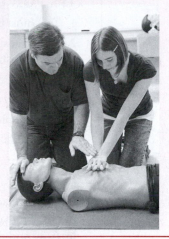

ACTIVITY Brainstorm No-Tech Presentation Aids

1 Work with a partner. Make a list of three or four no-tech visual aids you could use in a speech about the following topics.

EXAMPLE:

How to catch a mouse

I could bring in an actual mousetrap and a toy mouse to show how the trap works.

- Ventriloquism
- Getting rid of bedbugs
- Puppet shows
- Why we should boycott products tested on animals
- Other (choose your own): _____

2 Compare your lists of no-tech visual aids in small groups.

B. Low-Tech Presentation Aids

We are using the term "low-tech" to describe presentation aids that can be displayed or played using equipment other than computers. Examples of such aids are overhead transparencies, films, and audio recordings.

1. Overhead Transparencies

These are clear plastic sheets with text or images imprinted on them. The transparencies are projected onto a white screen or wall using an overhead projector, which enlarges the content so that audience members can see it clearly. Transparencies are very simple and inexpensive to prepare.

Overhead transparencies have several advantages.

- You can create text on a computer and print it out directly onto a transparency.
- You can also photocopy photos and drawings from books directly onto a transparency.
- You can write on transparencies with markers while you are speaking. This is helpful when you want to emphasize important information; for example, by drawing circles around key words or underlining key terms.

TIPS FOR USING TRANSPARENCIES

1. Text must be large enough to be seen from the back of the room.
2. Keep transparencies simple and uncluttered. Use them to display a few important points. Listeners will be distracted if transparencies are too complex.
3. Use the "Progressive Conceal/Reveal Method"
    a. Display information on the transparency little by little rather than all at once.
    b. Use a piece of paper or cardboard to cover the transparency.
    c. Gradually slide the paper or cardboard down to reveal each point you want your audience to see.

---

2. Films

If you have access to a TV and a DVD player, it can be very effective to show a film segment illustrating your subject. Many public libraries maintain collections of DVDs that you can borrow and use as aids in your speeches.

3. Audio

Audio recordings can be very effective presentation aids. Examples include:

- Musical compositions
- Instruments, such as drums beating
- Recordings of voices
- Sound effects (for example, doors slamming, bells ringing, tires screeching, wind blowing, ocean sounds)

If you do not have access to a computer or digital recorder, consider using older technologies such as CD or audiocassette players to play recorded audio segments. You can even try to produce your own sound effects!

TIPS FOR USING AUDIO OR VIDEO SEGMENTS

1. Keep segments short—no more than forty-five seconds for speeches of three to five minutes.
2. When possible, set up your audio or film segment before your audience arrives. Avoid making the listeners wait while you are looking for the segment you want to play. Always test your equipment before starting your speech!
3. Tell your audience what they are going to see or hear and why you are playing the segment.

    EXAMPLE A:

    In her speech "Techniques of Dog Training," one student explained that positive reinforcement was necessary in obedience training. She then played a brief video segment from a home movie showing her brother using positive reinforcement to teach their Doberman the basic obedience commands "Sit" and "Stay."

    EXAMPLE B:

    In his speech entitled "Autism," a student explained several characteristics of autistic adults. He then showed a segment from the movie *Rain Man*, in which actor Dustin Hoffman portrays an autistic adult.

    EXAMPLE C:

    In her speech "Creating a Family Legacy," a student played an audiotape of her grandmother describing life during the Great Depression in the 1930s.

C. Hi-Tech Presentation Aids

Hi-tech presentation aids are those that can be downloaded from the Internet or that require a computer in order to be displayed.

Downloadable Presentation Aids

1. Still Images

You can find thousands of photos, pictures, and illustrations on the Internet. Some databases include images that you can download free of charge. Be aware that it is illegal to download copyrighted images without getting permission or in some cases paying a fee.

To find an image:

a. Go to an image database site such as Google Images.

b. Type a search term in the search bar (be as specific as possible).

c. Click "Search."

d. Select an image that matches your needs and bookmark or download it so that you can access it easily during your presentation.

EXAMPLE A

You need a picture of a poisonous snake for a speech entitled "Medical Uses of Snake Venom." Enter "poisonous snakes" in the search box of the database you are using. In moments you will see hundreds of pictures of different poisonous snakes throughout the world. To limit the number of results, narrow your search further; for example, search for "rattlesnake" or "king cobra."

EXAMPLE B

In a speech to persuade the class that animal abusers should receive mandatory jail sentences, one student showed horrifying photos of abused animals. She found hundreds of photos on the topic by typing the words "animal abuse" in the search box of the image database.

2. Video Clips

On the Internet you can find an endless number of short segments ("clips") of movies, news reports, sports stories, comedy, and much more to enhance your speeches. Some sites (such as YouTube and Vimeo) feature videos created by nonprofessional filmmakers. You can search for video clips following the same procedure as you would for still photos. As with still photos, be careful about segments that require permission or a fee to download.

3. Audio Clips

You can find millions of musical and spoken audio samples on the Internet. In addition, there are many free mp3 files of sound effects online. Try doing a search for "free mp3 sound effects." Then search for the specific sound you want.

ACTIVITY 1   Select Audio and Video Clips

1 Work in small groups. Read the speech topics. List video and audio clips the speakers could try to locate to enhance their presentations.

EXAMPLE:

"How Smoke Detectors Work"

Video clip:	video of an accidental fire igniting in a kitchen, causing the smoke detector to sound
Audio clip:	alarm sound of an activated smoke detector
Audio clip:	beeping sound smoke detectors make when batteries need replacing

a. "My Skydiving Experience"

Video: _____

Audio: _____

b. "Teaching a Parrot to Talk"

Video: _____

Audio: _____

c. "Self-Defense Techniques"

Video: _____

Audio: _____

d. "The Zumba Craze"

Video: _____

Audio: _____

e. "Types of Burglar Alarms"

Video: _____

Audio: _____

2 Search online for clips that match the ones you described. Make a list of those you find. Note the Internet addresses. Share your findings with the members of your group.

Presentation Software

These days more and more speakers are using presentation software (e.g., PowerPoint® and Keynote®) to create dynamic presentations. If you are going to use this technology to your best advantage, you need to learn some basic information about creating great slides and delivering your speech with them.

There are three major aspects to creating effective presentation slides:

- Content (text and art)
- Color
- Font (type and size)

How to Design Great PowerPoint Slides

- Content (Text & Art)
- Color
- Font (Type & Size)

1. Content

Text and art are the most common elements of presentation slides.

- **Text.** Don't fill up a slide with too much text. Use a maximum of twenty words on a slide. If you have a lot of information, divide it among two or more slides.

One way to simplify text is to create keywords and easy-to-remember phrases.

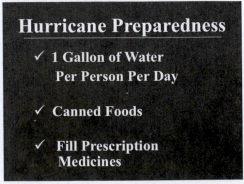

Hurricane Preparedness

Always prepare for a hurricane. It is important to have plenty of bottled water on hand just in case the water supply is contaminated.

A good rule of thumb is to have at least 1 gallon of water per person per day.

Be sure to have plenty of nonperishable canned foods. Also, be sure to fill doctors' prescriptions for medicines before the hurricane hits.

Ineffective Slide

Hurricane Preparedness

- ✓ 1 Gallon of Water Per Person Per Day
- ✓ Canned Foods
- ✓ Fill Prescription Medicines

Effective Slide

Another way to simplify text is to round off numbers.

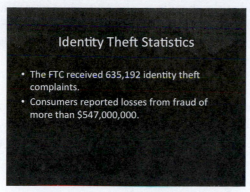

Ineffective Slide   **Effective Slide**

- **Art.** Clip art, pictures, and photographs can greatly enhance your message. Art can be entertaining or humorous. Just don't overdo it. Use a maximum of three pieces of art per slide, and keep illustrations simple.

  This sample slide shows a combination of text and clip art. Notice the short phrases and simple illustrations.

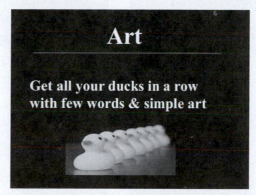

2. Color

Choose one color for the background of your slide, one color for titles, and one color for the text. Be consistent and use the same color combinations for all the slides in your presentation.

- **Background color.** Select a dark color (e.g., black or dark blue.) A dark background tones down the brightness of the projector light and focuses your audience's attention on the content of the slide.

- **Title and text color.** Select light colors that contrast well against a dark background. Shades of yellow or white show up best. Avoid using blues, greens, or reds for text or titles as they won't show up well.

3. Font Type and Size

You will need to choose a font for your slide titles, headings, and text. Most presentation software has dozens of fonts to choose from. Many are not effective for visual aids. Fancy, decorative, and cursive writing fonts are hard to read and can be very distracting. Use font types and sizes that are easy to see and easy to read.

Font Type

- If you prefer *serif* fonts (those that have little feet or tails on each letter), choose fonts such as Times New Roman, Bookman Old Style, or MS Reference Serif.
- If you prefer *sans-serif* fonts (no feet or tails on the letters), choose fonts such as Arial, Verdana, or MS Reference Sans Serif.
- Use the same font on all your slides throughout the entire presentation.

Font Size

- Make slide titles and main headings a minimum of 36 points. Subheadings should be a bit smaller than main headings and larger than text.
- Text should be a minimum of 24 points in size.
- Use uppercase and lowercase letters. Text that is set all in capital letters is difficult to read.

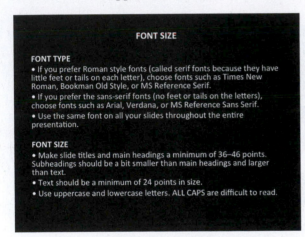

Ineffective Slide   **Effective Slide**

TIPS FOR USING PRESENTATION SOFTWARE

Delivering your speech with presentation software requires careful preparation. You need to be very familiar with your slides. It is important that you coordinate them with your words, maintain eye contact with your audience, and speak clearly—all at the same time! Follow these tips.

Face your Audience at All Times
Position the computer monitor so that it faces you. Look at your monitor to see which slide you're on. There is no need to turn around to look at the large screen.

Focus All of the Attention on YOU Occasionally
Black out the screen and your audience will automatically look at you. This will give you a chance to deliver other segments of your speech, make spontaneous comments, answer questions, and so on, without the audience being distracted by the continuous display of slides.

Use Presentation Slides Sparingly
Presentation software is most effective when the slides supplement your speech. Unfortunately, some speakers end up reading their speech to the audience as the slides are displayed. Avoid overloading your speech with too many slides. Remember: *You* are supposed to be the focus of the presentation, not your slides!

Back Up Your Slide Presentation

Murphy's Law states, "If anything can go wrong, it will." Despite all your hard work and practice, you might be horrified to discover that your equipment hasn't arrived or that the computer or projector doesn't work. There are many ways that technology can disappoint you. We recommend two safety nets:

- **Make copies of all your slides by printing them out on overhead transparency film.** If you are unable to use your presentation software for some reason, you may be able to use an overhead projector to display your transparencies in an emergency.

- **Print out your presentation.** Make a hard copy of your slide presentation. That way, if the electricity fails, you can still deliver your speech. Your notes and printed copies of your slides will act as your outline to trigger your memory.

ACTIVITY 2 **Identify Types of Presentation Aids**

1 Work in small groups. Read the examples of presentation aids for a speech to convince smokers to stop smoking. Identify each example as No (no-tech), Lo (low-tech), or Hi (hi-tech).

_____ a. Overhead transparencies showing a patient smoking in a hospital bed

_____ b. Hand-drawn cartoons showing smokers puffing and coughing outside an office building

_____ c. Pictures from a textbook showing the difference between a smoker's lungs and a nonsmoker's lungs

_____ d. An mp3 sound file of the hoarse, husky voice of a longtime smoker

_____ e. A downloaded video clip of actual lung-cancer surgery

_____ f. A cassette-tape recording of people coughing, gasping for air, or wheezing

_____ g. A YouTube video clip of a lung-cancer survivor breathing through an opening in her neck

_____ h. A slide presentation showing famous people who have died because of lung cancer caused by smoking

2 Work in groups. Choose three topics from the list below. Describe at least one no-tech, one low-tech, and one hi-tech aid for each topic.

how to make a great cup of coffee	the need to reduce highway speed limits
the benefits of eating apples	the health care crisis
drunk driving	global warming
the need for prison reform	boating safety
learning disabilities	interviewing for a job

3 Share your ideas with the rest of the class.

III. Presentation Preview

Many clubs and organizations schedule *poster display sessions*. Speakers set up their posters in a large room. They stand by their displays and speak informally with listeners in a relaxed and friendly environment. The audience has the opportunity to view a variety of posters and interact with different presenters.

In this chapter your goal will be to deliver a three- to four-minute presentation using either a poster display or presentation slides. The speech should be visually interesting, educational, and even entertaining. Your speech will focus on one of the content areas in this textbook, a topic your teacher assigns, or a topic you choose.

 ACTIVITY 1 Listen to a Model Poster Presentation

Listen to Shakira's informal poster presentation. Notice her effective use of visual aids.

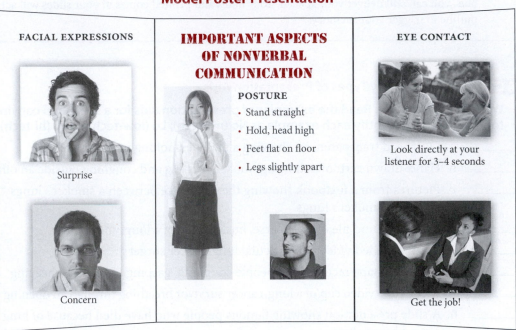

Model Poster Presentation

FACIAL EXPRESSIONS

Surprise

Concern

IMPORTANT ASPECTS OF NONVERBAL COMMUNICATION

POSTURE
- Stand straight
- Hold, head high
- Feet flat on floor
- Legs slightly apart

EYE CONTACT

Look directly at your listener for 3–4 seconds

Get the job!

Introduction
Attention Getter

Shakira:	Hi everyone! Are you ready to have some fun and learn something at the same time?
All Students:	Yes / sure / yeah.
Shakira:	Great. Let's begin.

Preview

My purpose is to review with you three important aspects of nonverbal communication: facial expressions, posture, and eye contact.

I'll begin with facial expressions. *[Shakira points to the left side of her poster, labeled Facial Expressions.]*

Body
Facial expressions are very important when listening and speaking to others. We use many facial expressions to show how we feel. For example, we smile when we are happy; we frown when we are sad. We should change our expressions while we speak and listen to others. Nobody wants to speak to someone who has no expression!

Let's play a little game to see how well you can use and identify different facial expressions. Choose a card from my bag and make the expression written on the card. Whoever guesses it correctly gets a prize! Who wants to go first?

Student 1:   I do!

Shakira: OK, choose a card and make the expression on it. [The volunteer silently reads the word on the card and makes an expression.]

Student 2:   Anger!

Student 1:   No, that's not it.

Student 3:   Fear!

Shakira: BINGO! That's right. You win a candy.

Shakira: OK, let's try another expression. Any volunteers?

Student 3:   I'll try!

Shakira: OK, choose a card. [Student 3 makes the expression on the card.]

Audience: Surprise!

Shakira: You're right! Here's a candy for all of you.

OK. Now that you are "experts" on facial expressions, let's move on and talk about posture. [Shakira points to the label Posture in the center of her poster.]

Your posture is the way you stand. Good posture conveys confidence. You should stand up straight and hold your head erect, like this girl. [Shakira points to a photo on the poster.] Now look at me. How is my posture?

Audience: Excellent.

Shakira: Thank you! Be sure to keep your feet flat on the floor with your legs slightly apart. Try balancing a textbook on your head. [Shakira points to an illustration of a male balancing a book on his head.] If you can do that without the book falling off, you know your posture is good!

Now you know how to practice good posture. Eye contact is the final concept I would like to talk about.

Eye contact is very, very important. Good eye contact shows you are prepared. It really encourages listeners to pay attention to you and to respect you. It also shows you are sincere and honest.

Make sure you look at everyone in your audience when you are speaking. Look directly at each person for three or four seconds, then move on to the next person.

So now you know about facial expressions, posture, and eye contact. Using these three aspects of nonverbal communication will be very important to you in real life. Let me explain how.

For example, if a friend, teacher, or your boss tells you about a serious situation, you would not want to have a blank expression on your face. That would tell them you don't care about the problem. You certainly wouldn't want to have a silly grin on your face. That would tell them you don't think the situation is important. You would want to use a serious or worried facial expression.

Eye contact and good posture are also important in real-life situations, for example, during a job interview. You will not make a good impression on an interviewer if you

(continued)

(continued)

slouch and look down at the floor. Standing or sitting with good posture and looking directly at the interviewer is more likely to help you get the position.

Conclusion
Summary

In summary, I have shared with you what nonverbal communication is and why it is important. I hope you now realize how important facial expressions, posture, and eye contact are when communicating with others.

Final Remarks

Remember, *a picture paints a thousand words**. Your nonverbal communication will make more of an impression on people than what you say!

* An image is more descriptive than words alone

Invite Questions

Now it's time for you to ask me some questions. Please don't be shy! Who has a question for me?

ACTIVITY 2 **Discuss the Model Poster Presentation**

Discuss these questions in small groups.

1. Was Shakira's attention getter effective? Why or why not?
2. What were her main points?
3. How did she involve the audience?
4. How did you know when she was about to discuss a different aspect of nonverbal communication?
5. How could Shakira's poster be improved?
6. In which real-life situations (beside job interviews) does Shakira's poster presentation apply?

ACTIVITY 3 **Listen to A Model Slide Presentation**

In the following model presentation, Shakira delivers a formal speech using a slide presentation. Listen to her speech and pay attention to her use of slides in each section.

Model Slide Presentation: Important Aspects of Nonverbal Communication

Introduction
Attention Getter

Shakira: Have you ever heard the expression, "It's not what you say, but how you say it?" How many of you know what this means? For those of you who may not, I will explain. It means that nonverbal communication is often more important than the actual words you say.

Preview

My purpose today is to review several important aspects of nonverbal communication and how they apply to you in real life.

First, I will discuss the value of using different facial expressions.

Second, I will urge you to have good posture.

Third, I will remind you to maintain good eye contact with your listeners.

Finally, I will explain how these aspects of nonverbal communication will help you in real-life situations.

Preview

1. Facial Expressions
2. Posture
3. Eye Contact
4. Application to Real Life

Transition

I will begin by speaking about facial expressions.

Body

Facial expressions are very important when listening and speaking to others. We use many facial expressions to show how we feel. We smile when we are happy; we frown when we are sad. We must change our expressions while we speak and listen to others. Nobody wants to speak to someone who has no facial expression. There are many facial expressions we can use to show emotions.

Let's play a little game. I will show you a slide of someone making a facial expression. See if you can identify their expression. When you think you know what it is, just call it out.

Let's play a game

(continued)

(continued)

Here's the first expression.

Audience: Unhappy / sad / upset.
Shakira: Yes, that's right.

Now for the second expression.

Audience: Happy.
Shakira: Right again!

Some people think animals show facial expressions too! What human emotion does this dog's expression remind you of?

Audience: Worry!
Shakira: I think so, too.

Transition

OK, you all did a great job identifying the facial expressions. Second, I will talk about posture.

Your posture is the way you stand. Good posture conveys confidence. You should stand up straight and hold your head erect. Look at me. How's my posture?

Audience: Excellent / great / good.

Shakira: Thank you. Be sure to keep your feet flat on the floor with your legs slightly apart.

[Shakira puts a book on her head and demonstrates good posture.]

If you can balance a book on your head without it falling off—like this—you know your posture is good!

[Shakira removes the book from her head and continues.]

Transition

Eye contact is the final aspect of nonverbal communication that I will talk about.

Eye contact is very, very important. It shows people that you have confidence in yourself and what you are saying, that you are prepared and that you want to relate to your audience. It really encourages listeners to pay attention to you and to respect you. It also shows you are sincere and honest.

Transition

Using facial expressions, having good posture, and eye contact will be very important to you in real life. I will now explain why.

If a friend, teacher, or your boss tells you about a serious situation, you would not want to have a bored expression on your face, like this fellow.

(continued)

(continued)

This bored expression tells people you don't care about their problem.

You would want to use a serious or worried facial expression, like this.

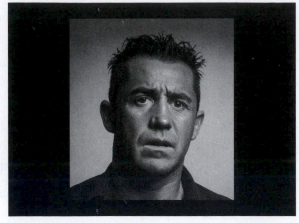

Now think about how important posture and eye contact are during a job interview. You will make a great impression on the interviewer if you stand tall and look directly at him.

Conclusion

Summary

In summary, I have shared with you three aspects of nonverbal communication and why they are important. I hope you now realize how important facial expressions, posture, and eye contact are when communicating with others.

Summary

- **Facial Expressions**
- **Good Posture**
- **Good Eye Contact**
- **Real Life Situations**

Final Remarks

Remember, *a picture paints a thousand words**. Your nonverbal communication might be more important than the words you use!

* *An image is more descriptive than words alone.*

A picture paints a thousand words.

Invite Questions

Well, now it's your turn to speak. Does anyone have any questions or comments?

ACTIVITY 4 **Discuss the Model Slide Presentation**

Discuss these questions in small groups.

1. How did the presentation slides enhance Shakira's speech?
2. Which slides were the most effective? Why?
3. How might Shakira's presentation slides be improved?
4. What advantages does a slide presentation have over a poster display?
5. What disadvantages does it have?

IV. Pronunciation Practice: *-s* as [s], [z], and [əz]

In English, the ending *–s* is used to form plural nouns, third-person present verbs, possessives, and contractions. The *–s* ending can have three different pronunciations. It can sound like [s] (as in *hats*), [z] (as in *dogs*), or [əz] (as in *roses*).

Pronounce -s ending as ...	After ...	Examples
[s]	the voiceless consonants [t], [θ], [p], [k], [f]	steps, bakes, Rafe's, that's, Seth's
[z]	the voiced consonants [d], [ð] (as in brea**the**), [b], [g], [v], [l], [r], [m], [n], [ŋ] (as in si**ng**), and vowels	lives, turns, plays, he's
[əz]	[s], [z], [ʃ] (as in wish), [tʃ] (witch), [ʒ] (as in beige), [dʒ] (as in edge)	buses, washes, speeches

ACTIVITY 1 Practice Saying -s Like [s].

Listen and repeat the short sentences. The final –s in the boldfaced words will sound like [s].

Plural Nouns	Third Person Verbs	Possessives	Contractions
1. Buy new **socks**.	6. He **smokes** a lot.	11. Don't eat the **cat's** food.	16. **Let's** eat.
2. Pet the **cats**.	7. Mom **makes** tea.	12. **Pat's** hat is blue.	17. **It's** true.
3. Fly **kites**.	8. It **tastes** good.	13. The **plant's** leaf fell.	18. **What's** that?
4. Study the **books**.	9. Sue **sleeps** late.	14. **Ralph's** friend left.	19. **That's** nice.
5. Read the **maps**.	10. He **jumps** high.	15. The **truck's** tire is flat.	20. **Jack's** here.

ACTIVITY 2 Practice Saying -s Like [z].

Listen and repeat the short sentences. The final –s in the boldfaced words will sound like [z].

Plural Nouns	Third Person Verbs	Possessives	Contractions
1. Play some **tunes**.	6. Sue **sings** well.	11. **Sue's** book is old.	16. **Here's** a pen.
2. Drive the **cars**.	7. He **sees** me.	12. My **friend's** house is red.	17. **When's** he coming?
3. The **tables** broke.	8. Dad **reads** a lot.	13. The **baby's** milk is sour.	18. **There's** a note.
4. Cover your **ears**.	9. It **smells** nice.	14. Our **teacher's** desk broke.	19. **He's** not home.
5. Send the **letters**.	10. The boy **listens**.	15. The **boy's** toy fell.	20. **She's** fine.

ACTIVITY 3 Practice Saying -s or -es Like the New Syllable [əz]

Listen and repeat the short sentences. The final -s or -es in the boldfaced words will sound like [əz].

Plural Nouns	Third Person Verbs	Possessives
1. Fix the **fences**.	6. He **wishes** for luck.	11. Change the **bus's** tires.
2. Mail the **packages**.	7. The bee **buzzes**.	12. The **witch's** hat is pointed.
3. Time the **speeches**.	8. Sam **catches** the ball.	13. Mr. **Jones's** pen is lost.
4. The **purses** are leather.	9. Dad **washes** his socks.	14. The **rose's** petals are red.
5. **Radishes** are red.	10. She **cashes** her check.	15. The **judge's** robe is black.

ACTIVITY 4 Identify the Sound of the -s Ending

Reread Shakira's slide presentation speech beginning on page 72. Circle twenty-four regular plural nouns, third-person verbs, possessives, and contractions. Write them in the chart.

[s]	[z]	[əz]

ACTIVITY 5 **Practice the Speeches**

Take turns reading the sample speeches aloud with a partner. Be sure to pronounce -s endings correctly.

V. Playing with Sayings: Sayings with -s Endings

ACTIVITY 1 **Learn the Meanings**

Read the following sayings. Check ✓ the ones you heard in the model presentations on pages 70 and 72. Refer back to the speeches if necessary.

_____ 1. **Actions speak louder than words:** It's better to do something than to just talk about it.
She makes promises she never keeps. She has never learned that *actions speak louder than words.*

_____ 2. **Go from rags to riches:** Go from being very poor to very wealthy.
The girl *went from rags to riches* when an aunt left her a fortune in her will.

_____ 3. **Hit the books:** To study.
If I don't *hit the books*, I will fail the class.

_____ 4. **A leopard can't (doesn't) change its spots:** People can't change their character or the way they are.
The day after being released from prison, the car thief stole another car. *A leopard doesn't change its spots!*

_____ 5. **A picture paints a thousand words:** An image is much more descriptive than words alone.
It was easier to e-mail my mom a picture of my new car rather than describe it. *A picture paints a thousand words.*

ACTIVITY 2 **Use the Sayings**

1 Fill in each blank with the saying that best fits the sentence.

EXAMPLE:

I have to _hit the books_ this weekend if I want to pass the test on Monday.

1. The homeless man went _____ when he won the lottery.

2. My cousin has always been rude and impolite. His girlfriend broke up with him because he was so unpleasant, but he's still just as nasty. I guess _____.

3. My friend talks about going back to school but never does it. I told her, "_____."

4. My classmate didn't want to _____, so he went to a party instead.

5. I always use visual aids in my speeches because I know that _____.

2 Practice reading your sentences in small groups. Be sure to pronounce the -s and -es endings correctly.

VI. Presentation Project: A Speech with Presentation Aids

Your project is to prepare and present a three- to four-minute speech using a poster display or presentation software.

STEP 1 | Choose a Topic

Your presentation can focus on an aspect of speech communication or any of the other topics presented in this chapter. Limit your topic to a few practical tips or ideas that would be helpful to the audience.

Possible topics related to speech communication include:

- How to develop self-confidence when speaking in public
- How to use effective body language
- How to use effective vocal characteristics
- How to rehearse a presentation
- How to outline information clearly
- How to develop presentation aids

STEP 2 | Plan Your Speech

A Review Shakira's sample presentations on pages 70 and 72.

B Read the following instructions for organizing your speech.

Introduction

1. Begin with an attention getter.
2. Preview your main points.

Body

1. Explain the first subtopic.
   - Use presentation aids.
   - Give examples.
   - Involve the audience.
2. Explain the second subtopic.
   - Use presentation aids.
   - Give examples.
   - Involve the audience.
3. Explain the third subtopic.
   - Use presentation aids.
   - Give examples.
   - Involve the audience.
4. Explain how the concepts relate to real life.
   - Work
   - School
   - Home

Conclusion

1. Summarize your main points.
2. Make final remarks.

Invite Audience Questions

C Read the Useful Language you can use to invite and then acknowledge questions. Place a check mark ✓ next to the expressions you like best.

USEFUL LANGUAGE: INVITING QUESTIONS

_____ Does anyone have any questions?

_____ Who has a question for me?

_____ Come on, don't be shy! Ask me questions!

USEFUL LANGUAGE: ACKNOWLEDGING QUESTIONS

_____ That's a great question.

_____ I'm so glad you asked that question.

_____ I bet everyone wants to know the answer to your question.

D Select a saying from page 79 to include in your speech. Write it here:

_____.

STEP 3 | Create Your Poster Display or Slide Presentation

A If you choose to use a poster display, decide whether to show the entire poster at once, as Shakira did, or whether to hide part of the content until you are ready to discuss it.

(a) Poster with some content hidden.

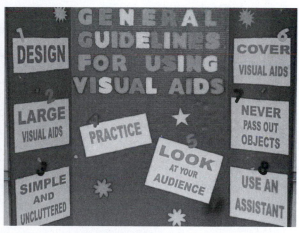
(b) Poster with all content displayed.

B If you select a slide presentation, create slides that make your information come alive and engage your audience. Review the tips for using presentation software on pages 65–69.

C Complete the following outline for your speech.

Speech Preparation Outline

Topic: _____

Introduction
Attention Getter

_____

_____

Preview

_____

First main point: _____

Second main point: _____

Third main point: _____

Importance of main points in real life

Transition

_____

Body
First Main Point (examples, explanations, presentation aids to be used)

_____

_____

Transition

_____

Second Main Point (examples, explanations, aids)

_____

_____

Transition

_____

Third Main Point (examples, explanations, aids)

_____

_____

_____

Transition

_____

How Concepts Relate to Real Life (examples, explanations, slides)

_____

_____

_____

Conclusion
Summary

_____

First main point: _____

Second main point: _____

Third main point: _____

Importance of these concepts in real life

Final Remarks

_____

_____

_____

STEP 4 | Prepare Note Cards

A Use the outline in Step 3 to prepare note cards for your speech. Label the cards:
- Attention Getter
- Preview
- 1st Main Point
- 2nd Main Point
- 3rd Main Point
- Relevance to Real Life
- Summary
- Final Remarks

B Fill in details from your outline. Use as many cards as you need.

C Write the Useful Language and the saying you selected on your note cards.

D Number your cards.

STEP 5 | Practice Your Speech

A Practice your speech with your note cards and poster or PowerPoint® slides. Record it and listen to it at least once. Make sure it is between three and four minutes.

B Complete the checklist. Is there anything you want to change or improve before you present it to an audience?

Speech Checklist	YES	NO
1. My introduction included an attention getter and a preview.	❏	❏
2. I created a poster or presentation slides.	❏	❏
3. I explained my main points using examples.	❏	❏
4. I explained how the main points apply to real life.	❏	❏
5. I involved the audience.	❏	❏
6. My conclusion included a summary.	❏	❏
7. I included a saying from the chapter.	❏	❏
8. I invited questions from the audience.	❏	❏
9. I included a Useful Language expression.	❏	❏
10. My pronunciation of words with -s and -es endings is correct.	❏	❏
11. My speech is between 3 and 4 minutes	❏	❏

C Practice again with your note cards and poster or presentation slides.

D Your teacher and/or your classmates may evaluate your speech. Study the evaluation form on page 233 so you know what your listeners expect to hear and how you will be evaluated. You may use the checklist to make final changes to your speech.

STEP 5 | Present Your Speech

A Relax, take a deep breath, and present your speech.

B Listen to your audience's applause.

CHAPTER 5
SPEAKING TO INFORM

Informative speaking is all around us. It is something most of us do every day. Whenever we give directions to someone, explain a problem to a mechanic, or describe an illness to a doctor, we are speaking to inform.

Any speech is informative if it presents information to an audience. A student report, a teacher's lecture, and a talk about fire safety at a neighborhood meeting are all examples of the types of informative speeches you are likely to hear or give.

CHAPTER CHALLENGE Your challenge in this chapter will be to learn how to present information simply and clearly so that listeners can understand and remember it easily. When you complete this chapter, you will know how to:

- analyze an audience
- choose and research a topic
- outline and organize information
- plan, prepare, and present a speech to inform.

I. Preparing for the Informative Speech

You build an informative speech the way you build a house. For both projects, you first need a blueprint, a vision of what you want to build. The steps for preparing an informative speech are:

- Analyzing your audience
- Choosing your topic
- Narrowing your topic
- Gathering information
- Preparing presentation aids
- Organizing your speech

If you follow these steps, or this blueprint, you will create an informative speech that is well organized, interesting, and memorable.

1. Analyze the Audience
2. Choose a Topic
3. Narrow the Topic
4. Gather Information
5. Prepare Presentation Aids
6. Organize Your Speech

A. Analyzing Your Audience

Start preparing for your informative speech by getting as much information about your audience as you can. Knowing about your audience will help you prepare a speech that is relevant and interesting to your listeners. Here's what you need to know:

1. Analyze the Audience

Age Range

What is the age range of your audience? What topics would interest them? If they are college age, an appropriate speech topic might be choosing a career. However, if they are middle-aged, a good topic might be planning for retirement.

Gender

What is the gender of your audience? If there are both men and women, choose a topic that is interesting to both. On the other hand, if there are only men or only women, you can choose a topic of specific interest to that group.

Occupation(s)

Is your audience made up of college students who also have jobs? If so, where do they work? What do they do? If members of your audience have occupations in common, you could build your speech on this shared background.

Economic Level(s)

What is the financial position of your audience? You would not, for example, try to inform the average college student about how to negotiate the purchase of a luxury yacht. However, it might be a great topic for a group of wealthy retirees.

General Background

Are your listeners married? Do they have children? What are their attitudes, habits, and religious beliefs? It would not be appropriate, for example, to talk to vegetarians about the best steak restaurants in Buenos Aires. Similarly, people who don't smoke would probably not be interested in a speech about different types of cigars. Your goal is to choose a topic that is of interest to everyone. In this class your classmates will be your audience for most speeches.

ACTIVITY 1 Survey Your Classmates

1 Work in groups of four or five students. Take turns reading the questions in the chart. All group members should answer each question. Use the chart to record your classmates' responses.

Personal Information Survey
1. How old are you? _____
2. Where were you born? _____
3. How long have you lived here? _____
4. Where else have you lived? _____
5. What languages do you speak? _____
6. What countries have you visited? _____
7. What is your major? _____
8. If you have a job, what do you do? _____
9. What is your marital status? _____
10. Do you have any children? How many? How old are they? ___
11. What are your special interests or hobbies? _____

2 Repeat Step 1 with a different group of students.

3 Now use the information you wrote in the chart to analyze your audience. Answer the questions. Discuss your answers with a partner.

    a. What are two topics that would be interesting and suitable for this audience?

    b. What are two topics that would be unsuitable?

B. Choosing Your Topic

2. Choose a Topic

After you have analyzed your audience, your next task is to select a topic that will interest your listeners and appeal to you as well. It's always a good idea to pick a topic that you know a lot about or that really interests you. Study these examples from an actual speech class.

Topic	Examples
• An experience you remember vividly	A student who had gone for a hot-air balloon ride while on vacation in Australia spoke enthusiastically about hot-air balloons.
• Something you care about deeply	A student who had come to the United States from Poland at the age of 18 gave an excellent speech about problems facing immigrants in a new country.
• Something you are skilled or experienced at doing	A Colombian student who was in business with her father buying and selling emeralds gave a terrific speech about emeralds.
• A subject you are knowledgeable about	A student who had been collecting stamps since he was 9 years old made an excellent speech about the history of the postage stamp.

ACTIVITY Brainstorm Topics

1 Think of personal interests, experiences, skills, or abilities you have. Write them in the chart. Explain why these would be good topics for a speech to inform.

Possible Topics	Reason
postage stamps	My hobby is stamp collecting.
skydiving	My parents own a skydiving school.
asthma	My little sister suffers from asthma.

2 Work with a partner. Share your topics and reasons. Find out if your partner would be interested in learning about the topics you selected.

C. Narrowing Your Topic

3. Narrow the Topic

The next step in your speech preparation is to narrow your topic. It is important to do this as it is impossible to say everything about a topic in a short speech. How do you narrow an informative speech topic effectively? Ask yourself these questions:

Is Your Topic Specific?

Limit your topic to one particular aspect. For example, the topic "Hurricanes" is too general, but the topics "Preparing for hurricanes" and "Dangerous effects of hurricanes" are specific. "Soccer" is too broad, but "The history of soccer" or "The basic rules of soccer" could be covered in a short speech.

Does Your Topic Contain Only One Idea?

Make sure your topic covers just one idea. For example, the topic "Choosing a hotel and buying a car in a foreign country" contains two ideas, but the topics "Choosing a hotel in a foreign country" or "Buying a car in a foreign country" contain one idea each.

Is Your Topic Achievable?

Make sure the audience is actually able to act upon, understand, or remember your information after your speech is over.

EXAMPLE A:

If you give a "how to" speech on "How to Weave a Persian Rug," your audience will not be able to weave a Persian rug after hearing your speech because the task is too complicated. However, the topic "How to Buy a Persian Rug" is achievable since your listeners would be able to use this information if they ever went shopping for a Persian carpet.

EXAMPLE B:

After hearing a speech called "Building a Personal Computer," most people would not be able to build a personal computer. However, they would be able to remember valuable information about "Using a Computer to Improve Your English Pronunciation."

ACTIVITY 1 Evaluate the Topics

1 Work with a partner. Indicate whether the topics are appropriate by labeling them as follows:

a. Too general

b. Contains more than one idea

c. Not achievable in a brief speech

✓ Good topic

EXAMPLES:

_____a_____ South America

_____c_____ How to become a concert pianist

_____✓_____ The significance of dreams

__b__ ✗ 1. Electronic watches and calculators

__a__ 2. Musical instruments

__c__ 3. How to fly an airplane

✓ __a__ 4. Applying for a bank loan

__a__ 5. Snakes

__✓__ 6. Life-saving uses of snake venom

__b__ 7. The history of Hawaii and Alaska

__✓__ 8. The use of marijuana in medicine

__✓__ 9. Chinese New Year traditions

__c__ 10. How to rebuild your car's engine

2.

2 Discuss your answers with the class.

ACTIVITY 2 **Narrow the Topics**

1 Work with a partner. Narrow the following topics in three different ways.

1. Dogs

   a. _____

   b. _____

   c. _____

2. Alaska

   a. _____

   b. _____

   c. _____

3. Learning a Foreign Language

   a. _____

   b. _____

   c. _____

2 Share your answers with the class.

D. Gathering Information

4. Gather Information

Now that you have analyzed your audience, chosen your topic, and narrowed it, you need to gather information so you can prepare your speech. Try to find more information about your topic than you can use. You will then be able to choose which information to include in your speech instead of having to "stretch" your facts to fill time. This extra knowledge may also be helpful when you answer questions after your presentation. There are two places to look for material for your speech:

- Within yourself: Write down what you already know about the topic.
- Outside yourself: Either interview people who know something about your topic, or do research in the library or on the Internet.

Interviews

One way to gather information is to interview people who know something about your topic. Search out experts in your school or community. Your peers, teachers, or acquaintances may also have knowledge about your topic.

Before you interview anyone, decide what questions you will ask. There are five basic types of questions that you can use:

1. **Open-Ended Questions** (general information questions requiring the respondent to elaborate):
   - How do you feel about the recent scandal in our city government?
   - What do you think about the new energy drink on the market?

2. **Yes/No Questions** (questions requiring a simple *yes* or *no* response):
   - Do you think the new mayor should be removed from office?
   - Has an airline ever lost your luggage?

3. **Scale Questions** (questions requiring the respondent to rank a topic on a scale):
   - How would you rate our city government?
     Poor   Fair   Average   Good   Excellent

4. **Directed Response Questions** (specific information questions requiring the respondent to provide the requested information):
   - Could you give me two reasons why students might cheat on tests?
   - Who is the mayor of New York City?

5. **Multiple-Choice Questions** (questions requiring the respondent to choose from two or more provided answers):
   - How many books does the average college graduate read in a year?
     _____ None   _____ One to ten   _____ Ten to twenty   _____ Over twenty

ACTIVITY 1   Practice Interviewing

1 Choose one of the topics below and prepare five different types of interview questions you could ask your classmates about it. Write your questions on the lines.

favorite places to go on vacation	favorite movies
weekend plans	sleeping habits

Topic: _____

a. _____ (Open-ended question)

b. _____ (Yes/No question)

c. _____ (Scale question)

d. _____ (Directed response question)

e. _____ (Multiple-choice question)

2 Work in small groups. Take turns asking one another your interview questions.

Library Research

Despite the popularity of the Internet, college and public libraries remain popular places to find information in books, magazines, newspaper articles, and journals. If you can't find what you're looking for, you can ask the reference librarian for help.

It's helpful to record every useful piece of information, fact, or quotation on a note card. Be sure to write down the important bibliographical information about your source. This includes:

- Author's name
- Author's credentials
- Title or name of the book, magazine, newspaper, or article; the publisher; and date of the publication

Recording this information on cards makes it easy to locate and cite your sources during your speech. Listeners like to know the source and reliability of a speaker's information. You also establish your own credibility as a speaker when you cite your sources.

Let's say you were preparing a speech about identity theft. You did your research and found many good sources of information. One of your bibliography cards might look like this:

BOOK TITLE:	*IDENTITY THEFT*
Author:	John R. Vacca
Credentials:	Security consultant and computer security official for NASA and the International Space Station Program; internationally known author of 30 books and 400 articles on Internet security.
Publisher:	Pearson Education, Inc. 2003
Quote:	"Identity theft is the appropriation of an individual's personal information to impersonate that person in a legal sense."

Here is a source citation from a student's speech about identity theft:

Some of you might be wondering, "What exactly is identity theft?" Internationally known author and security consultant John R. Vacca defines this crime in his book entitled Identity Theft, published by Pearson Education in 2003. He states, "Identity theft is the appropriation of an individual's personal information to impersonate that person in a legal sense."

TIP

Arrange your bibliography note cards in alphabetical order.

After your speech, a listener may ask for more information about one or more of your sources. You can then look through your note cards and quickly find information about your source's credentials.

Internet Research

Nowadays, the Internet is the most popular source of information about most topics. Use it wisely to help you gather information for your speeches. The last three letters of a Web page address ("URL") are called "extensions." URL extensions give you important information about the type of Internet site they represent. The following chart explains what some common extensions mean.

URL Extension	Types of Organizations	Example Sites

.gov	Government agencies, e.g.,
	    Immigration and Naturalization Service
	    Food and Drug Administration
	    NASA Space Agency
		
		www.ins.gov
		www.fbi.gov
		www.nasa.gov

.org	Nonprofit groups, e.g.,
	    Wikipedia
	    Science Digest
	    Central Intelligence Agency World Fact Book
		
		www.wikipedia.org
		www.sciencedigest.org
		www.cia-world-fact-book
		  .findthedata.org

.edu	Educational institutions, e.g.,
	    Harvard University
	    University of Virginia
		
		www.harvard.edu
		www.uva.edu

.mil	Military groups, e.g.,
	    The Army
	    The Navy
		
		www.army.mil
		www.navy.mil

.com or .net	Businesses or for-profit commercial sites, e.g.,
	    Dell Computers
	    American Telephone and Telegraph
		
		www.dell.com
		www.att.net

A Word about Wikipedia Wikipedia is a free, online encyclopedia. There are many advantages to using Wikipedia. It has easy-to-find, relevant information about virtually any subject, explained in clear, simple terms. Information in Wikipedia is often updated by the minute, so out-of-date content is quickly replaced. Wikipedia invites alternative viewpoints, so readers can get a complete picture of the current status of their topic. Entries include sources at the bottom of the page that can direct you to other useful websites, books, and so forth.

However, Wikipedia has disadvantages, also. As anyone can edit almost any page, readers can't always be sure of the accuracy of the information. Many entries lack detail. We advise readers to look for information in other sources besides Wikipedia. Compare the Wikipedia content with information you have or find elsewhere. As long as you are willing to confirm Wikipedia's accuracy, it is a great starting point for finding information about a subject.

Evaluating a Website You know how to search for material on the Internet. But how reliable is the material you find? Many websites provide inaccurate, biased propaganda disguised as "good" information. It is important to learn how to evaluate the quality of the websites you visit in order to decide if the information is trustworthy.

The following questions will help you sort out the "gems from the junk" on the Internet. Use the acronym PACO—Purpose, Authority, Content, Objectivity—to help you evaluate the quality of the website.

1. Purpose
   a. Is it commercial (written to sell something)?
   b. Is it persuasive (written to advance a cause or controversial policy)?
   c. Is it informative (written to educate the reader)?
   d. Is it a hoax (written to trick or fool the reader)?

2. Authority
   a. Who are the authors or sponsors of the website?
   b. What are the qualifications of the authors? (If you can't find any information about the author or sponsor, be suspicious about the information you find.)
   c. Do the authors have sufficient authority to write about the topic? (If so, then the information is most likely accurate.)

3. Content
   a. Is the content relevant to your topic or question?
   b. Is the information clearly presented?
   c. Is the information on the website up-to-date? (Look for the date the website was created. If it is not recent, the information might no longer be accurate.)
   d. Does the content contain spelling or grammatical mistakes? (Information written carelessly often contains inaccuracies.)
   e. Does the website provide a list of references? (A site with verifiable references is likely to have accurate information.)

4. Objectivity
   a. Is the content biased or objective? How do you know?
   b. How does the bias affect the usefulness of the information?

ACTIVITY 2 **Evaluate a Website**

1 Choose a topic from the list below and type it in the search bar of an Internet search engine. Select one of the sites from the list the search engine returns to you. Click on any links within the site to better evaluate the site's content.

preventing malaria	tax return preparation tips
treatment for depression	avoiding illness when travelling
causes of homelessness	motorcycle safety

2 Fill in the information about the site you selected.
   a. Topic: _____
   b. Website URL: _____
   c. What is the purpose of the site? _____
   d. Who wrote the information?

   _____

   e. Does the site provide links to other sites? Which ones?

   _____

   f. Does the information appear to be objective? How can you tell?

   _____

   g. How current is the information on the site? When was the site last updated?

   _____

   h. Did you find any careless errors on the site? If so, what types of errors?

   _____

3 Work in small groups. Discuss: Does the site you visited appear to be reliable? Why or why not? Refer to the elements in PACO.

A Word about Plagiarism

The *Longman Dictionary of American English* defines plagiarism as "the act of taking someone else's words, ideas, etc. and copying them, pretending that they are your own." In other words, plagiarism is stealing; it is a crime for which you could be expelled from your college or university. While many speakers realize the importance of giving credit to authors of books and newspaper or magazine articles, they often forget to cite sources when they use information from the Internet in their presentations. You will be guilty of plagiarism if you don't credit your Internet sources.

Citing Internet Sources

When citing Internet sources, be sure to specify the author's name when available, the website name, and the date. It is not enough to simply say, "According to the Internet" or "I found the following information on the World Wide Web." You must be more specific.

For example, here is an excerpt from an informative speech about identity theft. Notice how the speaker cited three Internet sources, using two in his introduction and the third in his transition to the body.

> **INTRODUCTION**
>
> In 2011, *The Washington Post* online reported that over 8.5 million Americans were identity-theft victims. In the same year, the United States Department of Justice website put the number at close to 12 million!
>
> What does this tell you? Clearly, identity theft is a serious crime affecting millions of people yearly.

> **TRANSITION TO BODY**
>
> I will begin by explaining how identity thieves are able to steal your personal information.
>
> I found this information on the official website of the Federal Trade Commission.

E. Preparing Presentation Aids

Always plan to include audio or visual aids in your speech to inform. As discussed in Chapter 4, these presentation aids help your audience to see and experience what you are talking about.

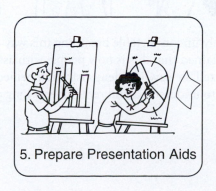

5. Prepare Presentation Aids

EXAMPLE A:

In a speech about the increasing population in the United States, a student prepared a poster with the following bar graph to help listeners see and remember statistics about population growth.

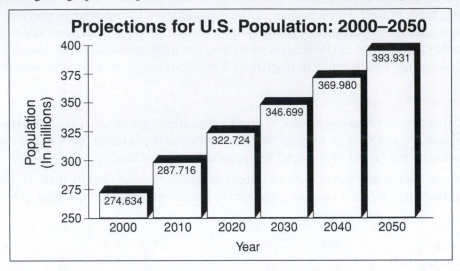

EXAMPLE B:

In a speech about asthma, a student conducted a demonstration that involved the whole class. She gave the audience drinking straws. She instructed them to hold their noses and to inhale and exhale through the drinking straw placed between their lips.

The students were extremely uncomfortable breathing this way and felt as though they would suffocate. The speaker explained that this is how people with asthma feel when attempting to breathe through a constricted airway. The demonstration helped the audience to "experience" the information as well as to understand and remember it long after the speech ended.

F. Organizing Your Speech

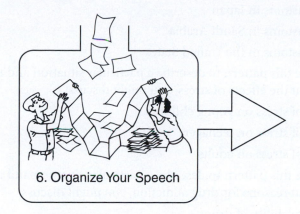

6. Organize Your Speech

Having completed your research and prepared visual aids, the next step is to organize your speech. As a reminder, a good informative speech includes the following components:

Attention getter	Summary
Preview	Final remarks
Body	Transitions

STEP 1 | Prepare the Body

First, prepare the body of your speech. Arrange the main points in a clear, logical manner. This involves choosing an organization pattern that fits your topic. Read about eight common organizational patterns below.

1. **Past-Present-Future.** Use this pattern to discuss how something once was, how it has changed, and how it will be in the future. For example, in discussing the evolution of the Olympic games, you might organize your information under the following three headings:

   I. The history of the Olympics

   II. The Olympics today

   III. The future of the Olympics

2. **Chronological Order.** Use this pattern to describe how events, activities, or processes happen by the hour, part of the day, week, month, or year. It can also be used to explain the steps in a process. For example, in speaking about making a speech, you might organize your information under the following headings:

   I. Choosing a topic

   II. Gathering information

   III. Making an outline

   IV. Presenting the speech

3. **Problem-Solution.** Use this pattern to speak about a specific problem and ways to solve it. (Note: A problem isn't always a negative situation like crime or child abuse. It can also be a positive situation, such as choosing a career or deciding where to go on vacation.) For example, in speaking about the problem of choosing the college that's right for you, you might present the following solutions:

   I. Read different college catalogues.

   II. Visit campuses of different colleges.

   III. Talk to people who attend various colleges.

   IV. Talk to teachers at the colleges you are considering.

4. **Location.** Use this pattern to divide a topic into different geographical locations. For example, in speaking about interesting marriage customs, you might use the following sequence:

    I. Marriage customs in Japan

    II. Marriage customs in Saudi Arabia

    III. Marriage customs in the United States

5. **Cause-Effect.** Use this pattern to describe a particular situation and its effects. For example, in speaking about the effects of stress, you might discuss:

    I. The effects of stress on young children

    II. The effects of stress on teenagers

    III. The effects of stress on adults

6. **Effect-Cause.** Use this pattern to describe a particular situation and its causes. For example, in speaking about reasons for drug addiction, you might discuss:

    I. The easy availability of drugs

    II. The need to escape from the pressures of work

    III. The lack of education about harmful effects of drugs

7. **Advantages-Disadvantages.** Use this pattern to talk about both positive and negative aspects of a topic in a balanced, objective manner. For example, in speaking about the death penalty for those convicted of first degree murder, you might discuss:

    I. Advantages of capital punishment

    II. Disadvantages of capital punishment

8. **Related Subtopics.** Use this pattern to divide one topic into different parts, or subtopics. For example, in speaking about false advertising, you might discuss:

    I. False advertising on television

    II. False advertising in magazines

    III. False advertising on the radio

ACTIVITY 1 **Recognize Organizational Patterns**

1 **Work with a partner. Indicate the organizational pattern of each speech summarized below by labeling them as follows:**

a. Past-Present-Future   e. Cause-Effect

b. Chronological Order   f. Effect-Cause

c. Problem-Solution   g. Related Subtopics

d. Location   h. Advantage-Disadvantage

EXAMPLES:

    _c_   In a speech about high school dropouts, Mary presented a series of suggestions for parents and teachers to follow in order to help teenagers do well in high school. She also suggested that students should help and encourage each other to graduate from high school, and presented research proving that schools that organize peer-counseling opportunities for students have reduced their dropout rates significantly.

    _f_   José also spoke about high school dropouts. He discussed some reasons why students drop out of school. He pointed out that some students don't receive encouragement at home, while others need money to help support their families, so they leave school to get jobs. Also, teen pregnancy causes many young women to drop out of high school as they have no one to help care for their babies.

    _____ 1. In a speech about looking for a job, Kim explained that the first thing to do is to prepare a résumé. The second thing to do is to find available job openings by doing online searches, reading the employment section in the newspaper, and networking with friends and family. Kim said the last thing to do is to schedule job interviews and pray a lot!

_____ 2. In a speech about casino gambling laws, Michelle chose three countries in which casino gambling is legal—the United States, Peru, and Switzerland. She then described the different laws governing casino gambling in each country.

_____ 3. In a speech about the evolution of the automobile, Jean described cars of sixty years ago and how hard they were to drive. She then talked about the automatic cars we have today with their many modern features. Finally, she said that someday cars would be driven by computers to reduce the number of accidents caused by human error.

_____ 4. In a speech about saving money, Hector said that saving money is a problem because most products are very expensive. He suggested that some good ways to save money are to comparison-shop for the best prices, buy things on sale, search for store coupons online, and substitute less expensive foods for more expensive ones.

_____ 5. In a speech about a day in the life of a teacher, Luisa talked about early-morning preparation, classroom teaching, and after-school activities.

_____ 6. In a speech about entertainment in his city, Claude talked about entertainment for music lovers, entertainment for art lovers, and entertainment for theater lovers.

_____ 7. In a speech about parrots as pets, Kimiko spoke about the drawbacks as well as the benefits of having parrots over other types of pets.

_____ 8. In a speech about hybrid cars, Aziz discussed how hybrid cars work, proper maintenance of hybrid cars, and safety aspects of hybrid cars.

_____ 9. In a speech about obesity in the United States, Nancy talked about how doctors define obesity. She then explained that many people are obese because they don't exercise, don't eat right, and lack the motivation to go on diets.

_____ 10. In a speech about diamonds, Antoine stated that diamonds are classified by the three Cs: cut, color, and clarity. He then explained each of these characteristics in more detail.

2 Discuss your answers in small groups.

ACTIVITY 2 Develop Outlines from Topics

1 Work in small groups. Choose one of the following topics for a speech to inform. Prepare three outlines for the body of the speech. Each outline should use a different organizational pattern and should include at least three main headings. (Use your imagination; be humorous if you like!)

being an only child	living alone
being married or being single	living with a roommate
owning a car or not owning a car	being a working student
living in a small town or village	getting fired from a job
living in a large city	traveling alone
having a boyfriend or girlfriend	having children
owning a pet	retiring
owning a home	renting an apartment

Topic: Ways to Survive with No Money
Organizational Pattern: Problem-Solution

    I. Ask friends to invite you to dinner every night.

    II. Save money in restaurants.

        A. Order hot water.

        B. Pour ketchup into the hot water to make tomato soup.

    III. Ask teachers to let you sleep in their offices to save on rent.

    IV. Borrow clothes from a friend.

2 **Share your outlines with the class.**

STEP 2 | Prepare a Preview

After deciding on an organizational pattern and determining the main headings in the body of your speech, you need to plan what you will say in your speech preview. This should be easy because you already determined what you will cover in the body of your speech. In the following examples, notice how the speaker clearly stated the purpose of the speech and numbered the subpoints. Thus, the audience knows exactly what the speaker is going to discuss.

EXAMPLE A:

My purpose today is to tell you what to do in the event of a hurricane. I will cover three important topics:

    A. First, how to prepare for a hurricane

    B. Second, what safety measures to take during a hurricane

    C. Third, what to do after the storm is over

EXAMPLE B:

This morning, I will discuss three interesting aspects of being left-handed:

    A. First, I'll explain why some people are born left-handed.

    B. Second, I'll discuss why left-handed people have more accidents than right-handed people.

    C. Third, I'll discuss how society discriminates against left-handed people.

STEP 3 | Prepare an Attention Getter

At the beginning of your speech, it is very important to grab your audience's attention and get them interested in what you have to say. There are several ways to do this.

1. **Ask Your Audience a Series of Rhetorical Questions.** Rhetorical questions are asked for dramatic effect; no answers are expected. The following rhetorical questions were used to open a speech about the process of getting a tattoo:

    What can cost ten dollars or a thousand dollars?
    What can be every color of the rainbow?
    What can be with you as long as you live?
    What can you wear on your arm, your cheek, your leg, or even your back?

2. **Tell a Story.** People love to listen to a story. They want to find out what it is about. This story was used to open a speech about the Gold Museum in Bogotá, Colombia:

    A guard took me into a square room with no lights. The room was so black, I couldn't even see my own feet. All of a sudden, a hidden electric wall closed behind me. There was no way out. I thought I was in a tomb. All at once, bright lights came on. I was surrounded by gold on all four sides!

3. **State a Surprising Fact.** The statement below was used to introduce a speech about the billion-dollar business of bartering. The speaker talked about ways to trade skills, services, or products to get almost anything you want without cash:

   You can get almost anything you want without cash! And you can begin today!

4. **State a Well-known Quotation.** This quotation from William Shakespeare's *Hamlet* was used to open a speech about the disadvantages of borrowing:

   Neither a borrower nor a lender be, for loan oft loses both itself and friend.

STEP 4 | Prepare a Summary

As explained in Chapter 3, every speech needs a summary of the information presented. Remind your audience of what you said by repeating the main points covered in the body of your speech.

EXAMPLE A:

Well, I've given you some very important information today. You now know how to prepare if a hurricane is coming, what safety measures to take during the storm, and what to do after the hurricane is over.

EXAMPLE B:

As you can see, the Olympic Games are very important to people all over the world. I hope that today you learned some interesting information about the history of the Olympics, the Olympics today, and the future of the Olympic Games.

STEP 5 | Prepare Memorable Final Remarks

Again, as you learned in Chapter 3, every speech needs an ending that leaves the audience with something to think about. Like attention getters, memorable final remarks can take the form of rhetorical questions, stories, surprising facts, or quotations. Many famous public speakers have used effective quotations.

EXAMPLE A:

Former presidential candidate Robert F. Kennedy ended one of his speeches with this quotation from the playwright George Bernard Shaw: "Some men see things as they are and ask 'Why?' I dare to dream of things that never were, and ask 'Why not?'"

EXAMPLE B:

Civil-rights leader Martin Luther King Jr. ended his famous "I Have a Dream" speech with words from an old spiritual song: "Free at last, free at last, thank God Almighty, we are free at last."

STEP 6 | Prepare Transitions

Transitions make it easy for your listeners to follow your plan for your speech. They remind your audience where you've been and indicate where you're going.

Think of transitions in a speech as "signposts" along a highway as you travel from one city to another. For example, let's say that you are en route from Miami to Disney World in Orlando, Florida. After driving for an hour, you see a sign that says "Welcome to Ft. Lauderdale." Shortly after that you see another sign that says "Orlando, 200 Miles." You know where you've been and how far you are from your destination. The signposts reassure you that you are on the right road, and they help you to stay on track.

Just as signposts on a highway are important, so are transitions in a speech. Transitions tell your audience that something new or important is about to happen in your speech.

Transition after the Introduction. Every speech needs a transition after the introduction. For example, look at the model presentation "Look Out for Lightning" on page 102. After the introduction, the following transition signals the first section of the body:

So to begin, let's look at why people get killed or hurt by lightning.

Transitions within the Body. Transitions are also needed between each section of the body. Such transitions generally consist of two separate sentences that provide two important functions: to review the information just presented and to preview the next section. There are two easy ways to do this:

- Review the previous subtopic; then preview the next subtopic. For example:
  I have talked about how to analyze the audience. Next I will talk about how to choose a topic.

- Review the previous subtopic; then ask a rhetorical question. For example:
  I have talked about how to analyze the audience. Now, how do you choose a great topic?

Transition Before the Conclusion. You should also include a transition before the conclusion. This last transition acts as a signal that the speech is about to end. Notice how the following transition links the body and the conclusion:

Now that you know how to stay safe during an earthquake, our investigation about earthquake safety is complete.

II. Presentation Preview

Your goal in this chapter is to present a speech to inform about a topic that interests you.

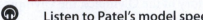

ACTIVITY 1 Listen to the Presentation

Listen to Patel's model speech. Notice the following components:

- Attention getter
- Preview
- Body
- Summary
- Memorable final remarks
- Transitions to connect the components

Patel's Presentation: Look Out for Lightning!

INTRODUCTION
Attention Getter

It might be beautiful to watch, but it can kill you! Every year it kills at least sixty people in the United States and causes brain damage in hundreds of others. What do you think I'm talking about? I'm talking about lightning.

Preview

Today, I'm going to talk about three aspects of lightning. Listen carefully, because the information I give you might save your life!

First I'll explain the reasons why people get struck by lightning, both outdoors and indoors.
Second, I'll teach you how to avoid being struck by lightning while outside.
And third, I'll share expert advice about safety tips to follow indoors during a storm.

So to begin, let's look at why people get killed or hurt by lighting.

BODY

First, people get hit by lightning outdoors because they get caught in a storm and can't get to a safe place. Another reason people get struck is that they wait too long before getting to a safe place. And third, some people get hit because they don't wait until it's safe to leave their shelters.

Believe it or not, people can also get struck by lightning inside their homes. You might wonder, "How can lightning get into my house?" Well it can! There are two main ways. It can strike the house directly, or it can strike wires or pipes that extend outside the building and be transmitted inside by those wires or pipes. If you're using any electrical appliances or plumbing fixtures during a storm, you're at risk.

Now you understand how people get hit by lightning. So how can you avoid being a victim of a lightning attack? First, let's talk about what to do if you're outside.

The most important thing is to have a lightning safety plan and decide in advance where you'll go if you get caught in a storm. The safest place is inside a fully enclosed building. If there's no building close by, then get inside a car or truck with a hard top and stay there until it's safe to come out.

Second, you should monitor the weather, especially during the summer, the peak season for lightning strikes. Look for signs of a storm before planning an outdoor activity. If you see any flashes of lightning, you shouldn't go out.

Third, as soon as you hear thunder, get to a safe shelter. Remember this slogan: "When thunder roars, go indoors!" Let me show you a lightning safety poster I found online at the National Weather Service website.

[Patel shows this poster.]

Finally, the fourth bit of advice to avoid being hurt by lightning is to stay inside your safe shelter for at least thirty minutes after the thunder finally stops. Don't come out one minute before that! *It's better to be safe than sorry!*

* *It's best not to take risks*

Transition You now know how to avoid being hit by lightning if you're caught outside in a storm. Let's continue by learning safety tips to follow if you're indoors during a lightning storm.

First, don't use any electrical appliances. For example, don't use an oven to prepare food. Turn off your computer, and don't talk on a phone with a telephone cord. It's safe to use a cordless phone or a cell phone, though. Be sure to unplug electrical equipment such as lamps, televisions, toasters, and stereos before the storm arrives. And whatever you do, don't touch any electrical cords during the storm.

Second, experts from the National Weather Service advise people to avoid running water during a storm. That means don't take a shower or bath, don't wash your hands, and don't wash any dishes.

Transition Now that you know how to stay safe indoors during a lightning storm, our investigation into lightning safety is complete.

CONCLUSION

Summary You should now understand three important facts about lightning safety: first, why people get struck by lightning; second, how to avoid being struck by lightning outdoors; and third, safety tips to follow indoors during a thunder storm.

Final Remarks Keep in mind, *an ounce of prevention is worth a pound of cure.* You'll live a long and happy life if you follow the experts' advice. [Patel holds up his poster again.] Remember: When thunder roars, stay indoors!

* *It's easier to prevent a problem than to fix it.*

ACTIVITY 2 Model Presentation Discussion

Discuss these questions in small groups.

1. Was Patel's attention getter effective? Why or why not?
2. What information did Patel include in his preview?
3. What organizational pattern did Patel use in the body of the speech?
4. How did Patel phrase his transitions? Were they effective? Why or why not?
5. Which words did Patel use to list his suggestions in each part of his speech?
6. How could Patel have reworded his summary?
7. Were Patel's final remarks effective? Why?
8. What other audio or visual aids might enhance this speech about lightning?
9. Was this a good topic for a speech to inform? Why or why not?

ACTIVITY 3 Outline Patel's Speech

1 Work with a partner. Using the model speech as a guide, complete the outline below.

Patel's Informative Speech Outline

Introduction

I. It might be beautiful to watch, but it can kill you! Every year it kills at least sixty people in the United States and causes brain damage in hundreds of others. What do you think I am talking about? I am talking about lightning.

II. Today, I am going to talk about three aspects of lightning.

    A. _____

    B. _____

    C. _____

Transition: So to begin, let's look at why people get killed or hurt by lightning.

Body

I. Why people are injured or killed by lightning

    A. Outdoors

        1. _____

        2. _____

        3. _____

    B. _____

        1. _____

        2. _____

Transition: Now you understand how people get hit by lightning. So how can you avoid being a victim of a lightning attack? First let's talk about what to do if you're outside.

II. Outdoor safety tips during a lightning storm

    A. _____

B. _____

    1. _____

    2. _____

C. _____

    1. Fully enclosed building

    2. _____

    3. _____

D. _____

Transition: You now know how to avoid being hit by lightning if you're caught outside in a storm. Let's continue by learning safety tips to follow if you're indoors during a lightning storm.

III. _____

A. Don't use any electrical appliances

    1. Don't use oven

    2. _____

    3. _____

       a. Cordless phones are safe

       b. _____

B. _____

    1. Lamps

    2. _____

    3. _____

    4. _____

C. Don't touch any electrical cords during the storm.

D. Avoid running water/plumbing

    1. _____

    2. _____

    3. _____

Transition: _____

_____

_____

Conclusion

I. You should now understand three important facts about lightning safety.

A. _____

B. _____

C. _____

II. Keep in mind, an ounce of prevention is worth a pound of cure. You'll live a long and happy life if you follow the experts' advice: _____!

2 Work in small groups and compare your completed outlines.

III. Pronunciation Practice: Phrasing and Pausing

A phrase is a group of words that convey meaning. A pause is a brief moment during which a speaker is silent. In spoken language, sentences are divided into phrases through the use of pauses. Speakers use pauses to convey or emphasize meaning and to take a breath!

ACTIVITY 1 Sentence Practice

Listen and repeat the sentences. Be sure to pause between the phrases marked by slashes.

1. I don't agree / and I won't change my mind!
2. My dog barks at people / when they knock on the door.
3. Mr. Brown / our neighbor / is very nice.
4. Dr. Stevens / our dentist / cancelled my appointment.
5. I bought a red blouse / a blue tie / and white socks.

ACTIVITY 2 Practice Sentences from the Model Speech

1 Listen and repeat the sentences. Insert slashes where you hear a pause.

EXAMPLE:

When thunder roars / go indoors!

a. It might be beautiful to watch but it can kill you!

b. So to begin let's look at why people get hurt by lightning.

c. They get caught in a storm and can't get to a safe place.

d. They don't wait until it's safe to leave their shelters.

e. First let's talk about what to do if you're outside.

f. Decide in advance where you'll go if you get caught in a storm.

g. Believe it or not people can also get struck by lightning inside their homes.

h. It's safe to use a cordless phone or cell phone.

i. It's better to be safe than sorry.

j. You'll live a long and happy life if you follow the experts' advice!

2 Take turns reading the sentences to each other in small groups. Be sure to pause where you inserted slashes.

IV. Playing with Sayings: Sayings with Pauses

ACTIVITY 1 Learn the Meanings

Read the following sayings. Check ✓ the ones you heard in the Model Presentation on page 102. Refer back to the speech if necessary.

_____ 1. **What will be, will be:** As we can't predict the future, we must wait to see what happens. Sue was expecting a baby. She wondered if it would be a boy. Then she told herself, *what will be, will be.*

_____ 2. **All that glitters is not gold:** Something that looks great doesn't always have value. I bought a sparkling diamond ring that turned out to be fake. *All that glitters is not gold!*

_____ 3. **It's better to be safe than sorry:** It's safer to be careful than to take unnecessary risks. High-wire walkers and aerial acrobats use safety nets to catch them in case they fall. *It's better to be safe than sorry!*

_____ 4. **Where there's a will, there's a way:** When you really want something, you will find a way to make it happen.
Abraham Lincoln was very poor but became president of the United States. *Where there's a will, there's a way!*

_____ 5. **An ounce of prevention is worth a pound of cure:** It's easier to take steps to prevent a problem than to fix it later.
I exercise and eat right to stay healthy because I know that *an ounce of prevention is worth a pound of cure.*

ACTIVITY 2 Practice the Sayings

1 Work with a partner. Take turns reading the sayings aloud. Each saying should be spoken with two phrases. Circle the phrases.

EXAMPLE: (It's better to be safe) (than sorry.)

a. All that glitters is not gold.

b. What will be will be.

c. Where there's a will there's a way.

d. An ounce of prevention is worth a pound of cure.

e. It's better to be safe than sorry.

2 Read the sayings to each other again. Be sure to pause between the phrases.

ACTIVITY 3 Use the Sayings

1 Think of a situation in which you can use each of the sayings in Activity 1 and write about it on the lines. Begin each sentence with one of the phrases below:

I told my friend …	This (experience) taught me …	I always remember …
I learned that …	Now I know that …	
I remind myself …	You should / shouldn't …	

EXAMPLES:
- I learned that all that glitters is not gold when the beautiful used car I bought didn't start.
- I always remember to wear my seat belt in the car because it's better to be safe than sorry.

a. _____

b. _____

c. _____

d. _____

e. _____

2 Work in small groups. Take turns reading your sentences to each other. Be sure to pause between the phrases.

V. Presentation Project: A Speech to Inform

Your project is to prepare and present a four- to five-minute speech to inform. The body of your speech should have three main sections.

STEP 1 | Choose a Topic

Choose a topic that you find interesting and know something about. Make sure it is narrow, specific, and achievable! You might choose any of the example topics mentioned throughout the chapter or another one.

STEP 2 | Plan Your Speech

A Review your completed outline of Patel's informative speech on page 102. Pay attention to the parts of his speech.

B Read the guidelines for organizing your speech.

Introduction
1. Begin with an attention-getting opener.
2. Preview the main sections in the body of your speech.

Body
1. Include three main sections.
2. Provide supporting information.
   a. cite sources
   b. give supporting details
   c. use presentation aids
3. Include transitions.

Conclusion
1. Summarize the main sections of your speech.
2. Make final remarks your audience will remember.

C Read the Useful Language you can use when citing your sources. Place a check mark ✓ next to the expressions you like best.

USEFUL LANGUAGE: CITING SOURCES

_____ According to _____.

_____ I found this information (online) at _____.

_____ Experts at _____ say _____.

_____ A recent article in _____ states _____.

D Complete the following outline for your speech.

Informative Speech Preparation Outline

Title: _____

Introduction

  I. Attention Getter

     _____

     _____

  II. Preview

     _____

     First: _____

     Second: _____

     Third: _____

Transition to Body: _____

_____

Body

  I. _____

     (Cite sources, give supporting details, use presentation aids)

     _____

     _____

     _____

     _____

Transition: _____

_____

  II. _____

     (Cite sources, give supporting details, use presentation aids)

     _____

     _____

     _____

Transition: _____

_____

  III. _____

     (Cite sources, give supporting details, use presentation aids)

     _____

     _____

     _____

(continued)

(continued)

Transition to Summary: _____

Conclusion

   I. Summary

        _____

        First: _____

        Second: _____

        Third: _____

  II. Final Remarks

        _____

        _____

E Prepare at least one presentation aid.

F Select a saying from page 106 to include in your speech. Write it here:
_____ .

STEP 3 | Prepare Note Cards

A Use the outline above to prepare note cards for your speech. Label the cards:

- Attention Getter
- Preview
- Transition to Body
- Body
- Main Section I
- Transition to Main Section II
- Main Section II
- Transition to Main Section III
- Main Section III
- Transition to Summary
- Summary
- Final Remarks

B Fill in important details from your Speech Preparation Outline. Use as many cards as you need.

C Add Useful Language and a saying from page 106 to your notes.

D Number your cards.

STEP 4 | Practice Your Speech

A Practice your speech with your note cards and presentation aid(s). Record it and listen to it at least once. Be sure it is between four and five minutes.

B Complete the speech checklist. Is there anything you want to change or improve before you present it in class?

Speech Checklist	YES	NO
1. My introduction included an attention getter and a preview.	❑	❑
2. I included three main sections in the body of the speech.	❑	❑
3. I included transitions.	❑	❑
4. My conclusion included a summary and final remarks.	❑	❑
5. I included a saying from the chapter.	❑	❑
6. I included a presentation aid.	❑	❑
7. I included a Useful Language expression.	❑	❑
8. My phrasing and pausing are correct and clear.	❑	❑
9. My speech is four to five minutes long.	❑	❑

C Practice again with your note cards and presentation aid.

D Your teacher and/or your classmates may evaluate your speech. Study the form on page 234 so you know how you will be evaluated. You may use the items on the form to make final changes to your speech.

STEP 5 | Present Your Speech

A Relax, take a deep breath, and present your speech.

B Listen to your audience's applause.

CHAPTER 6
UNDERSTANDING INTERPERSONAL COMMUNICATION

Interpersonal communication occurs any time people exchange messages—when they express their opinions, ask and answer questions, share how they feel, or talk about what they like and dislike. Whenever we talk to friends, parents, children, teachers, employers, waiters, doctors, salesclerks—in short, anyone—we are communicating interpersonally.

CHAPTER CHALLENGE Your challenge in this chapter will be to learn techniques of effective interpersonal communication that will help you feel confident about yourself and your interactions with others. When you complete this chapter, you will be able to:

- avoid many miscommunications and misunderstandings with others
- avoid jumping to conclusions and making assumptions
- use a variety of communication styles
- prepare for a successful job interview
- plan and participate in a job-interview role play

113

I. Perceptions and Interpersonal Communication

We all have beliefs—some correct, some incorrect—about other people and their values. Likewise, other people have perceptions and attitudes about us. These perceptions often affect our interpersonal exchanges. For example, one person might think you are friendly; another might label you as unfriendly and be reluctant to communicate with you. Someone might insist you are shy while another person is sure you are outgoing! The following activities will enable you to better understand and appreciate the contrasting perceptions and feelings of your classmates. At the same time, you might be surprised to learn that no two people perceive you in the same way.

ACTIVITY 1 **Learn How Others Perceive You**

Work in small groups.

1. Choose a group leader.

2. On a blank sheet of paper, write:

> I think that most people in this group see me as _____
>
> and _____ ; however, I really am
>
> _____ , _____ , and
>
> _____ .

3. Fill in the blanks with adjectives or descriptive phrases. Don't let anyone see your responses and don't write your name on the paper.

4. Give your paper to the group leader.

5. As the leader reads each statement, try to guess who wrote each one. Explain your reasons.

6. When everyone has finished guessing, identify which statement you wrote.

7. As a class, discuss whether you were surprised by what any of the group members wrote. If so, what surprised you? Why? Do you think people perceive you differently from how you perceive yourself? If so, why?

ACTIVITY 2 **Share Your Perceptions**

1 Select a coin from your country that you feel represents you as a person. Possible reasons for choosing the coin might be its:

value	size	shape
color	inscription	picture

2 Bring the coin to class. Sit in a large circle with your classmates. Take turns stating your reasons for selecting the coin.

3 Select a classmate to whom you would like to give your coin. Possible reasons for choosing a classmate might be:

- A feeling that you are very similar to that person
- A feeling that you are very different from that person
- A desire to better understand that person
- An appreciation of that person's contributions to the class
- A desire to encourage that person
- A desire for the person to change something about himself or herself
- A characteristic of the coin that reminds you of the person

4 Give your coin to the classmate you selected. Don't speak until all students have given away their coins.

5 Discuss the following questions with the class:

a. What was your reason for giving your coin to the recipient you selected?

b. How did you feel if you received coins?

c. How did you feel if you didn't receive any coins?

d. Why do you think you received (didn't receive) coins?

e. What have you learned about your classmates from this exercise?

f. What have you learned about yourself from this exercise?

g. What situations in life are similar to this exercise?

II. Avoiding Miscommunications

Misunderstandings happen to everyone. They occur between friends, coworkers, and family members. Communication breakdowns can be as harmless as showing up for an appointment a half-hour early or as inconvenient as waiting in the rain for two hours for someone who never shows up. They can be as devastating as a broken relationship or a divorce. They can even be a matter of life and death. For example, a failure to communicate fuel shortages and other mechanical problems has been the cause of some airline disasters.

A. Why Miscommunications Happen

Miscommunications often occur because listeners assume they understand what a speaker means when, in fact, the speaker had intended a completely different meaning from what was understood. Read the following examples.

EXAMPLE 1: SUSANA'S STORY

Susana was generally too shy to speak up in her psychology class, but one day, she finally found the courage to ask her professor a question during a lecture. Before answering her, the professor said, "Now that's an unusual query." Susana felt insulted as she believed her professor was implying that her question was foolish. She tearfully told the story to her speech communication professor, who was sure the psychology teacher hadn't intended to insult Susana. Susana's speech teacher convinced her to ask the professor what he really meant. He assured Susana that he intended his comment to be a compliment. He meant that her question was intelligent and insightful.

EXAMPLE 2: PEGGY AND ANNE'S STORY

Peggy was expecting a package and knew she would not be home to accept it. She asked the delivery service to leave the parcel with her neighbor, Anne. Happy to help, Anne brought the small package to Peggy's home after dinner. Peggy exclaimed, "I'm sure glad you didn't know what was in the box. Those are the diamond earrings my daughter sent for my birthday."

Anne's first reaction was to feel offended. She assumed Peggy was implying that she was dishonest and that she would have stolen the package if she had known it was valuable. She was very angry with Peggy.

However, after a couple of days, Anne realized she might have misinterpreted Peggy's remarks. She wisely called Peggy and told her, "I hope you're enjoying the earrings. By the way, why were you glad I didn't know what was in the box?" Peggy replied, "Because had you known, you might have been unwilling to be responsible for such a valuable package." Anne was extremely relieved to learn that Peggy hadn't meant she was untrustworthy. Had Anne not made the effort to clear up the misunderstanding, she might have ended her friendship with Peggy without Peggy ever knowing why.

Both Susana and Anne effectively cleared up a miscommunication by asking the other speakers to clarify what they had meant. If you are upset or confused about somebody's message, ask yourself, "Could I be misinterpreting what was said?" Getting the answer is as simple as saying, "I'm not sure what you meant. Would you please explain?"

ACTIVITY 1 Compare Your Understanding with a Speaker's Intent

1 Work with a partner. Read this information about Donna.

Donna was level-headed and giddy. She was kind and silly.

Donna was tiny but so large that everyone admired her.

2 What is your first impression of the information? Write it below.

_____

_____

3 Discuss your impression with the class. Did you think the words were contradictory or nonsensical?

Think about this: With today's meaning of some words, this message does indeed sound like nonsense. However, in early English, many of the words had different definitions from what they mean today.

- *Giddy* used to mean "enthusiastic" or "divinely possessed," derived from the same root as *God*.
- *Silly* once meant "happy," coming from the German word *soelig*.
- *Large* meant "good-hearted" or "generous."

If you substitute these definitions, the description means:

> Donna was level-headed and enthusiastic. She was kind and happy.
>
> Donna was tiny but so generous that everyone admired her.

Now that the words make more sense, you are less likely to reject them, call them nonsense, or criticize the author. If people made a consistent effort to look beyond a speaker's actual words to find out the speaker's intent, misunderstandings would occur much less frequently!

ACTIVITY 2 Describe a Miscommunication

1 Think of a miscommunication you have had with someone.

2 Work in small groups. Take turns describing the miscommunications. Discuss the following questions:

  a. Why did the miscommunication occur?

  b. How might the miscommunication have been avoided?

  c. Was the misunderstanding resolved? If so, how? If not, what could be done now to resolve it?

B. Jumping to Conclusions and Making Assumptions

The tendency to jump to conclusions and make assumptions when we don't have enough information is a great barrier to interpersonal communication. It can create animosity between people, cause hardship or embarrassment, and even destroy friendships.

ACTIVITY 1 Think about How Assumptions Are Made

1 Read the following story.

> A man went for a walk one summer day and met a friend whom he hadn't seen or heard from in over twenty-five years. The man greeted his friend, who was holding a child's hand, and asked, "Is this your daughter?" The friend replied, "Yes." The man asked the little girl, "What's your name?" The child replied, "It's the same as my mommy's." The man replied, "You must be Elizabeth."

2 Write your answer to the following question: The man hadn't seen or heard from his friend in twenty-five years. He didn't know that his friend was married or had any children. How could he possibly have known his friend's daughter's name?

_____

(The correct answer is at the end of the chapter on page 134. Did you jump to a conclusion without realizing it?)

ACTIVITY 2 Test Your Ability to Evaluate Evidence

1 The following activity, called the "Inference/Observation Confusion," was created to test people's ability to evaluate evidence.[1] Work in small groups. Read and follow the instructions in the box.

---

[1] This test has been administered to thousands of students for over fifty years! It was included in an unpublished PhD dissertation written by William V. Haney of Northwestern University in 1953.

Instructions

Read the following sample story. Assume that all the information presented in it is accurate and true. Read it carefully because it has ambiguous parts designed to lead you astray! There is no need to memorize the story. You can refer back to it whenever you wish.

Next, read the statements about the story. Decide whether you consider each statement to be true (T), false (F), or uncertain (?). "T" means that the statement is *definitely true* based on the information presented in the story. "F" means that the statement is *definitely false*. "?" means that the statement may be either true or false and that you cannot be certain based on the information presented in the story. If any part of the statement is doubtful, mark it "?". Answer the statements in order; do not go back to change an answer later. Don't reread any statements after you have answered them.

Sample Story

You arrive home late one evening and see that the lights are on in your living room. There is only one car parked in front of your house, and the name "Harold R. Jones, MD" is spelled in small gold letters on one of the car's doors.

Statements about Sample Story

1. The car parked in front of your house has lettering   T   F   ?
   on one of its doors.

2. Someone in your family is sick.   T   F   ?

3. No car is parked in front of your house.   T   F   ?

4. The car parked in front of your house belongs   T   F   ?
   to a man named Smith.

2 Discuss your answers to the statements about the sample story. Then check the answers on page 134. Did you make any mistakes due to incorrect assumptions?

3 Now begin the actual test. Remember: Mark each statement in order. Don't skip around or change answers later!

Story

Babe Smith has been killed. Police have rounded up six suspects, all of whom are known gangsters. All of them are known to have been near the scene of the killing at the approximate time that it occurred. All had substantial motives for wanting Smith killed. However, one of these suspected gangsters, Slinky Sam, has been positively cleared of guilt.

Statements about Story

1. Slinky Sam is known to have been near the scene   T   F   ?
   of the killing of Babe Smith.

2. All six of the rounded-up gangsters were known   T   F   ?
   to have been near the scene of the murder.

3. Only Slinky Sam has been cleared of guilt.   T   F   ?

4. All six of the rounded-up suspects were near the scene   T   F   ?
   of Smith's killing at the approximate time it took place.

5. The police do not know who killed Smith. T F ?

6. All six suspects are known to have been near the scene of the foul deed. T F ?

7. Smith's murderer did not confess of his own free will. T F ?

8. Slinky Sam was not cleared of guilt. T F ?

9. It is known that the six suspects were in the vicinity of the cold-blooded assassination. T F ?

4 Form a large circle with the entire class. Reread the instructions at the top of page 118. Work together as an entire class to answer the questions. Have one student record the class's answers.

5 Discuss the following as a class:

   a. Was everyone in agreement? Why or why not?

   b. Did some students try to convince others to change their responses? How? Were they successful?

   c. Did anyone change his or her responses based on the class discussion?

   d. Which small group got the most correct answers?

   e. Which small group jumped to the most conclusions?

   f. Did the entire class do better on the test than the small groups? Why, in your opinion?

   g. What real-life situations relate to this activity?

III. Interpersonal Communication Styles

> *There are three possible broad approaches to the conduct of interpersonal relations. The first is to consider one's self only and ride roughshod over others. The second is always to put others before one's self. The third approach is the golden mean. The individual places himself first but takes others into account.*
>
> — Joseph Wolpe, MD, *The Practice of Behavior Therapy*

Dr. Joseph Wolpe (1915–1997) was a South African psychiatrist who was a pioneer in behavior therapy. He described three interpersonal communication approaches. The first is called the "aggressive" style. The second is called the "submissive" style. The third approach is the one Dr. Wolpe recommended above all the others. He referred to it as the "assertive" style.

People who use the aggressive style of communication appear to be somewhat belligerent. They deliver their messages in loud, often hostile voices conveying the impression that they believe their opinions and feelings are more important than anyone else's. Intentionally or unintentionally, aggressive communicators tend to embarrass, insult, or intimidate their listeners in order to get their way.

People who use the submissive style of communication appear to put themselves last and seem to consider themselves inferior to others. This style encourages others to disregard their needs and to take advantage of them. Intentionally or unintentionally, submissive communicators often don't get what they want because they don't stand up for themselves.

In contrast, people who use the assertive communication style appear to have a healthy self-image. They express their wishes clearly and directly, thus conveying the impression that they expect their rights to be respected and that they, in turn, respect the rights of others. Assertive speakers appear to be positive, fair, and self-confident.

The following chart summarizes the messages conveyed by the three interpersonal communication styles.

Style	Characteristic
Aggressive	I'm important. You're not important.
Submissive	I'm not important. You're important.
Assertive	We're both important.

Being aware of these three interpersonal communication styles will help you recognize your usual style and that of the people you know. With practice, you can become more skillful at using an assertive style in your interactions with others. The following examples illustrate how people with submissive, aggressive, and assertive styles of interpersonal communication might respond to different situations.

EXAMPLE A:

A smoker asks if you object to his or her smoking in your car. You are allergic to smoke.

Aggressive response: "Yes, I most certainly do object. You are very rude and inconsiderate to even consider subjecting me to secondhand smoke. I refuse to allow smoking in my car."

Submissive response: "I'm allergic, but no problem. It's fine if you really want to."

Assertive response: "Thank you for asking. I'd prefer you didn't. It really bothers me. Would you like me to pull over so you could smoke a cigarette outside? I'd be happy to stop whenever you like."

EXAMPLE B:

You're next in line at a checkout counter and are in a hurry to leave. Somebody says, "Excuse me, I'm late for an important meeting. May I go ahead of you?"

Aggressive response: "Absolutely not! Go to the end of the line like everybody else!"

Submissive response: "Um, I'm in a hurry too, but sure, OK."

Assertive response: "Actually, I'm also in a hurry. I have to say no, but thank you for asking."

ACTIVITY 1 **Identify Communication Styles**

For each response to the following situations, circle the letter of the communication style used.

A = aggressive   B = submissive   C = assertive

1. You are in a restaurant and order your meal with a plain baked potato. The potato is served to you with butter and sour cream.

   a. You reprimand the server for not paying better attention to your order and for not checking the food before serving it.   A   B   C

   b. You remind the server that you had requested a plain potato and politely ask him or her to bring you another one.   A   B   C

   c. You either eat the potato as is or leave it uneaten on your plate without mentioning the error.   A   B   C

2. While you are waiting in line to buy movie tickets, someone cuts in front of you.

    a. You say nothing, hoping someone behind you will complain.   A   B   (C)

    b. You admonish the person for being rude and loudly tell him or her to wait like everyone else.   A   (B)   C

    c. You say that you had arrived first and point out the end of the line in case the person hadn't realized his or her mistake.   (A)   B   C

3. Your teacher returns your exam after grading it. He or she marked an answer wrong that you're sure is correct.

    a. You wait until after class and then show your teacher the exam. You explain that you don't understand why your answer was marked wrong and ask if it could be an oversight on his or her part.   A   (B)   C

    b. When you notice the error, you interrupt the lecture. Waving your exam in the air, you say, "You made a mistake grading my paper. I want you to correct it right now."   (A)   B   C

    c. You rationalize that the question was only worth three points and decide not to bring the error to your teacher's attention.   A   (B)   C

ACTIVITY 2   **Practice Different Communication Styles**

1   **Work with a partner. Think of aggressive, submissive, and assertive responses to each situation. Write them in the spaces provided.**

    a. After waiting for your car to be serviced at the dealership, you are informed by the service manager that it's ready. You go outside prepared to drive away. The car hasn't been washed, and the mechanics have left the windows and floor mats filthy. Handing you the keys, the service manager thanks you for your business.

       1) Aggressive response: _Why the matsisfilthy._

       2) Submissive response: _Than you have a nice day without any repone frome me._

       3) Assertive response: _Than you for the serice, but could pedle make the mats_

    b. A delivery person brings you a pizza loaded with anchovies, mushrooms, and sausage. You specifically ordered one with double cheese only.

       1) Aggressive response: _Sorry I don't want it._

       2) Submissive response: _Than you for deliver with tipes_

       3) Assertive response: _I take and I than him without tipe and I explan to him that and I trout it after I pay to him._

c. You and a friend are seated in a crowded movie theater. All the seats are taken. The loud conversation of the couple sitting next to you is distracting.

1) Aggressive response: _Shut up, Please._

2) Submissive response: _I try to move to anther Place it is possiable without saying anything._

3) Assertive response: _You have a good conversation and that help me improv my Englis, but could please be ctil quiet_

d. Your roommates are pressuring you to move with them into a more expensive apartment. You really can't afford to pay more rent; besides, you like your current apartment. You're worried that they'll resent you if you don't agree to their request.

1) Aggressive response: _Dont go stay with me I cant pay alot._

2) Submissive response: _I do what ever he want and I borrow many to pay for the apartment_

3) Assertive response: _I explan to hom I cant pay for the expensive apartment and I hope him to hepe by stay with me._

e. You are standing in line at the supermarket. Someone cuts in front of you. You are annoyed and feel the person should wait in line like everyone else.

1) Aggressive response: _hay you have to be in the line like everyone._

2) Submissive response: _waw good job you are smart_

3) Assertive response: _Excuse me all of we are in the line waiting for our turn. could you please wait fou your turne thank you_

2 Compare your responses in small groups.

ACTIVITY 3 **Practice Being Assertive**

1 Think of ten situations in which you might be reluctant to speak up or take action. Choose from the following situations or use your own ideas.

- Speaking up about receiving a lesser product or service than you expected
- Sending back improperly prepared food in a restaurant
- Calling attention to an overcharge in a bill
- Declining an invitation to a social event or for a date
- Saying "no" to unwanted houseguests
- Asking a friend to return money that he or she borrowed
- Speaking up if someone cuts in front of you in line
- Returning a defective product to a store
- Speaking up to a colleague who calls you by a nickname you don't like
- Saying "no" to a friend's request to borrow a favorite possession

2 Rank the situations you chose from 1 to 10, 1 being the situation in which it is most difficult for you to assert yourself. Write your choices below.

Rank	Situation
1	
2	
3	
4	
5	
6	
7	
8	
9	
10	

3 In small groups, discuss your rankings and how you will respond the next time you face each situation.

ACTIVITY 4 **Role-Play Being Assertive**

1 Work with a partner. Choose a situation from Activity 3.

2 Review what you would like to say and how you would like to act in that situation.

3 Role-play the situation with your partner. Practice responding assertively.

4 Present the role play to the class.

IV. Interpersonal Communication during a Job Interview

A job interview is a meeting between a job applicant and a person of authority working for the company or business. The meeting occurs because the business has a job opening. People apply for the job; the company decides whom it will hire. Good interpersonal communication skills are particularly important when you are being interviewed for a job.

Interview Questions

Questions and answers between the applicant and the employer form the basis of most job interviews. Employers ask applicants a series of questions to decide who would be the best person for the job. Most job interviews will also provide an opportunity for applicants to ask the employer questions about the job or company.

ACTIVITY 1 **Employer or Applicant?**

1 Work in small groups. Read the following list of questions. On the line next to each one, write E if this is a question an employer might ask. Write A if it is a question an Applicant might ask.

_____ 1. Tell me about yourself.	_____ 11. What is your greatest strength?
_____ 2. Is there a chance for promotion?	_____ 12. What are your career goals?
_____ 3. Please tell me about the benefits.	_____ 13. What languages can you speak?
_____ 4. When might I expect to hear from you regarding the position?	_____ 14. How do you feel about working overtime?
_____ 5. What salary do you expect?	_____ 15. What salary do you offer?
_____ 6. What motivates you?	_____ 16. What are your weaknesses?
_____ 7. Why would you like to work for us?	_____ 17. To whom would I report?
_____ 8. What is the sick leave policy?	_____ 18. How do you get along with others?
_____ 9. How did you do in school?	_____ 19. Why should we hire you?
_____ 10. Why do you want this job?	_____ 20. Are there opportunities for overtime?

2 Formulate other questions that employers and applicants might ask. Add them to the chart.

3 Discuss your questions with the class.

ACTIVITY 2 **Summarize Your Abilities, Personal Qualities, and Expectations**

1 Write a few brief sentences describing your abilities, personality traits, and expectations from your ideal job. You will use this information later in developing responses to interview questions.

EXAMPLES:

a. I have good interpersonal communication skills.

b. I'm an excellent problem solver.

c. I have a strong work ethic.

d. I'm motivated by opportunities for personal growth.

Some key words and expressions to consider include:

challenging	collaboration	initiative	listening
planning ahead	organization skills	decision making	counseling others
friendly coworkers	counseling people	writing	perseverance
maturity	good judgment	outgoing	flexible
creative	reliable	honest	punctuality

Key Achievements:

_____

_____

Strengths:

_____

_____

Weaknesses:

_____

_____

Career Goals:

_____

_____

Personality Traits:

_____

_____

Abilities:

_____

_____

What Motivates You:

_____

_____

Expectations:

_____

_____

Complete the Questions

1 Work with a partner. How would you answer the following questions in a real interview? Formulate answers with your partner. Whenever possible, use your responses from Activity 2. (Suggestions for answering the questions are provided in brackets.)

a. Tell me about yourself. [Talk about a couple of your current activities.]

b. What is your greatest strength? [Talk briefly about your best skill and give an example.]

c. How did you handle a difficult situation? [Describe a difficult situation you handled well.]

d. What would you like to improve about yourself? [Choose a weakness that many people have. Explain how you are working to improve it.]

e. What are you looking for in a job? [Talk about one or two things; explain why they're important to you.]

f. What are your career goals? [Talk about your future career plans and how they relate to the job.]

g. What motivates you? [Mention specific skills you are motivated to use.]

h. Why do you want to work for us? [Impress the interviewer with what you know about the company. Talk about the merits of the company or business.]

i. Why should we hire you? [Sell yourself. Explain how your skills fit the needs of the company.]

j. Do you have any questions for me? [Review the questions from Activity 1, page 124.]

2 Discuss your responses in small groups.

Job-Interview Behavior

The impression you make on your interviewer will be based on more than your answers to the interview questions. A large part of making a good impression results from your interpersonal communication, appearance, and behavior. These include your clothing, posture, body language, and facial expressions. (Review pages 16–20 in Chapter 2.)

ACTIVITY 4 **Categorize the "Dos" and "Don'ts"**

1 Work with a partner. Read the following job interview behaviors. Then write them in the "Dos" and "Don'ts" chart on page 127.

Know the exact location of the interview.	Arrive a bit early.
Wear revealing clothes.	Be thorough in your responses.
Smoke if you like and are invited to do so.	Chew gum.
Ask when a decision about the job will be made.	Accept a cup of coffee if offered.
Maintain good eye contact.	Answer questions honestly.
Be prepared for typical interview questions.	Wear lots of jewelry.
Give the impression that salary is the most important issue.	Treat everyone you meet with courtesy and respect.
Ignore the secretary and the receptionist.	Slouch in your seat.
Act as though you are desperate for employment.	Show enthusiasm.
Make negative comments about a previous job.	Criticize a previous coworker.
Use informal language such as "yeah" and "hey."	Dress conservatively.
Be prepared to ask intelligent questions.	Use the interviewer's first name.
Turn off your cell phone.	Offer a firm handshake.[2]
Complain about your previous boss.	Pay attention to personal grooming.

---

[2]Due to cultural beliefs, it may not be proper for some women to shake hands with a male. In that case, greet politely and smile. If the male has already offered his hand, smile and explain that you are unable to shake hands.

"Dos" and "Don'ts" of Job Interviewing	
Dos	**Don'ts**

2 Think of other "Dos" and "Don'ts" of job interviewing. Add them to the appropriate column of the chart.

3 Discuss all the "Dos" and "Don'ts" in small groups.

V. Presentation Preview

Your goal is to work with a partner and role play a four- to five-minute mock job interview. You will play the role of either the interviewer or the applicant. Then you and your partner will switch roles.

ACTIVITY 1 **Listen to a Model Job Interview**

Listen to Yolanda's interview with Mrs. Manning. Pay attention to Mrs. Manning's questions and Yolanda's answers.

Model Job Interview

Mrs. Manning: Hello, I'm Mrs. Manning. Are you here for an interview?

Yolanda: Yes, Mrs. Manning. My name is Yolanda Sole. I'm here to interview for the part-time bookkeeper position you advertised in the newspaper.

Mrs. Manning: It's nice to meet you, Miss Sole. Please have a seat. Did you have any trouble finding the office?

Yolanda: No trouble at all. I left early to beat the traffic and my car's GPS directed me perfectly!

Mrs. Manning: I'm happy to hear that. So, Miss Sole, please tell me a little about yourself.

Yolanda: Well, I'm originally from Mexico and moved here three years ago. I'm majoring in math at the University and hope to become an accountant.

Mrs. Manning: That's good. Why do you feel you are qualified for this job?

Yolanda: Well, I'm very good with numbers. I earned A's in algebra, calculus, and statistics. I'm very careful when I do math calculations, and I pay close attention to details. Oh, and of course I have excellent computer skills.

Mrs. Manning: What languages do you speak?

Yolanda: I speak Spanish, Portuguese, and English. My father is Mexican and my mother is Brazilian. I would be able to communicate with many of your customers who don't speak English.

Mrs. Manning: You have an interesting background. Let me ask you, Miss Sole, what do you consider to be your greatest strength?

Yolanda: I firmly believe in the saying, *A stitch in time saves nine*. I don't like to procrastinate. When something must be done, I do it right away. I don't wait until a little problem becomes a big one that is much harder to fix.

* *Fixing a small problem immediately prevents a bigger problem later*

Mrs. Manning: Thank you. And what do you consider to be your weaknesses?

Yolanda: Actually, I can think of two. I'm a little shy and nervous about speaking in public. I'm currently taking a speech class to help with that. Also, I'm maybe too much of a perfectionist. I get impatient with people who make mistakes. I'm working on being more flexible and patient with others.

Mrs. Manning: That sounds like an honest answer. Tell me, why do you want to work for us?

Yolanda:	As I mentioned, I hope to become an accountant. Working as your bookkeeper would be very interesting and motivating for me. It would give me excellent experience to help me when I study accounting.
Mrs. Manning:	Well, Miss Sole, I have all the information I need. Do *you* have any questions?
Yolanda:	Yes, Mrs. Manning, I have two. The newspaper said the job was part-time in the afternoons. Is it five days a week?
Mrs. Manning:	No, Miss Sole. It's three afternoons a week from 1:00 to 5:00 p.m. Is that a problem?
Yolanda:	No, that's perfect. I can schedule my classes in the morning. I also wonder, when can I expect your decision about the job?
Mrs. Manning:	Well, Miss Sole, you seem very mature and responsible. You won't be like some workers who wait for *the cat to be away so the mice can play*! I see I can trust you to work with minimal supervision. Congratulations! The job is yours. Please be here Monday at 1:00 p.m.
Yolanda:	Oh, thank you, Mrs. Manning! It was very nice meeting you. I'll see you on Monday!

* *Ignore one's duties when no one is watching*

ACTIVITY 2 Model Job-Interview Discussion

Discuss these questions in small groups.

1. Which of Yolanda's responses was the most effective? Why?
2. Could Yolanda have improved any of her responses? How?
3. What questions would you have asked Mrs. Manning about the job?
4. Were you surprised that Yolanda was offered the job immediately? Why?

VI. Pronunciation Practice: Intonation in Sentences with Two or More Word Clusters

Intonation refers to the use of melody and the rise and fall of the voice when speaking. It helps you convey your message effectively. For example, falling intonation at the end of a statement can mean that you have finished speaking. If you use rising intonation at the end of an utterance, you might unintentionally confuse your listeners into thinking that you have more to say.

The same is true in sentences that contain two or more word clusters (grammatical phrases or clauses). If your voice drops after the first word cluster, your listeners may think you've finished speaking. To make it clear you have more to say, you should use a slightly upward intonation on the last stressed syllable of the first cluster and a downward intonation at the end of the sentence.

ACTIVITY 1 Sentence Practice

Listen and repeat the sentences. Be sure to use correct rising and falling intonation.

1. I don't like cookies ⌣↗ but I love cake. ↘
2. He's good at math ⌣↗ but not spelling. ↗↘
3. I'll play golf with you ⌣↗ but not your friend. ↘

4. I need an umbrella ⌣↗ so I don't get wet. ↗
5. I bought a blouse ⌣↗ and a pair of shoes. ↗
6. Let's go to the beach ⌣↗ if it's sunny and hot. ↗
7. Do your homework ⌣↗ before you go to the party. ↗
8. I couldn't finish my project ⌣↗ because I was sick. ↗
9. It doesn't matter if you arrive in the morning ⌣↗ or at night. ↗
10. When their parents are away ⌣↗ the teenagers don't behave well. ↗

ACTIVITY 2 **Practice Sentences from Model Interview**

Work with a partner. Read the following sentences from the model job interview to each other. Be sure to use a slight upward intonation after the last stressed syllable in the first word cluster and a downward intonation at the end of the sentence.

1. I left early to beat the traffic ⌣↗ and my car's GPS directed me perfectly! ↗
2. I'm originally from Mexico ⌣↗ and moved here three years ago. ↗
3. I'm majoring in math at the University ⌣↗ and hope to become an accountant. ↗
4. As I mentioned ⌣↗, I hope to become an accountant. ↗
5. When can I expect your decision ⌣↗ about the job? ↗

VII. Playing with Sayings: Sayings with Two-Word Clusters

ACTIVITY 1 **Learn the Meaning**

Read the following sayings. Check the ones you heard in the Model Job Interview on page 128.

_____ 1. **What goes around, comes around:** Good deeds bring good things; bad deeds bring bad things.
I loaned jumper cables to a stranger when her car wouldn't start; then when I had a flat tire, a stranger changed it for me. *What goes around, comes around!*

_____ 2. **When the cat's away, the mice will play:** When an authority isn't around to supervise, others will do as they please.
The students threw books at each other when the teacher left the room. *When the cat's away, the mice will play!*

_____ 3. **When it rains, it pours:** When one event finally happens, a lot of similar events quickly follow.
The teenager had no babysitting jobs for a month. All of a sudden four families offered her jobs on the same night. *When it rains, it pours.*

_____ 4. **When in Rome, do as the Romans do:** In an unfamiliar situation, behave like those around you.
When the tourist saw the crowd stand for the National Anthem during the football game, he stood up too. *When in Rome, do as the Romans do.*

_____ 5. **A stitch in time saves nine:** Fixing a small problem when it first occurs prevents it from becoming more difficult or expensive later.
I called a roofer to fix a small leak before the dripping water caused a lot of damage. *A stitch in time saves nine.*

ACTIVITY 2 Use the Sayings

1 Work in small groups. Read the following situations. Write the saying from Activity 1 that best applies.

a. The teenagers had a party and wrecked the house when their parents left them alone for a weekend.

_____

b. My car broke down, my computer "died," my dog got sick, and I lost my wallet—all in the same week!

_____

c. Lara's car was leaking oil. She never fixed the problem. She drove her car with no oil until the engine was destroyed.

_____

d. My classmate wouldn't let me borrow his cell phone when I needed to make a call; when he asked for a favor two weeks later, no one would help him.

_____

e. My Japanese friend always removes her shoes before entering her house. When I visit her, I take off my shoes, too.

_____

2 In small groups, tell about a personal experience that matches one of the sayings in Activity 1. Have your other group members guess which saying it matches. Remember, each saying consists of two clusters of words. Make sure your intonation rises on the last stressed syllable of the first cluster and then falls at the end of the saying.

EXAMPLE:

Experience: Our office supervisor was out of the office for the day. We did very little work that day. We just sat around drinking coffee, playing video games, and checking our e-mail.

Saying: *When the cat's away ⌇, the mice will play ⌇.*

VIII. Presentation Project: Job-Interview Role Play

Your project is to role play a four- to five-minute job interview with a partner. You will have a chance to play the roles of both the employer and the applicant.

STEP 1 | Decide on a Job

Work with a partner. Each of you should select a job to apply for. Choose from the list or use your own idea.

salesperson in a shoe store	salesperson in an electronics store
waiter/waitress in a restaurant	nurse in a hospital
manager of a bookstore	library assistant
secretary in a law office	assistant in a travel agency
camp counselor	restaurant host/hostess
bank teller	supermarket cashier
doctor's office receptionist	teacher's assistant
airline/cruise line reservationist	tour guide
ticket taker in a theatre	toll collector on a highway

STEP 2 | Choose the Interviewer's Questions

A Review the questions that employers typically ask during an interview. (See Activity 3 on page 126.)

B Select five questions to ask. Be sure that you and your partner select different questions.

STEP 3 | Plan the Applicant's Responses

A Review the suggestions for answering interview questions. (See Activity 3 on page 126.)

B Plan how to answer your partner's five questions from Step 2.

STEP 4 | Plan the Interview

A Review the Model Job Interview on page 128.

B Read the following guidelines for organizing your job-interview role play.

Beginning the Interview
1. Employer and applicant greet each other.
2. Employer and applicant establish rapport with a brief conversation.

The Interview
1. Employer asks applicant the interview questions.
2. Applicant responds to interview questions.
3. Applicant asks interviewer questions.

Ending the Interview
1. Applicant inquires when a decision will be made about the position.
2. Employer and applicant make closing conversation.
3. Employer and applicant express appreciation for the interview to each other.

C Read the Useful Language you can use when the interviewer invites questions. Place a check mark ✓ next to the expressions you like best.

USEFUL LANGUAGE: RESPONDING TO AN INTERVIEWER'S INVITATION FOR QUESTIONS

Employer asks, "Do you have any questions about the job?"

Interviewee replies:

_____ As a matter of fact, I do. Please tell me . . .

_____ Yes, I have one. What . . . .

_____ Thank you. I have a couple. My first question is . . . .

STEP 5 | Practice Your Job Interview Role Play

A Practice your role play with your partner at least three times. Record it and listen to it at least once.

B Complete the interview checklist. Is there anything you want to improve before you present your role play in class? (Note: The checklist is for the "applicant" only. The "interviewer" will not be evaluated.)

Speech Checklist	YES	NO
1. I opened the interview with a greeting.	☐	☐
2. I made brief conversation.	☐	☐
3. I prepared responses to five questions.	☐	☐
4. I answered questions specifically and thoroughly.	☐	☐
5. I asked the employer questions about the job.	☐	☐
6. I appeared friendly and courteous.	☐	☐
7. I maintained good eye contact and posture.	☐	☐
8. I dressed appropriately for the interview.	☐	☐
9. I asked when a decision would be made about the job.	☐	☐
10. I shook hands and thanked the employer for the interview.	☐	☐
11. My intonation is clear and correct.	☐	☐
12. The interview is between four and five minutes.	☐	☐

C Your teacher and/or your classmates may evaluate your interview. Study the form on page 235 so you know how you will be evaluated. You may use the items on the form to make final changes to your responses.

STEP 6 | Present Your Interview

A Relax, take a deep breath, and present your interview.

B Listen to your audience's applause.

Answers to Activity 1, Part 2, Page 117

The man's friend was a woman named Elizabeth.

Answers to Activity 2, "Test Your Ability to Evaluate Evidence," Part 1, Pages 117–118

1. T—The story clearly states there were gold letters on one of the car's doors.
2. ?—We don't know this for sure. This is an assumption due to seeing a doctor's name on the car.
3. F—This is false. The story clearly states there is a car parked in front of the house.
4. ?—We don't know who the car belongs to. Maybe the car was just sold to Smith or Harold R. Jones leases the car.

CHAPTER 7

LISTEN TO LEARN

Listening is one of the most important activities we engage in. People spend close to 50 percent of their waking time listening; for college students, the number is almost 90 percent. Most people realize that it is important to listen carefully when teachers lecture, friends talk, parents or advisers provide information, bosses explain things, or radio commentators report the news. The exercises and activities in this chapter will help you improve your ability to listen effectively in all these situations.

CHAPTER CHALLENGE This chapter is full of exercises and activities to help you improve your ability to listen effectively in a variety of situations. When you complete this chapter, you will be able to:

- identify bad listening habits and learn to overcome them
- practice critical thinking while you listen to information
- listen for main ideas and details in a message
- present an impromptu, "thinking-on-your-feet" speech

I. Listening Self-Evaluation

Have you ever told a friend, child, parent, spouse, or anyone at all, "You don't listen!"? Has anyone ever told you in frustration, "Why don't you listen?" Chances are you have experienced both of these situations. Why is this? Why aren't people better listeners? Before we examine this question more closely, it's important to objectively evaluate your own listening skills and target the specific areas you would like to improve.

ACTIVITY Find Out How Well You Listen to Others

1 Work individually. Complete the "Listening Self-Evaluation" below.

Listening Self-Evaluation

Check ✓ the box that best describes your listening habit in each situation.				
Listening Habit	**Often**	**Sometimes**	**Seldom**	**Never**
a. When I don't agree with what someone is saying, I tend not to listen carefully.				
b. I pay attention to a speaker's appearance and don't listen to what the person is saying.				
c. When someone is speaking, I tend to think about what I want to say, not what the speaker is saying.				
d. When I am not interested in the topic being discussed, I tend not to listen carefully.				
e. I stop listening when I think I know what someone is going to say.				
f. At times my mind is somewhere else when I really should be listening.				
g. When I don't like or trust the speaker, I tend to block out what is being said.				
h. When someone criticizes me, I tend to become annoyed or defensive and don't listen carefully to what the speaker is saying.				
i. I pretend to be listening when I am not listening at all.				
j. I tend to focus on specific details of what a speaker is saying rather than on the main ideas or general purpose of the message.				
k. I tend to look at other people or objects in my surroundings rather than directly at the person speaking.				
l. I tend to hear what I want to hear or expect to hear instead of what the speaker is actually saying.				
m. I tend not to concentrate on what a speaker is saying if there is noise or other distractions.				

n.	When I haven't been listening to someone speaking to me, I admit I wasn't listening and ask the speaker to repeat what he or she said.				

2 Work in small groups. Take turns discussing your responses to the different questions.

3 Think of situations in which you may have been guilty of not listening well. Share these examples with your group.

4 Share your examples with the class.

II. Bad Listening Habits and Their Cures

Now that you have evaluated how well you listen to others, you probably realize you have some room for improvement! The following section describes some of the most common ineffective listening habits and how to overcome them.

A. Being Distracted by a Speaker's Appearance or Delivery

Habit: Some people don't listen to what a speaker is saying because they are concentrating on the person's speech patterns, gestures, posture, clothes, or appearance.

Example: A friend of John's father was explaining how to apply for a job with his company. John was so busy admiring the man's gold watch and expensive suit that he forgot to listen to what he was being told.

Cure: Concentrate on what the speaker is saying, not on how he or she looks or sounds. You can miss important information by thinking about a person's appearance or delivery style instead of paying attention to the speaker's words.

B. Deciding the Topic Is Boring

Habit: Some people decide in advance that they will be bored by what a speaker is going to talk about and use this prejudice as an excuse not to listen.

Example: The president of a local bank came to speak to a group of college students about inflation. Emma decided that she wasn't interested in the topic and would be bored, so she read a newspaper during the speech. The banker gave excellent suggestions about fighting inflation and saving money. All of Emma's friends thought it was a great speech with a lot of useful information. But she missed out because she wasn't listening.

Cure: Never take the attitude: "I have to sit through another boring talk." Even if you are not interested in the topic at first, remember that some of the information could be important or interesting. Make an effort to listen for information that you could use later. Adopt the attitude: "I may as well listen since I'm already here."

C. Faking Attention

Habit: Some people pretend to be listening, but their minds are on other things. They might be looking directly at the speaker and even nodding their heads in agreement when, in fact, they are actually daydreaming, thinking about their own problems, or planning a shopping trip. The speaker thinks the listeners are polite and interested when they are really not paying attention.

Example: Margaret Lane, author of a *Reader's Digest* article entitled "Are You Really Listening?" describes how faking attention cost her a job. An editor who was interviewing her for a job on a newspaper described his winter ski trip. She wanted to impress him by talking about a camping trip in the same mountains and started planning her own adventure story. The editor suddenly asked, "What do you think of that?" Ms. Lane (not having listened to him) answered, "Sounds like fun!" The annoyed editor replied, "Fun? I just told you I was in the hospital with a broken leg."

Cure: Don't just pretend to pay attention. Be sincere and take a real interest in the person speaking to you. If you are too busy to listen, ask the speaker to speak with you later, when you can really take the time to listen.

D. Being Distracted by Surroundings

Habit: Some people allow themselves to be distracted by their surroundings. They might look out the window or at the wall, play with a pencil or hair clip, or observe how people in the room are dressed.

Example: One student failed a math test because she wasn't listening when the teacher told the class to be prepared for a quiz the following day. She was busy looking at a broken window shade and thinking that it was a shame that no one had bothered to fix it.

Cure: Concentrate! Refuse to allow distractions to take your mind off the speaker. Develop the ability to stay focused.

E. Concentrating on Unimportant Details

Habit: Some people concentrate on specific details and miss the speaker's main points. Notice how the student missed the adviser's main points in the example below.

Example: Adviser: On Friday May 10, Miss Martin, the Director of Financial Aid, spoke about applying for a scholarship.
Student: May 10 was a *Thursday*, not a *Friday*.
Adviser: I'll now summarize this important information for you.
Student: It's not *Miss* Martin, it's *Mrs.* Martin.
Adviser: Write to the address I gave you and send the application.
Student : What address? What application?

Cure: When listening, pay attention to the general purpose of the message rather than to insignificant details. Listen for the main point of the talk first; then take note of any supporting facts.

F. Reacting Emotionally to Trigger Words

Habit: Some people ignore or distort what a speaker is saying because they react emotionally to "trigger words"—words, phrases, or names that cause positive or negative emotional reactions. When this happens, their ability to listen decreases because they allow their emotions to take over.

Example A: Mia, a student from Argentina, was listening to her economics professor discuss the economy in South America. As soon as he mentioned Buenos Aires, Mia became homesick and started to think about her friends and family still there. The mention of Buenos Aires caused her to have a pleasant emotional reaction. However, pleasant or not, the trigger *Buenos Aires* caused Mia to stop listening to the lecture.

Example B: Several students have reported that "terrorism" or "biological warfare" are their emotional trigger words. Upon hearing newscasters say these words, they become so preoccupied with the possibility of a terrorist attack that they stop listening to the rest of the newscast even when the commentator has started to discuss other topics.

Cure: Identify the trigger words that affect you. They may be names of certain people or any topic such as "poverty" or "music." Once you determine what your triggers are, it will be easier to remain objective and to concentrate on a speaker's message.

ACTIVITY 1 **Identify the Problem**

1 Work with a partner. Next to each example, write the letter of the bad listening habit demonstrated.

a. Being distracted by the speaker's appearance or delivery

b. Deciding the topic is boring

c. Faking attention

d. Being distracted by surroundings

e. Concentrating on unimportant details

f. Reacting to emotional triggers

_____ 1. A Mexican tour guide was explaining the history of Chapultepec Castle to some American tourists. One of the tourists loved to hear the way Spanish speakers roll the letter *r* and paid more attention to the guide's pronunciation than to his explanation.

_____ 2. Linda got a phone call from her friend Gregorio. As Gregorio was talking, Linda kept saying, "Really?" and "I see" to make Gregorio think she was listening. Linda was really working on her crossword puzzle.

_____ 3. Akiko's physical education teacher was explaining how to use CPR to save the life of a heart attack victim. As the teacher was speaking, Akiko was saddened by the memory of her grandfather, who had recently died of a heart attack. All she could think about was how much she missed him.

_____ 4. Your friend is teaching you how to use his new camera. You want to learn to use the camera, but you notice he also just bought an expensive stereo system with four speakers. While he is talking, you are looking at his new stereo, wishing you could afford one too.

_____ 5. Chung, a Korean student, told us that whenever someone mentions Korea, he gets homesick. He immediately thinks of his family in Seoul and starts to miss them terribly. He gets so emotional about being so far from his family that he doesn't listen to the speaker or follow the rest of the conversation.

_____ 6. A counselor was speaking about college graduation requirements. Lena decided that she didn't need to listen and would look up the information in the college catalogue. She wrote a letter to her boyfriend instead of listening to the speaker. She missed valuable information about new requirements that were not printed in the catalog.

_____ 7. Your aunt is not a stylish dresser. You never really listen to what she says because, when you see her, you can't stop thinking about her mismatched, out-of-style clothes.

_____ 8. A group of people were listening to a librarian review a book at their local library. One man was concentrating on remembering the exact ages and birthdays of all the book's characters; unfortunately, he missed much of the librarian's fascinating description of the novel's general plot.

_____ 9. Your academic adviser was explaining how to apply for financial aid or scholarships. You noticed that she bites her nails. You started thinking how ugly her nails looked and that she should stop biting them.

_____ 10. The school nurse was explaining the schedule for receiving free flu shots. She mentioned how many people get the flu each year. You were trying to remember the exact statistic and missed the information about when and where the flu shots would be administered.

2 **Discuss your responses with the class.**

ACTIVITY 2 **Explore the Effects of Bad Listening**

1 **Work in small groups. Take turns describing a situation in which you demonstrated one of the poor listening habits listed on pages 137–138. Include your answers to these questions:**

- What was the consequence of your "bad" listening habit?
- How can you improve this habit in the future?

2 **Take turns describing a recent experience in detail. While one student is talking, the other group members should purposely demonstrate one of the bad listening habits described.**

3 **After each member of the group has had a turn, discuss the following:**

- As a listener, how was your ability to listen affected by using the bad listening habits?
- As a speaker, how did you feel while your group members were demonstrating bad listening habits?

4 **Choose a member of your group to summarize the experiences of the group for the class.**

ACTIVITY 3 **Identify Personal Trigger Words**

1 **In the chart below, write the names of people or other subjects that trigger strong emotions in you.**

	Negative Triggers	Positive Triggers
People		
Other Subjects		

2 **Discuss your responses in small groups. How do your classmates react when they hear your triggers?**

ACTIVITY 4 **Play Telephone**

1 All students line up in the front of the room or at their desks.

2 Your teacher will whisper a saying or quote to the first student. That student will whisper the saying to the next student, who in turn will whisper the saying to the next person in line, and so on.

3 The last person in the line will announce the saying aloud.

4 Discuss the following questions as a class:

- Did the original saying that your teacher told the first student change?
- Why did it change?
- What could the listeners have done to prevent the message from changing?

ACTIVITY 5 **Retell the Story**

1 Your teacher will ask four students to leave the room. They are not allowed to listen at the door!

2 Your teacher will read a brief, humorous anecdote or story from a newspaper or periodical such as *Reader's Digest*.

3 Your teacher will then call in the first student from outside the room and ask one of the students in the room to retell the story.

4 The second student from outside will be called in. The first student will tell this student the story.

5 Repeat this procedure with the third and fourth students.

6 When the fourth student has finished relating the story to the class, the teacher will reread the original story.

7 Analyze how the story has changed from the original version. Discuss the following questions with the class:

- Have details been added to the original story? Which ones?
- Have details been omitted from the original story? Which ones were left out?
- Have details been distorted or completely changed? If so, how?

III. LISTENING SKILLS

Listening is not a simple activity, especially in a second or foreign language. It involves a wide range of skills, many of which you will need to use in all your classes. It is beyond the scope of this text to teach all of the necessary listening skills. However, this section provides practice in the following common ones:

- Comprehending main ideas and details
- Taking notes: Outlining main ideas and supporting details
- Distinguishing between facts, opinions, and inferences
- Evaluating what you hear
- Following oral directions

A. Listening for Main Ideas and Details

Your challenge in the following two exercises will be to practice listening for main ideas and specific details. You will need to listen carefully in order to remember the ideas and details long enough to answer a series of questions about the passages you hear.

1 Listen to the passage "Lying: Studies in Deception."

2 Based on the information you heard, write "T" if a statement is true and "F" if it is false.

_____ a. The ability to lie well is not a simple skill to learn.

_____ b. An expert can easily detect a good liar.

_____ c. Many companies and government agencies use polygraph tests each year.

_____ d. Most experts agree that polygraph or lie-detector tests are reliable.

_____ e. People have only recently become interested in attempting to detect lies.

3 Listen to the passage again.

4 Based on the information, complete the multiple-choice questions below by circling the correct responses.

a. The researcher who has studied lying is _____.

   1) an anthropologist from California.

   2) a police officer from New York.

   3) a psychologist from California.

b. Lie-detector tests are also called _____.

   1) polygraph tests.

   2) standardized tests.

   3) psychological profiles.

c. Who uses lie-detector tests? (Circle all correct responses.)

   1) Police departments

   2) Federal agencies

   3) Private companies

d. How often are lie-detector tests used?

   1) A million times a year

   2) A million times every five years

   3) A thousand times a year

e. How can lie detectors be fooled? (Circle all correct responses.)

   1) Closing one's eyes

   2) Using drugs

   3) Hypnosis

5 Discuss these questions as a class.

a. Do you think the "donkey tail" method of detecting liars was a good one? Why or why not?

b. Why was it assumed that the real liars would be the ones without soot on their hands?

c. Do you know of any other methods of detecting liars? If so, what are they?

ACTIVITY 2   Listen for Main Ideas and Details

1 Listen to a passage about daydreaming.

2 Based on the information you heard, write "T" if a statement is true and "F" if it is false.

_____ a. Almost everyone daydreams or fantasizes daily.

_____ b. Daydreaming is a perfectly normal and enjoyable activity.

_____ c. It is not normal for children to engage in fantasy play.

_____ d. Although daydreaming has several advantages, it can be harmful.

3 Listen to the passage again.

4 Based on the information, decide if the statements are true ("T") or false ("F"). Correct the false statements.

_____ a. Men daydream more than women.

_____

_____ b. Older people daydream a lot about the past.

_____

_____ c. Daydreaming helps children develop reading skills.

_____

_____ d. Daydreaming puts people to sleep when they are bored.

_____

_____ e. People have both realistic and unrealistic daydreams.

_____

_____ f. Most daydreaming occurs in company.

_____

5 Discuss these questions as a class.

a. What are the advantages of daydreaming? The disadvantages?

b. When do you daydream or fantasize the most?

c. What types of daydreams do you have?

ACTIVITY 3 Fill in the Supporting Details in the Outline

1 Listen carefully to a passage about the heart. The headings have been supplied in the outline below. Fill in the supporting details.

I. **Two general facts about the heart**

A. _____

B. _____

II. **Living beings with four-chambered hearts**

A. _____

B. _____

1. _____

2. _____

3. _____

C. _____

(continued)

(continued)

III. Four chambers of the heart

A. _____

B. _____

C. _____

D. _____

IV. Heart functions

A. Functions of auricles

   1. _____

   2. _____

B. Functions of ventricles

   1. _____

   2. _____

2 Work with a partner and compare your responses.

ACTIVITY 4   Fill in the Main Headings in an Outline

1 Listen carefully to a passage about umbrellas. The details have been supplied in the outline below. Fill in the main headings.

I. _____

A. Latin word

B. Comes from *umbra*

C. Means "shade"

II. _____

A. First person to use an umbrella

B. Tied palm leaves together for shade

III. _____

A. Large

B. Heavy

C. Ribs made of whalebone

D. Canvas-covered ribs

IV. _____

A. Lightweight

B. Compact

C. Ribs made of aluminum

D. Waterproof material covers ribs

V. _____

A. Bus

B. Train

C. Cab

2 Compare your answers with a partner's.

ACTIVITY 5 **Outline Main Headings and Supporting Details**

1 Before you listen, try to predict three major headings that might be included in the body of a speech entitled "Sleep Deprivation in Night-Shift Workers."[3]

a. _____

b. _____

c. _____

2 Listen carefully to the body of the speech and fill in the missing main headings and supporting details in the outline below.

   I. _____

      A. _____

      B. Difficulty concentrating

      C. _____

      D. _____

  II. _____

      A. Gastrointestinal disorders

      B. _____

      C. _____

 III. Causes of sleep deprivation

      A. _____

      B. Run errands

         1. _____

         2. _____

      C. Set appointments

         1. _____

         2. auto repair

         3. home repair

      D. _____

  IV. _____

      A. Make sleeping a priority

         1. _____

         2. _____

            a. 7:00–11:00 a.m.

            b. _____

      B. _____

         1. Create an environment conducive to sleeping

            a. _____

            b. _____

---

[3]Night-shift workers are people who don't work during daytime hours. They usually work between 10:00 p.m. and 6:00 a.m.

2. _____

    a. _____

    b. making grocery lists

3. _____

4. Avoid alcohol

5. _____

3 Discuss your responses in small groups.

B. Distinguishing between Facts, Opinions, and Inferences

Your challenge in this section will be to practice critical thinking and listening. You will need to listen carefully to be able to identify whether the statements you hear are facts, opinions, or inferences. Before attempting the activity below, review the following information.

Characteristics of Facts

- Are known to be true
- May be based on something that has definitely happened
- May be based on direct observation
- Do not readily change unless proven false
- Are objective and unbiased

Characteristics of Opinions

- Cannot be proven true or false
- Are subjective
- May be based on personal experiences
- Are often based on personal likes and dislikes

Characteristics of Inferences

- Are assumptions made without direct observation (**Example**: An observer sees a person running from the scene of a robbery. The observer didn't actually witness the robbery but infers that the person running committed the crime.)
- Are assumptions made when we lack complete information (**Example**: The police report the robber was tall and heavy. The listener infers that the person was a man.)
- Are assumptions based on connections we make among diverse pieces of information (**Example**: A man waving a gun runs past a woman on the street. A necklace falls out of his pocket. The woman infers that the man has just committed a robbery.)
- Can be proven or disproven (**Example**: The police report the robber was tall and heavy. The listener infers the robber was a man. Eventually, an investigation by police will prove whether the robber was male or female.)

ACTIVITY **Identify Facts, Opinions, and Inferences**

1 You will hear ten short passages. After each passage you will hear three short statements. Based on the information presented, decide whether the statements are facts, opinions, or inferences. Check ✓ the appropriate box.

EXAMPLE:

You will hear, "Richard is a popular male name. Rick, Richie, and Dick are common nicknames for boys and men named Richard."

Example Statements:	Fact	Opinion	Inference
a. Many boys are named Richard.	☑	☐	☐
b. Rick is a nicer name than Dick or Richie.	☐	☑	☐
c. Girls are not usually named Richard.	☐	☐	☑

Explanation:
a. This is a fact. The passage directly states that Richard is a popular male name.
b. This is an opinion. Some people might like Rick the best; others might prefer Richie or Dick.
c. This is an inference. The passage does not mention anything about girls. While it would be highly unusual, parents could name their daughters Richard.

Statement	Fact	Opinion	Inference
1. a.	☐	☐	☐
b.	☐	☐	☐
c.	☐	☐	☐
2. a.	☐	☐	☐
b.	☐	☐	☐
c.	☐	☐	☐
3. a.	☐	☐	☐
b.	☐	☐	☐
c.	☐	☐	☐
4. a.	☐	☐	☐
b.	☐	☐	☐
c.	☐	☐	☐
5. a.	☐	☐	☐
b.	☐	☐	☐
c.	☐	☐	☐
6. a.	☐	☐	☐
b.	☐	☐	☐
c.	☐	☐	☐
7. a.	☐	☐	☐
b.	☐	☐	☐
c.	☐	☐	☐
8. a.	☐	☐	☐
b.	☐	☐	☐
c.	☐	☐	☐
9. a.	☐	☐	☐
b.	☐	☐	☐
c.	☐	☐	☐
10. a.	☐	☐	☐
b.	☐	☐	☐
c.	☐	☐	☐

Listen to Learn **147**

🎧 **2** Listen to the passages again. Discuss your responses with the class.

C. Evaluating What You Hear

Your challenge in the following exercise will be to practice critical thinking and listening. You will need to carefully consider the information presented and evaluate the questions you hear in order to answer them correctly.

ACTIVITY Practice Verbal Comprehension and Reasoning

🎧 **1** Listen to ten questions. Write the answer to each question immediately after hearing it. Think carefully before responding.

a. _____

b. _____

c. _____

d. _____

e. _____

f. _____

g. _____

h. _____

i. _____

j. _____

D. Following Oral Directions

Your challenge in this exercise will be to follow a series of instructions provided verbally. You will need to listen carefully to be able to accomplish the tasks you are asked to perform.

ACTIVITY Follow the Directions

🎧 **1 Listen to the directions one at a time. Follow the instructions.**

a. 2   5   17   20   24   100   59

b. red   blue   chair   green   desk   table   black   seven   twenty

c. W   B   X   E   Z   C   U

d.

e. ○   △   ▭   □

f. apple   pear   corn   carrot   banana   paper   squash

g. _____

h.

i. ▭▭▭ (rectangle divided into sections)

j. _____
_____
_____

🎧 **2 Listen to the directions again. Work with a partner. Compare your responses.**

3 Discuss the following questions:

a. How many directions did you follow perfectly?

b. Which ones did you do incorrectly? What part of the directions did you misunderstand?

IV. Presentation Preview

Your challenge is to present an impromptu speech on a topic you have just been given. You will have approximately a minute to collect your thoughts and organize your ideas before beginning.

ACTIVITY 1 Listen to the Presentation

🎧 Listen to Simon's Model Impromptu Speech.

Simon's Model Speech: Good and Bad Addictions

INTRODUCTION   I'll bet everyone in this room is an addict or knows one! That's right, I said *addict*.

Attention Getter   Before you get angry with me for calling you addicts, please let me explain.

(continued)

(continued)

Preview   My topic is addictions. When we hear this word, we usually think of harmful substances like drugs, alcohol, or tobacco. We forget there are many other kinds of addictions. I'd now like to talk about different types of addictions, some good and some bad!

BODY   First, I will talk about some bad addictions.

Alcoholism is a dangerous addiction. People who are alcoholics become very dependent on drinking. They might drive while drunk and hurt themselves or innocent people. Alcohol also causes physical problems like liver problems. It is a very unhealthy addiction.

Another addiction which is bad for your health is related to food.

Some people are addicted to food. They can't stop eating junk food or lots of sweets like ice cream and chocolate. Food addicts eat too much food for their body type. Food addictions can also be very unhealthy. Overeating can cause obesity, heart problems, diabetes, and many other health problems.

The last bad addiction I will talk about isn't physically unhealthy, but it gets lots of people into trouble.

I am talking about an addiction to shopping. Shopping addicts buy things they don't need or want. They never seem to have enough clothes, DVDs, or shoes, for example. Shopping addicts often can't afford what they buy, and they get into debt. Sometimes the shopping addiction gets so bad that shopping addicts have to declare bankruptcy and ruin their credit.

Now, I will tell you about some good addictions!

First, EXERCISE! Many people are addicted to exercising. They wake up early each morning before work or school and work out in the gym. They never miss a day because exercise makes them feel so good. They are simply addicted to it!

Hobbies can be another good addiction. I have friends who are "addicted" to photography, stamp collecting, and scrapbooking. They work on their hobbies every single free minute they have. Being creative makes them feel good about themselves. Their hobbies relax them and take their minds off the stress of work and school.

Reading is the other good addiction I would like to mention. I am a reading addict! I like science fiction and biographies about famous athletes. I read when I am riding the bus; I read when I am waiting in line; I read when I am waiting in a doctor's office for an appointment. Reading helps my vocabulary; it teaches me many new things. I can never be bored if I am reading a good book.

CONCLUSION   As you can see, not all addictions are bad. Anyone who thinks they are is *barking up the wrong tree*. So find a good addiction and tell people with pride, "I am an addict!"

* *To be wrong about something*

Thanks so much, everyone, for listening to my speech.

1 Work with a partner. Fill in the main headings and subheadings of Simon's skeleton outline.

Body

    I. _____

        A. _____

        B. _____

        C. _____

    II. _____

        A. _____

        B. _____

        C. _____

2 Compare your results in small groups.

ACTIVITY 3 **Model Speech Discussion**

1 Review the following speech organization patterns. (See Chapter 5, pages 97–98.) Don't forget, it is also possible to combine patterns.

Past-Present-Future	Cause-Effect
Time	Effect-Cause
Problem-Solution	Related Subtopic
Location	Advantage-Disadvantage

2 Discuss these questions in small groups.

    a. Was Simon's attention getter effective? Why or why not?

    b. How did Simon preview the body of his speech?

    c. What pattern did Simon use to organize his speech on addictions?

    d. What other organization patterns could be used for this topic?

    e. What subtopics could be used for each organization pattern you suggested?

    f. What other good and bad addictions could Simon have mentioned if he had had more time?

    g. Was Simon's conclusion effective? Why or why not?

V. Pronunciation Practice: Linking

Linking means connecting the last sound of one word to the first sound of the next word. It is a necessary feature of fluent, spoken English. There are two situations in which English speakers regularly use linking:

1. When one word ends with a consonant sound and the next word begins with a vowel sound, the two words are linked and pronounced as one word.

   EXAMPLES:
   - *Pat is tall* sounds like "Pa tis tall."
   - *We like apples* sounds like "We li kapples."

2. When the same consonant sound ends one word and also begins the next word, that sound should not be pronounced twice. It should be pronounced one time, often with a slightly lengthened articulation.

   EXAMPLES:
   - *Warm milk* sounds like "warmilk."
   - *Get ten* sounds like "geten"

ACTIVITY 1 Link Consonants to Vowels

Listen and repeat the following sentences. Be sure to link the words in each phrase so that the phrase sounds like one word.

1. It's open.   ("Itsopen.")
2. Make a wish.   ("Mayka wish.")
3. Kiss Aunt Alice.   ("Kisauntalice.")
4. Let's eat now.   ("Letseat now.")
5. Leave it alone.   ("Leavitalone.")

ACTIVITY 2 Pronounce Double Consonants as One

Repeat the following sentences. Be sure to pronounce the identical consonant letters in the adjacent words as one sound.

1. Get two tickets.   ("Getwo tickets.")
2. Stop pushing me   ("Stopushing me.")
3. It's less serious.   ("It's leserious.")
4. My mom made lemon pie.   ("My momade lemon pie.")
5. Will Linda be there?   ("WiLinda be there?")

ACTIVITY 3 Practice Sentences from the Model Speech

1 Work with a partner. Read each of the following sentences.

2 Determine where linking should take place. Draw a curved line under letters that should be linked.

EXAMPLE: My topic is addictions. ("My topicisaddictions.")

a. Alcoholism is a dangerous addiction.

b. They wake up early each morning before work or school and work out.

c. Their hobbies take their minds off the stress of work and school.

d. I can never be bored if I am reading a good book.

e. Tell people with pride, "I am an addict!"

3 Read the sentences to each other. Remember:

- Link the final consonant sound in a word to the vowel sound of the next word.
- Link the consonant ending one word to the consonant beginning the next word if they are the same.

VI. Playing with Sayings: Sayings with Linking

ACTIVITY 1 Learn the Meanings

Read the following sayings. Check ✓ the ones you heard in the Model Speech on page 149.

_____ 1. **You can't teach an old dog new tricks:** It's difficult to change habits or ideas that people have had for a long time.
My grandfather refuses to learn how to use a computer; I guess *you can't teach an old dog new tricks.*

_____ 2. **A drop in the bucket:** A very small or insignificant amount.
You might think a dollar donation is just a *drop in the bucket,* but every dollar counts!

_____ 3. **Give (him) an inch and he'll take a mile:** Some people will take advantage of you if you are generous to them.
If you loan her your car for an hour, she'll drive it for a week. *Give her an inch and she'll take a mile.*

_____ 4. **Land on one's feet:** To be lucky or successful, often after having difficulty.
She takes unnecessary risks but always seems to *land on her feet.*

_____ 5. **Bark up the wrong tree:** To make a wrong choice; to be wrong about something you believe.
If you think I am guilty, *you are barking up the wrong tree.*

ACTIVITY 2 Use the Sayings

Work with a partner. Fill in each blank with the saying that best fits the sentence.
EXAMPLE:
Although he never studies, he always manages to <u>land on his feet</u> and pass his exams.

1. It may take you a few weeks to find a job, but I know that you will

_____.

2. I offered my son a little help with his research paper. He expected me to write it for him.

_____.

3. One can of donated food is _____ when there are thousands of hungry, homeless people.

4. You are _____ if you think you will get the job with no college degree.

5. My mom doesn't know how to ride a bicycle. I offered to teach her, but she said

_____.

1 Work with a partner. Read each of the sayings.

2 Determine where linking should take place. Draw a curved line under letters that should be linked in the spoken phrase.

EXAMPLE:

You can't teach an old dog new tricks. (You canteachanoldog new tricks.)

a. A drop in the bucket

b. Give him an inch and he'll take a mile.

c. Land on one's feet

d. Barking up the wrong tree

3 Read the sayings aloud to each other. Be sure to use linking as appropriate.

VII. Presentation Project: Impromptu Speech

An impromptu speech is a speech you make without advance preparation. You have no prior notice of the topic, nor do you have much, if any, time to prepare notes.

However, good impromptu speakers know many different ways to organize their thoughts on the spur of the moment. They have the ability to quickly review possible organizational patterns as soon as they hear their topic. Being familiar with such patterns will:

- help you choose the best way to organize your ideas for your specific topic;

- make it easier for you to think of things to say and examples to present.

Your challenge is to make a two- to three-minute impromptu speech on a topic your teacher will give you just before your speech. You might be assigned any of the following topics or another one:

travel	stress	punctuality
friends	hobbies	working students
rules	customs	free speech
habits	manners	communication
a story in the news	siblings	parents
holidays	responsibilities	prejudice
curfews	torture	technology
shopping	laws	heroes

STEP 1 | (In advance of your speech): Review Organizational Patterns

A Review patterns of speech organization (Chapter 5, page 97–98).

B Review Simon's Model Speech on page 149.

STEP 2 | (After learning your topic): Plan Your Speech

A Choose an organizational pattern that fits your topic.

B Plan the body of your speech. (Create a mental outline.)

C Think of an attention-getting opener.

TIPS FOR IMPROMPTU SPEAKING

1. Stay calm and begin slowly in order to give yourself time to think. Remember, the audience is not expecting a perfectly prepared speech.

2. Don't get nervous or confused if you forget what you want to say. Pause briefly, organize your thoughts, and continue speaking as if nothing happened.

3. Finish gracefully by thanking your audience. Never conclude by saying "That's it," "I'm finished," or "I can't think of anything else."

D Study the following guidelines for impromptu speaking.

Introduction
1. Begin with an attention-getting opener.
2. State your topic.
3. Preview the organizational pattern you plan to use.

Body
Develop your topic with:
- Examples
- Facts
- Stories
- Reasons
- Other types of details

Conclusion
1. Conclude with memorable remarks.
2. Thank the audience for listening.

E Read the Useful Language you can use to state your topic and preview your impromptu speech. Check ✓ the expressions you like best.

USEFUL LANGUAGE: PREVIEW STATEMENTS

_____ This morning I will share some (advantages and disadvantages) of . . .

_____ My topic is _____. I will describe how (it is different in Japan, Korea, and China).

_____ I'm going to talk about _____, and explain (quick steps you need to know to get started).

F Try to use a saying from page 153 in your speech.

G Your teacher and/or your classmates may evaluate your speech. Study the evaluation form on page 236 so you know exactly how you will be evaluated.

STEP 3 | Present Your Speech

A Relax, take a deep breath, and gather your thoughts.

B Present your speech.

C Listen to your audience's applause!

PROBLEM-SOLVING GROUP DISCUSSIONS

Much of what we do in life involves solving problems and making decisions. A large amount of problem solving takes place in group settings. Therefore, we are often expected to work as part of a group. To make the most effective choices and find the best solutions, we need to use an organized approach to problem solving and decision making. Used in the right way, group problem solving can be the most effective way of solving problems.

Group problem solving is an important part of speech communication. In this chapter you will learn how to communicate effectively as a member of a small group, both as a leader and as a participant.

CHAPTER CHALLENGE Your challenge is to plan and prepare for a problem-solving discussion about a problem that interests all the members of a small group. When you complete this chapter, you will be able to:

- prove a serious problem exists
- explain the causes of the problem
- brainstorm possible solutions to the problem
- evaluate the solutions and choose the best ones
- research a topic and contribute to a problem-solving discussion about it

I. Brainstorming

"Brainstorming" is an important technique that you will need to use when discussing a problem and figuring out ways to solve it. Brainstorming involves producing many ideas, then narrowing down the list and choosing the best ones. During the group brainstorming process everyone should feel free to contribute as many ideas as possible. You should not criticize anyone's ideas by saying "That will never work," "Forget that idea. It's silly," and so forth. As you brainstorm, follow the guidelines in this section.

A. Generating Ideas

As stated above, the purpose of brainstorming is to generate as many ideas as possible for the group to evaluate. Follow these suggestions at the start of a group brainstorming session:

- Choose a "recorder" to list the group's ideas.
- Think of as many ideas as you can. Anyone may contribute ideas at any time. The more ideas, the better.
- Say anything about the topic that pops into your head. Don't worry if an idea seems ridiculous or silly.
- Do not evaluate ideas at this point. Even "bad" ideas may trigger better ones from someone else.
- Remember: The more ideas, the better. Everyone in the group should participate.

B. Evaluating the Ideas

After making a list of all the group's ideas, it is time to discuss the ideas and choose the best ones. Start by eliminating the ideas that are the least popular. Follow these steps:

- Group members read through the entire list of ideas.
- Each member selects two favorite ideas.
- The group's recorder crosses out all ideas that no one selected.
- Group members then discuss the pros and cons of the remaining ideas and choose the one (or ones) they like best.

ACTIVITY 1 Practice Brainstorming in Small Groups

1 Work in small groups. Read the following situations and choose one for brainstorming practice.

a. Three students are living together. One is a vegetarian. She eats dairy and fish but not meat. The second one is allergic to all dairy products. The third one hates fish. The roommates would like to eat dinner together at least once a week.

b. Micah is always asking his friend Tom to borrow Tom's only jacket and tie. Micah often returns the clothes late or dirty. Tom can never think of an excuse not to loan Micah his clothes.

2 Brainstorm several main courses that all three roommates can eat for dinner or excuses that Tom can give Micah for not loaning him his clothes. Use your imagination, and be as silly as you like. Try to think of at least ten ideas.

EXAMPLE:
Tom might say, "A homeless man needed my jacket and tie to apply for a job."

3 Choose a recorder to list everyone's ideas.

4 Follow the steps for evaluating ideas in B above.

Practice Brainstorming in Large Groups

1 The recorders from the groups in Activity 2 should write their groups' two or three best ideas on the board.

2 As an entire class, evaluate all of the small groups' ideas and narrow the list down to the best two or three. Use the guidelines described in B. Evaluating the Ideas, page 158.

II. Identifying Topics for a Problem-Solving Discussion

Many discussions are not productive because the participants wander from point to point without any plan. In order to have a successful problem-solving discussion, you have to have a logical and organized plan.

Before you begin, you need to identify a problem that interests all group members. The discussion will be much livelier if all participants feel personally involved and committed to solving the problem.

ACTIVITY **Practice Identifying Problems**

1 Come to class prepared to suggest problems that you think would be of interest to the group.

2 In small groups, brainstorm and make a list of specific problems for each category in the "Problems for Group Discussion" chart that follows. An example is provided in each category.

Problems for Group Discussion	
Campus Problems	**State Problems**
limited access for disabled students	insufficient funding for education
Community Problems	**National Problems**
an unsafe intersection	illiteracy
City Problems	**International Problems**
lack of affordable housing	water pollution

III. Path to Successful Problem-Solving Group Discussions

The following path to successful problem solving will help you organize a group discussion into a logical sequence of events so that all participants can agree on one or more solutions to a problem.

A. Prove the Problem Exists

Present evidence that your group's problem truly exists.

1. Find statistics.
2. Refer to your own personal experiences or the experiences of people you know.
3. Quote expert sources.
4. Give specific incidences of the problem that have been reported in the news.

EXAMPLE:

Childhood obesity is a national problem in the United States.

- According to a news story in the *New York Times* on April 20, 2012, over 40 percent of children in New York City public schools are overweight or obese.
- According to the U.S. Department of Health and Human Services (2011), more than one-third of children are overweight or obese.
- My own family provides further proof of the problem. Two of my nieces and three of my nephews are obese. Furthermore, I have observed that most of their friends are overweight, also.
- The Centers for Disease Control reports (9/15/2011) that the childhood obesity rate has tripled in the past thirty years.

B. Describe the Consequences of the Problem

Describe the future effects or consequences if the problem is not solved.

1. Explain how people or society in general might be affected.
2. Share the results of your research.
3. Share personal opinions.

EXAMPLE:

There will be many serious effects if the problem of childhood obesity is not solved.

- The American Cancer Society (2006) reports that childhood obesity increases the risk for many types of cancer in adulthood.
- A higher percentage of adults will be obese.
- The Mayo Clinic reports (August 2, 2011) more people will have physical problems in adulthood such as diabetes and high blood pressure, causing much human suffering.
- Billions of dollars will be spent to solve medical problems caused by obesity. Medical insurance premiums will become higher, and people will have to pay more out-of-pocket medical expenses.
- There will be lower productivity due to increased absenteeism from work.
- A report in *The New England Journal of Medicine* (March 2005) warns that obese children will have shorter life spans than their parents.
- The Boys and Girls Club of America (2009) warns there will be a shortage of physically fit people to serve in the military.
- According to the American Academy of Child Psychiatry (March 2011), more children will suffer from anxiety and depression.

ACTIVITY Practice Brainstorming for Consequences of a Problem

1 **Work with a partner. Brainstorm the consequences of the problem "High School Dropouts." (Dropouts are students who stop attending classes and fail to graduate from high school.) Come up with at least five consequences. Write them below.**

If the problem of high school dropouts continues,

a. *juvenile delinquency will increase in many neighborhoods.*

b. _____

c. _____

d. _____

e. _____

2 **Share your ideas in small groups.**

C. Explain the Causes of the Problem

Present reasons why the problem came about.

1. Share the results of your research.
2. Share personal opinions.

EXAMPLE:

There are many causes of childhood obesity.

- Children have diets high in fat, salt, and sugar.
- The *Journal of Childhood and Obesity* (2011) reports that eating fast food is a major cause.
- Children do not get enough exercise.
- Pollution and/or crime make it unsafe for children in some areas to play outside.
- The KidsHealth Organization (2011) states that children spend too much time watching TV and playing video games.
- Many schools do not require children to participate in any physical fitness activities.

ACTIVITY Practice Brainstorming for Causes

1 Work with a different partner. Brainstorm causes of the problem of high-school dropouts.

2 Share your ideas in small groups.

D. Present Possible Solutions to the Problem

Brainstorm ways this problem might be solved.

1. Present suggestions made by authorities and concerned individuals.
2. Give your opinions about how to solve the problem.

EXAMPLE:

There are several solutions to the problem of childhood obesity.

- Pressure local schools to offer daily physical education classes. On 8/2/11 the National Institute of Child Health advised that sixty minutes of physical activity daily can help children overcome obesity.
- Pressure the schools to put more emphasis on good nutrition.
- Encourage parents to limit their children's TV and video-game time.
- Encourage parents to substitute low-fat, healthier foods for junk food.
- Pressure local law enforcement officers to better patrol public playgrounds so that children and their parents are not afraid to use them.
- Make it illegal for restaurants to supersize meals.
- Make it illegal for children under age 18 to enter fast-food restaurants unless accompanied by an adult.
- Encourage parents and schools to teach children about the importance of good nutrition.

ACTIVITY Practice Brainstorming Solutions

1 Work with a partner. Brainstorm possible solutions to the problem of high-school dropouts.

2 Share your solutions in small groups.

E. Select the Best Solutions

1. Ask the following questions as you evaluate each proposed solution. (If you can answer yes to the first question and no to the second, you may have found a winning solution!)
   - Will this solution eliminate any of the causes?
   - Will this solution create more problems?
2. Select the best solution(s). Remember: While some solutions may not be perfect, they might still be the best solutions to the problem.

EXAMPLE:

The possible solution that children under age 18 should not be allowed in fast-food restaurants without an adult is not effective.

1. It won't solve the problem.
   - There are many other sources of unhealthy foods and soft drinks for children under 18.
   - Parents will accompany their children to the fast-food restaurants just as they do now.
2. It will create more problems.
   - Children will break the law by getting fake IDs or being untruthful about their age.
   - Older teens will prey on younger children by charging them a fee to accompany them into the restaurant.

ACTIVITY Evaluate Causes and Solutions

1 Read the following scenario.

Problem

Hundreds of cats are roaming free throughout the campus of your school. They approach people and expect to be fed. They pounce on unsuspecting birds and eat them. They spray everywhere and leave their awful scent. They have frequent cat fights and make a lot of noise. They are a terrible nuisance. This is a serious problem because students and faculty are afraid to walk from one building to the next.

Consequences or Future Effects

The cats will spread disease. Teachers will look for jobs at other schools. Enrollment at the school will drop as students decide to go to another school. People who have been attacked or made ill by the cats will file lawsuits.

---

2 Divide the class into two groups, A and B. The groups will take turns sitting in a circle and brainstorming for ten minutes while the other group observes.

3 Group A should brainstorm to identify causes of the cat problem while Group B observes.

4 A recorder should write Group A's ideas on the board.

5 The entire class should eliminate the least popular ideas by following the process described in Evaluating the Ideas, page 158.

6 Group B should brainstorm to identify solutions to the problem while Group A observes.

7 The class should repeat steps 4 and 5 for Group B's list of solutions.

8 Discuss the following questions as a class:

a. Did both groups successfully brainstorm ideas? Why or why not?

b. Did group members work well together? Did everyone participate?

c. How can group members work more effectively together in the future?

IV. Path to Being an Effective Group Leader

Every successful group discussion needs an effective group leader. All group leaders should follow the guidelines in this section.

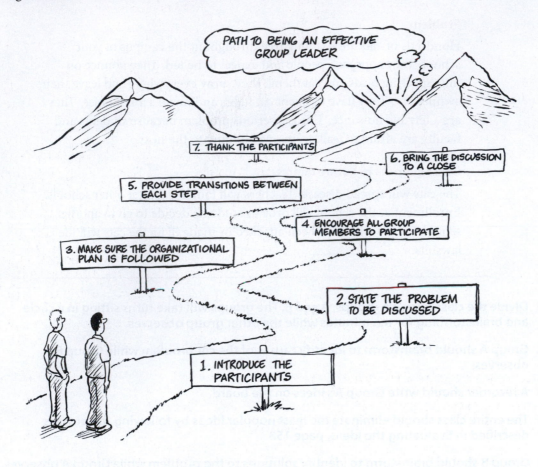

A. Introduce the Participants

Introduce the members of the group to one another and to the audience, if there is one.

B. State the Problem to Be Discussed

This is similar to introducing a speech by providing a preview and an attention-getting opener, as discussed on page 100 of Chapter 5: Speaking to Inform.

- Introduce the problem to be discussed.
- Briefly explain the organizational plan to be followed.

C. Make Sure That the Organizational Plan Is Followed

Make certain the group follows the organizational plan and does not skip steps. If a group member goes off on a tangent, it's your job to get him or her back on track. For example:

- "Let's get back to that point later."
- "That's an interesting comment, but let's finish what we are currently discussing."

D. Encourage All Group Members to Participate

To encourage shy group members to speak, you might call on them by name and ask:

- "Helena, what do you think about that?"
- "Do you have any information to add, Ben?"

E. Provide Transitions between Each Step

Summarize each step in the discussion before going on to the next step.

EXAMPLE:

Now that we've discussed the future effects of childhood obesity, let's move on and talk about the causes of the problem.

F. Bring the Discussion to a Close

After an agreed-upon time limit, conclude the discussion. This is similar to providing a summary and memorable concluding remarks for a speech.

G. Thank the Participants

After concluding the discussion, be sure to thank the participants by name for their time and hard work.

V. Path to Being a Responsible Group Member

In addition to having an effective group leader, every group discussion needs responsible and enthusiastic participants who are committed to the discussion's success.

The following path to being a responsible group member will help assure an animated and productive group discussion.

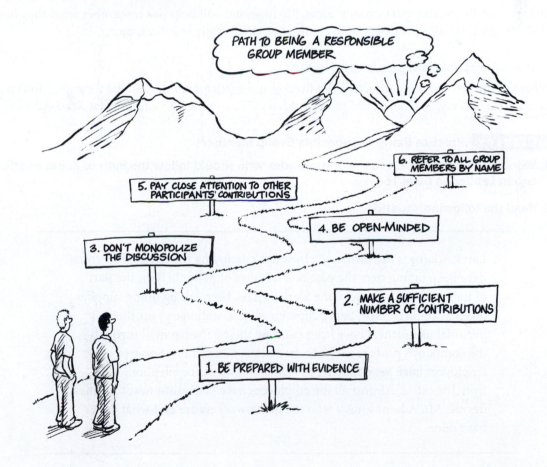

A. Be Prepared with Evidence

Prepare for the discussion by researching quotations, facts, statistics, and examples. Write possible contributions for each step of the discussion on note cards so that you can refer to them as needed during the discussion.

B. Make a Sufficient Number of Contributions

Contribute often during each step of the discussion. Your comments should be brief. Talk when you have a thought to share or a question to ask or when you feel a point needs to be clarified.

C. Don't Monopolize the Discussion

Don't interrupt other group members while they are speaking. Give all participants a chance to speak and express themselves.

D. Be Open-Minded

Acknowledge other people's opinions and their right to express them. If you disagree with someone's opinion, let the person express the idea completely without interrupting. If you want to introduce a contrary point of view, do so politely. For example, you could start by saying, "I see your point. However, ..."

E. Pay Close Attention to Other Participants' Contributions

Listen carefully to other participants' ideas. Taking notes will help you remember what they have said. The group leader may ask you to summarize each step in the discussion.

F. Refer to All Participants by Name

Whether you refer to them directly or indirectly, use participants' names. For example, don't point to Marisela and say, "I'd like to add to what *she* said." Say, "I'd like to add to what *Marisela* said."

ACTIVITY Practice Being Responsible Group Members

1 Work in small groups. Choose a group leader, who should follow the Path to Being an Effective Group Leader on page 164.

2 Read the following situation.

> Larry Adams is the owner of a business employing thirty people. Profits have been falling over the past year because of petty theft on the part of the employees. Some of the workers have been taking home supplies (such as staplers, tape, paper clips, envelopes, stationery) for their personal use. Others have been running their personal mail through the company's postage meter to save money on stamps. Some of the employees have been making personal long-distance telephone calls from the office. Almost all the employees have been dishonest to some degree. Mr. Adams knows who the guilty workers are and what they have done.

3 Discuss the question: What are the possible ways that Mr. Adams might deal with this situation? Brainstorm as many different options as you can and write them below. Be sure to follow the Path to Successful Problem Solving on page 160 and the Path to Being a Responsible Group Member on page 165.

a. _____

b. _____

c. _____

d. _____

e. _____

4 Share your solutions with the entire class. Designate one student as "recorder" to write all the ideas on the board.

5 Choose another student to lead a class discussion about solutions to Mr. Adams's problem. The entire class should eliminate the least popular ideas by following the process described in B. Evaluating the Ideas, page 158. After the least popular solutions are crossed out, discuss the remaining ones and choose the best two or three solutions to Mr. Adams's problem.

VI. Presentation Preview

You and your group members will have the task of choosing a problem that exists in society and participating in a problem-solving discussion about it.

ACTIVITY 1 Listen to a Model Discussion

 Listen to the Model Discussion called "Childhood Obesity: A National Problem." Take notes. Be sure to list all the proposed solutions that the group members brainstorm.

MODEL DISCUSSION: Childhood Obesity: A National Problem

INTRODUCTION BY GROUP LEADER	**Shai:**	Good morning everyone. Before we get started, I'd like to introduce the members of our group. Allow me to present Yanni, Andres, Tomiko, and Martin. We'll be discussing a very serious problem that exists in the United States. It's the problem of childhood obesity.
Group Leader Transition	**Shai:**	We'll start by proving this is a very real and widespread problem affecting millions of children. Who'd like to begin?
PROVE THE PROBLEM EXISTS	**Tomiko:**	I will. I found out that more than one-third of American children are overweight or obese. This is according to a 2011 report published by the U.S. Department of Health and Human Services.
	Yanni:	That's a lot of kids, Tomiko! I found research on this topic from the National Institutes of Health. In 2011 they reported that childhood obesity has reached epidemic proportions and is still rising.
	Shai:	That goes along with what I found, Yanni. On September 15, 2011, the Centers for Disease Control reported on their website that the childhood obesity rate has tripled in the past thirty years.
	Andres:	That's really scary. I also got information from the CDC website. I learned that different states have different childhood obesity rates. I'd like to show you a visual aid of a U.S. Obesity Map. The light gray states have a childhood obesity rate of 20 percent; the medium gray states have a rate of 25 percent; and the dark gray states have a rate of 30 percent or more.

(continued)

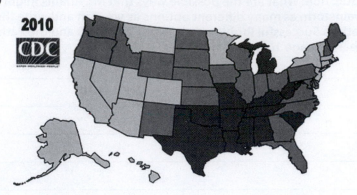

2010

Shai:	That's a great map, Andres.
Andres:	Thanks.
Shai:	Martin, you've been very quiet. Would you like to add anything before we move on?
Martin:	Not really.
Shai:	Does anyone have anything else to add? No? OK, then let's continue with our discussion.

Group Leader Transition

Shai:	Thank you all for helping to prove that the obesity problem exists. Let's now describe some possible consequences if this serious problem isn't solved.

[Tomiko raises her hand.]

DESCRIBE CONSEQUENCES OF THE PROBLEM

Shai:	Yes, Tomiko. What do you have?
Tomiko:	Well, for one thing, if this problem isn't solved soon, these overweight kids are going to have serious physical problems in adulthood.
Martin:	Like what?
Tomiko:	Good question, Martin! Well, childhood obesity can lead to heart disease, high blood pressure, and strokes later in life. It also leads to the need for hip and knee replacements and lots of other health problems. I got this information from a Mayo Clinic report dated August 2, 2011. Here, this diagram shows many of the health problems that are caused by childhood obesity.

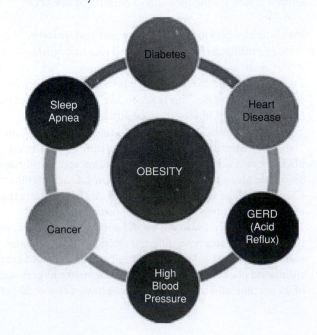

Yanni:	On top of that, I read that many children will have shorter life spans than their parents if this problem isn't solved.
Andres:	You know, I read that too. And all those health problems could lead to lots of other problems. For example, if all these obese children grow up to be obese adults, medical insurance premiums for everyone may become higher in the future.
Yanni:	That's true. In 2010, the Center for American Progress warned that childhood obesity is already contributing greatly to rising health care costs.
Andres:	That's terrible. I read about another consequence on the website of the Boys and Girls Club of America. It warns that in the future, there could be a shortage of physically fit people to serve in the military. That could be a big problem for the United States.
Shai:	Those are all good points. Does anyone have anything to add before we move on?
Yanni:	I do. I didn't get this from research, but I think that if adults have so many health problems caused by obesity, they'll miss a lot of work.
Shai:	That makes a lot of sense, Yanni. What I read supports what you just said. Because of all the lost work time, U.S. workers won't produce as much. That's another economic consequence of obesity.
Tomiko:	I have one other piece of information to share.
Shai:	Sure. Go ahead, Tomiko.
Tomiko:	In March 2011, the American Academy of Child Psychiatry reported that obese children are more likely to suffer from anxiety and depression. This can cause them to have emotional problems and do poorly in school.
Shai:	I never thought of that. It's an excellent point. Martin, would you like to tell us what you found?
Martin:	Everyone already said exactly what I was going to say.

Group Leader Transition

Shai:	OK. We've described many consequences of the childhood obesity problem. Now let's discuss some of the causes. Who'd like to begin? [Martin raises his hand.] OK, Martin, great.

EXPLAIN THE CAUSES OF THE PROBLEM

Martin:	Well, many kids just eat too much. And their family members eat too much. They all copy each other. It's like the saying we learned, *birds of a feather flock together*. This photo proves it!

* People with similar interests like to associate with one another

Shai:	I see what you mean. I read something similar in the *Journal of Childhood and Obesity*. It reported that eating in fast-food restaurants is a major cause of childhood obesity.

(continued)

(continued)

Andres:	That's why parents have to do a better job of making sure their children eat healthy meals.
Shai:	Andres, that is very important, but it's not a cause. Let's talk about how parents can help when we get to the solutions step of the discussion. Right now we need to stay on track and explain the causes of the problem.
Andres:	You're right, Shai. Sorry, I got carried away! It isn't just fast foods that cause the problem. In general, research shows that many children have diets high in fat, salt, and sugar.
Yanni:	That's true. My little niece is overweight. Her parents let her drink soda instead of milk. They feed her ice cream, cake, and lots of salty fried foods.
Tomiko:	So, we can say that parents are part of the cause of this problem. They encourage bad habits that lead to obesity.
Yanni:	Not only that—many parents don't set a good example for their kids. They're overweight also. The photo that Martin presented earlier also shows this.
Shai:	You all make some really good points. Other than poor diets, are there any other causes of childhood obesity?
Tomiko:	Yes. Lots of kids don't get enough exercise because they spend too much time watching TV and playing video games.
Shai:	Right, and another reason kids don't get enough exercise is that many schools don't have recess or outdoor fitness activities.
Andres:	I also read that many communities have high crime rates. It's not safe for children to play outside.
Shai:	Wow, we have lots of causes for the problem. Would anyone like to share any other causes? No? Then it's time to move on.

Group Leader Transition

Shai:	We've proven that childhood obesity is a very serious problem; we've described its consequences; and we've explained its causes. Now we're ready to propose some solutions to the problem. Andres will be our recorder. Andres, please write our solutions on the board as we propose them.

POSSIBLE SOLUTIONS TO THE PROBLEM

Shai:	Who has a solution? [Tomiko raises her hand.] Yes, go ahead, Tomiko.
Tomiko:	*The handwriting is on the wall.* To solve the childhood obesity problem, children have to improve their diet and exercise.
Martin:	That's easy to propose. But how can we make that happen?
Shai:	That's exactly what we need to brainstorm. Who has an idea?
Andres:	I know one solution to getting children to exercise more. Parent groups need to pressure schools into offering daily physical education classes.
Tomiko:	That's right. In fact, on August 2, 2011, the National Institutes of Health advised that sixty minutes of physical activity daily can help children overcome obesity.
Shai:	OK. So in addition to pressuring schools to offer gym class every day, we also need to get parents to limit their children's TV and video-game time so that they play outside more.
Martin:	But what if they live in a high-crime area and don't want to go outside?
Shai:	Well, then we need to pressure local police to patrol the neighborhoods and playgrounds so it's safe for children to play outside.
Tomiko:	Not only that—parents also need to stop giving in to their kids when they want junk food. They should give their children low-fat, healthier foods.
Martin:	Like what?
Yanni:	Well for starters, kids can eat whole-wheat crackers instead of chips. They can eat fruit instead of cake or ice cream. They can drink milk or juice instead of soft drinks. This photo shows a variety of healthy foods children can eat instead of junk food.

* *It's obvious something bad is going to happen.*

Andres:	Parent groups could also pressure schools to put more emphasis on good nutrition.
Yanni:	That's true. Schools usually listen when enough parents complain about something. And here's another idea. My sister suggested that it should be illegal for restaurants to supersize meals.
Martin:	That's a dumb idea.
Shai:	Excuse me, Martin. Please be respectful of your group members. Now is not the time to criticize anyone's ideas. Right now, let's just think of as many ideas as we can. We'll evaluate the possible solutions in the next step of the discussion.
Andres:	I think it should be illegal for fast-food restaurants to serve children under 18 unless they're accompanied by an adult.
Yanni:	Hmm. I never heard that idea before. I guess *necessity is the mother of invention!* Personally, I think parents need to be better role models for their children. They need to exercise and eat healthy foods too.

* Difficult
situations
inspire
people to
think of
unique
solutions

Group Leader Transition

| Shai: | OK, everyone. We have a lot of possible solutions. Now let's evaluate them. Everybody please go up to the board. Put a check mark next to your two favorite solutions. Andres will cross out ideas that don't receive any check marks. |

EVALUATE THE SOLUTIONS AND CHOOSE THE BEST ONES

[The discussion stops here.]

ACTIVITY 2 **Conclude the Model Discussion**

1 Work as an entire class. Different students should call out the solutions from the Model Discussion that they wrote in their notes. A recorder should list them on the board.

2 The class should brainstorm other solutions for the recorder to add to the list.

3 All students should go to the board and put check marks next to their two favorite solutions.

Problem-Solving Group Discussions **171**

4 The recorder should eliminate solutions that received no check marks.

5 The class should discuss the remaining solutions and choose the best one(s).

ACTIVITY 3 Analyze the Model Discussion

Discuss these questions as a class.

1. Was the model discussion well organized? Why or why not?
2. Did the group leader do a good job? Why or why not?
3. Did all group members research their topic? How do you know?
4. Do you believe the problem is as serious as the group described? Why or why not?
5. Did all group members stay on track? How do you know?
6. Who was an unproductive group member? In what way was this member unproductive?

VII. Pronunciation Practice: Stress within Words

Every word of more than one syllable has a syllable that is emphasized more than the others. These stressed syllables receive more force and are louder than the others.

In some words, it is possible to predict where the stress will fall. For example, many two-syllable nouns and verbs are spelled alike. However, when spoken, these noun/verb pairs are pronounced differently. Most of the nouns are stressed on the first syllable and the verbs on the second syllable.

ACTIVITY 1 Practice Words

Listen and repeat the following words. Be sure to stress each word on the correct syllable.

Stress the First Syllable	Stress the Second Syllable	Stress the Final Syllable
apple	al**low**	guaran**tee**
table	va**nil**la	after**noon**
yesterday	to**mor**row	recom**mend**
elephant	ac**cep**tance	seven**teen**
president	com**ple**tely	intro**duce**

ACTIVITY 2 Practice Noun/Verb Pairs and Sentences

Listen and repeat the noun/verb pairs and sentences. Be sure to stress the nouns on the first syllable and the verbs on the second syllable.

Nouns		Verbs	
1. **pre**sent	(a gift)	pre**sent**	(to give; to show)
2. **pro**ject	(an assignment)	pro**ject**	(to predict; to anticipate)
3. **con**vict	(a criminal)	con**vict**	(to find guilty)
4. **ob**ject	(a thing; a purpose)	ob**ject**	(to be against)
5. **des**ert	(a hot, dry, sandy land mass)	de**sert**	(to abandon)

6. I **object** (v) to the ugly **object**. (n)
7. He will **present** (v) you with a **present**. (n)
8. We **project** (v) that the **project** (n) will be good.
9. Please don't **desert** (v) me in the **desert**. (n)
10. The jury will vote to **convict** (v) the ex-**convict**. (n)

ACTIVITY 3 Speech Practice

🎧 **A** Listen again to the Model Discussion on pages 167–171. Circle the first ten words stressed on the first syllable, the first ten words stressed on the second syllable, and the six words stressed on the third syllable.

B Complete the following chart with the twenty-six words you circled from the Model Discussion. The first three are done as an example.

Words Stressed on First Syllable		Words Stressed on Second Syllable		Words Stressed on Third Syllable
national		obesity		introduce

C Practice pronouncing these words aloud with a partner.

VIII. Playing with Sayings: Sayings with Multisyllabic Words

ACTIVITY 1 Learn the Meanings

Read the following sayings. Check the ones you heard in the Model Discussion. Refer back to pages 167–171 if necessary.

_____ 1. **Necessity is the mother of invention:** When you really need to solve a problem, you will figure out a way to do it.
The artist couldn't afford expensive paper, so he painted on old envelopes. *Necessity is the mother of invention.*

_____ 2. **All that glitters is not gold:** Something that looks great doesn't always have value.
Movie stars appear to lead exciting lives, but many of them are very unhappy. *All that glitters is not gold.*

_____ 3. **The handwriting is on the wall:** Something bad is about to happen; it's obvious that there is a problem.
The company didn't pay its employees last week. *The handwriting is on the wall*—the company is about to go out of business.

_____ 4. **Birds of a feather flock together:** People with similar characters and interests tend to associate with one another.
Jenny hangs around with smart people. She must be smart, too, because *birds of a feather flock together.*

_____ 5. **Leave well enough alone:** Allow something to stay as it is so you don't make it worse.
I thought about revising my essay, but decided to *leave well enough alone.*

A Work with a partner. Complete each of the following statements with the saying that best fits the context.

1. My eyeglass frames broke, so I used a paper clip to hold my glasses together. After all,
   _____.

2. The recipe has turned out fine in the past, so you should
   _____.

3. My friend dislikes school and complains constantly about having to study.
   _____. It looks like she is going to drop out of school.

4. My beautiful, shiny new car turned out to have all kinds of problems. I learned that
   _____.

5. His son likes to play chess. Because _____, he will probably
   join the chess team.

B Complete the following chart with the twenty-six two-, three-, and four-syllable words from the sentences in part A. Note: Seventeen are stressed on the first syllable; nine are stressed on the second syllable.

Words Stressed on the First Syllable	Words Stressed on the Second Syllable

C Practice reading the sentences from part A aloud. Be sure to pronounce the multisyllabic words correctly.

IX. Presentation Project: Problem-Solving Group Discussion

There are many problems in society. Your project is to participate in a fifteen-to-twenty-minute discussion about one of them. You should pretend that you are discussing the topic with no audience watching you.

STEP 1 | Choose a Topic

A Work together in groups of four or five students. Brainstorm possible discussion topics. Use your own paper to record your group's ideas or choose one of the following.

illegal immigration	animal abuse	underage drinking
credit card fraud	credit card debt	cheating on exams
illegal music downloads	child abuse	gang violence
computer hacking	homelessness	nursing home abuse
paparazzi	juvenile delinquency	shoplifting
teenage pregnancy	police brutality	illegal internet gambling

B As a group, evaluate the topics and choose the three you all like best.

C Working independently, go online or use a library to find some information about the topics your group selected.

D Meet again as a group in class. Brainstorm the merits of each topic and choose one for your discussion.

STEP 2 | Plan for Your Discussion

A Choose a group leader.

B Read the steps your discussions should follow.

Introduction
1. The group leader introduces the topic.
2. The group leader describes how the discussion will be organized.

Body
Step 1: Prove the problem exists.
Step 2: Describe the consequences or future effects of the problem.
Step 3: Describe the causes of the problem.
Step 4: Propose various solutions to the problem.
Step 5: Evaluate the solutions and choose the best ones. Discuss the questions:
- Does the proposed solution eliminate one or more causes of the problem?
- Does the proposed solution create new problems?

Conclusion
1. The group leader brings the discussion to a close after fifteen or twenty minutes.
2. The group leader thanks the participants.

C Read the Useful Language you can use during the discussion. Place a check mark ✓ next to the expressions you like best.

USEFUL LANGUAGE FOR GROUP LEADER:
Encouraging Participation

_____ You've been very quiet, [name of person]. What did you find?

_____ We haven't heard from you, [name of person] How do you feel about
_____?

_____ [Name of person], you haven't said anything yet. Please share your findings with the group.

USEFUL LANGUAGE FOR PARTICIPANTS:
Feedback and Reinforcement

_____ That's really scary [interesting, disturbing].

_____ Good point, [name of person].

_____ You really gave this a lot of thought, [name of person].

_____ I agree with you, [name of person].

D Research your group's topic on your own. Be prepared to participate in a problem-solving discussion about it in class on the scheduled date.

E Select a saying from page 173 to include during the discussion. Write it here:

_____

STEP 3 | Prepare Discussion Note Cards

A Group Member Note Cards

1. Prepare at least one note card for each step of the discussion. Label the cards:
   - Proof the Problem Exists
   - Consequences of the Problem
   - Causes of the Problem
   - Possible Solutions to the Problem
   - Pros and Cons of Each Solution

2. Add important details from your research notes.

3. Number your cards.

4. Add Useful Language from this page and a saying from page 173 to your notes.

B Group Leader Note Cards

1. Prepare the following note cards:
   - Introduction + Preview
   - Transition to Prove the Problem Exists
   - Transition to the Consequences of the Problem
   - Transition to Causes of the Problem
   - Transition to Possible Solutions to the Problem
   - Transition to Evaluate Solutions and Choose the Best Ones
   - Conclusion

2. Number your cards.

3. All group members should include at least one presentation aid.

STEP 4 | Review Your Notes

A Read your notes aloud several times to become familiar with them.

B Complete the discussion checklist. Is there anything you want to change or add to your notes before the scheduled discussion?

Discussion Checklist	YES	NO
1. I included information proving the problem exists.	☐	☐
2. I included information about the consequences of the problem.	☐	☐
3. I included information explaining the causes of the problem.	☐	☐
4. I included several possible solutions to the problem.	☐	☐
5. I can give at least two sources for my information.	☐	☐
6. I have sufficient information to contribute to a fifteen- to twenty-minute discussion.	☐	☐
7. I included a saying from the chapter.	☐	☐
8. I included a presentation aid.	☐	☐
9. I included my personal opinions and examples.	☐	☐
10. I completed the group-member note cards.	☐	☐
11. I completed the group-leader note cards (group leader only.)	☐	☐
12. My pronunciation of words with more than one syllable is correct.	☐	☐

C Your teacher and/or your classmates may evaluate your participation in the discussion. Study the form on page 237 so you know how you will be evaluated. You may use the items on the form to make final changes to your notes.

STEP 5 | Participate in the Group Discussion

A Relax, take a deep breath, and join in the discussion.

B Listen to your audience's applause.

CHAPTER 9

SPEAKING TO PERSUADE

We use persuasive language all the time. Whenever we ask a friend to lend us money, ask our teacher for a higher grade, try to convince a sibling to lose some weight, or coax a parent to buy us something, we are speaking to persuade.

Any speech is persuasive if its purpose is to convince others to change their feelings, beliefs, or behaviors. A salesperson trying to convince someone to buy a product, a political leader trying to get someone to vote a certain way, and a teacher lecturing about why a history class should be required are all speaking to persuade.

CHAPTER CHALLENGE Your challenge in this chapter will be to learn how to plan and organize information for a speech to persuade. Your goal will be to convince the audience to agree with your persuasive claim. When you complete this chapter, you will know how to:

- choose a persuasive topic
- determine the specific purpose for the claim
- analyze your audience
- plan, prepare, and present a speech to persuade

I. Preparing for the Persuasive Speech

As with the informative speech, you build a persuasive speech step by step. The path below will help you create persuasive presentations that are interesting and effective. The steps for preparing a persuasive speech are:

1. Choosing your topic
2. Determining your specific purpose
3. Analyzing your audience
4. Gathering information
5. Preparing presentation aids
6. Organizing your speech

1. Choose a Topic

2. Determine the Specific Purpose

5. Prepare Visual Aids

4. Gather Information

3. Analyze the Audience

6. Organize the Speech

A. Choosing Your Topic

1. Choose a Topic

As with your previous speeches, your first question may be, "What should I talk about?" This section provides several suggestions for choosing appropriate topics for your persuasive speech.

Choose a Topic That Really Interests You

It is easy to think of ideas if you choose a topic that you feel strongly about.

EXAMPLE:

A student who had a brown belt in karate gave a speech entitled "Everyone Should Learn Karate as a Form of Self-Defense."

Suggest a Change That Isn't Too Large

It is much easier to convince listeners to adjust their opinions, feelings, or behavior a little than to persuade them to adopt a radically different point of view.

EXAMPLE:

It would be unrealistic to try to persuade a very religious person to convert to a different faith. However, you might be able to convince the person to read a book about different religious customs.

Choose a Topic That Is Controversial

Do not choose a point of view that most people already agree with.

EXAMPLE:

The topic "English Is Spoken All Over the World" is not controversial. However, "Everyone Should Learn English as a Second Language" and "English Should Be Required in Brazilian Schools" are topics that could be disputed since many people might disagree with these opinions.

ACTIVITY 1 Evaluate the Topics

Read the list of persuasive claims. Label each claim as follows:

a. Too general
b. Not controversial
c. Calls for an unrealistically large change
✓ Clear and specific

EXAMPLES:

_____a_____ The legal drinking age should be lowere

_____✓_____ The legal drinking age should be 18 year

_____c_____ Everyone should go skydiving this week

_____b_____ It is unhealthy for babies to drink alcoh

_____ 1. Homosexual couples should be allowed

_____ 2. Small children should not be left unatter

_____ 3. Highway speed limits are too high.

_____ 4. First time shoplifters should receive life i

_____ 5. Exercise is good for you.

_____ 6. Supermarkets should not be allowed to s

_____ 7. Driving under the influence of alcohol is

[Handwritten notes on sticky note:]
1. can't in b
2. a we don't know the age.
3. a we don't specific limit
4. c.
5. b
6. c
9. b
10. a

_____ 8. Testing cosmetics on animals should be banned.

_____ 9. Eliminate red meat from your diet.

_____ 10. Children's TV watching should be limited.

Be as Specific as Possible

EXAMPLE:

The topic "Mothers should not work while their children are young" is not specific. Is it all right for mothers to work in the home? How old should their children be before their mothers may work outside the home? Would part-time work be acceptable? The following two persuasive claims are more specific:

- Mothers should not work outside the home until their children attend kindergarten, *or*
- Mothers should not work outside the home until their children start high school.

ACTIVITY 2 Formulate Persuasive Claims for Topics

1 Work in small groups. Look over the following general topics. Take turns presenting your opinions about them. If you have a strong opinion about one, you may have found a good topic for your persuasive speech.

capital punishment	cloning (of animals or humans)
arranged marriages	legalization of marijuana
required college courses	smoking in public places
gun control	the legal drinking age
living together before marriage	euthanasia
working mothers	violence on TV
stem cell research	highway speed limits
animal experimentation	

2 Choose two or three of your favorite general topics. Formulate three specific persuasive claims for each general topic and write them on the lines.

EXAMPLE:

General Topic: Required College Courses

Specific Persuasive Claims:

- Students should not be required to take math classes in college.
- All students should be required to take three semesters of a foreign language in college.
- Required courses should be abolished at all public universities.

a. General Topic: _____

Specific Persuasive Claims:

(1) _____

(2) _____

(3) _____

b. General Topic: _____

    Specific Persuasive Claims:

    (1)_____

    (2)_____

    (3)_____

c. General Topic: _____

    Specific Persuasive Claims:

    (1)_____

    (2)_____

    (3)_____

3 Share your specific persuasive claims with the class. Invite suggestions for additional specific claims related to the general topics you chose.

B. Determining Your Specific Purpose

2. Determine the Specific Purpose

The general goal of persuasive speaking is to convince your listeners to change something. To accomplish this goal, you must first decide what you want them to change—a belief, an opinion, or their behavior.

Changing an Audience's Belief about the Truth of Something

In this case, your specific purpose is to convince the audience of one of the following:

- A reported fact is either true or false.
- Something will or won't happen.
- An event was represented accurately or inaccurately.

EXAMPLES:
- The defendant committed (or did not commit) a crime.
- Capital punishment is (or is not) a deterrent to crime.
- There is (or is not) life after death.

Changing an Audience's Opinion about the Value of Something

In this case, your specific purpose is to convince the audience that something is:

- Good or bad
- Important or unimportant
- Fair or unfair
- Better or worse (than something else)
- Helpful or not helpful

- It is fair (or unfair) for foreign students to pay higher tuition than American-born students.
- Required math courses in college are important (or unimportant).
- Dogs make better (or worse) pets than cats.
- New York is more (or less) interesting for tourists than San Francisco.

ACTIVITY 1   Differentiate Facts from Opinions

This activity is designed to help you understand the difference between statements of fact and statements of opinion. Understanding this distinction will help you to determine your specific purpose.

1 Work alone for five or ten minutes. Follow these steps:

   a. Think of any place (city, state, country, continent, etc.) in the world beginning with the first letter of your first name. (For example, Pablo chose Panama.)

   b. Think of two objective, indisputable facts about the place. ("Panama is in Central America." "Panama is an isthmus.")

   c. Now think of a product, an animal, or an object beginning with the first letter of your first name. (Pablo chose perfume.)

   d. Think of two subjective opinions about the product, animal, or object. ("Perfume makes people more attractive." "Perfume smells nice.")

2 Now work with the whole class. Take turns saying your four statements to the group. After each statement, the class should call out "Fact" or "Opinion." If your classmates disagree, your teacher will lead a discussion to figure out the reason for the disagreement. (You might be surprised to find that something you stated as a fact turned out to be an opinion.)

Changing an Audience's Behavior

In this case, your specific purpose is to convince your listeners:
- To do something they are not doing now.
- To stop a behavior they currently practice.

EXAMPLES:
- You should donate blood at the campus blood drive.
- You should stop drinking coffee.
- You should limit the amount of TV you watch to a maximum of one hour daily.
- You should learn to scuba dive for a hobby.

ACTIVITY 2   Identify the Specific Purpose

1 Work with a partner. Write the letter of the specific purpose next to each persuasive speech topic.

   a. Change an audience's belief about the truthfulness of something

   b. Change an audience's opinion about the value of something

   c. Change an audience's behavior

   _____ (1) Everyone should learn to give artificial respiration.

   _____ (2) Airplane travel is the safest way to travel in the United States.

   _____ (3) Soccer is a more exciting sport than baseball.

   _____ (4) All cigarette advertising should be prohibited.

   _____ (5) Lower highway speed limits save lives.

_____ (6) Homosexual marriages should be legal nationally.

_____ (7) History is a better major than biology.

_____ (8) You should donate at least fifty dollars a year to your favorite charity.

_____ (9) Alcoholic beverages should not be sold on Sunday.

_____ (10) Parrots make wonderful pets.

2 **Compare your responses in small groups.**

C. Analyzing Your Audience

3. Analyze the Audience

Audience analysis was discussed on page 86 of Chapter 5: Speaking to Inform. It is especially important in persuasive speaking. You need to know how your audience members feel and why they feel a certain way in order to prepare an effective persuasive speech.

You can expect your listeners to feel one of three ways about the topic you choose for your persuasive speech. They might:

Agree. If your audience already agrees with your belief or point of view, you must choose a different topic for your speech.

Be Indifferent. If your audience doesn't care about your topic, you must find out why they are indifferent to it. In your speech, you need to:

- Interest them in your topic
- Convince them that it is important
- Persuade them to adopt your opinion

Disagree. If your listeners do not agree with your point of view, they probably have definite reasons for feeling the way they do. You must find out why they disagree with your opinion in order to convince them that their reasons are incorrect or unreasonable.

ACTIVITY **Analyze Your Audience**

1 **Select one of the claims you wrote in Activity 2, page 182.**

2 **Work in small groups. State your claim. Your classmates should respond by saying if they agree, disagree, or are indifferent.**

3 **Change groups. Survey the members of the new group. Repeat this step if there is time.**

4 **Analyze your classmates' responses. Report to the class whether your claim would be suitable for a persuasive speech in your class.**

D. Gathering Information

4. Gather Information

The next step is to collect the information you need to create your speech. You can do this in three ways:

1. Write down what you already know about your topic.

2. Think about your own related observations or experiences.

3. Gather additional necessary information by:
   - conducting research;
   - interviewing experts or people who have an interest in your topic.

When you are looking for information for a persuasive speech, the editorial pages of newspapers can be especially useful. They often include articles and letters that express different opinions about current controversial topics. The Internet may be of particular value as well: Often there are links to websites in which different opinions about the topic are expressed.

Whenever you quote specific people or use information from newspapers, magazines, books, or the Internet in your speech, be sure to tell your audience the source of your information. This will make your evidence and arguments more believable. You will also gain the respect of your listeners by showing them that you are a responsible researcher.

E. Preparing Presentation Aids

As discussed in Chapter 4, presentation aids make your speech more interesting. They can be very powerful persuasive tools. An audience is more likely to be convinced if they can actually see the importance of what you are describing.

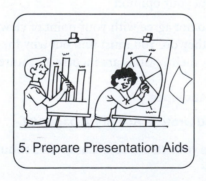

5. Prepare Presentation Aids

EXAMPLE A:

In a speech to persuade a class to donate money to a charity that helps children with disabilities, this picture affected the audience emotionally and thus made them want to make a donation.

EXAMPLE B:

In a speech to persuade a class to complain to university officials about polluted lakes on campus, one student held up a large bottle of dirty brown water with a dead fish in it. He explained that the dead fish came from one of the nearby lakes. This convinced the students that his speech presented a serious problem.

F. Organizing Your Speech

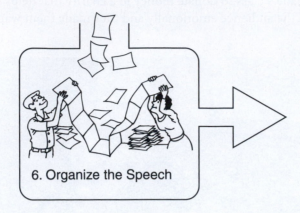

6. Organize the Speech

The next step is to organize your speech. A good persuasive speech includes the following components:

1. Opener building on areas of agreement with audience
2. Statement of persuasive claim
3. Preview of persuasive points
4. Body
5. Summary
6. Memorable concluding remarks
7. Transitions

1. Prepare an Opener Building on Areas of Agreement

The introduction to a persuasive speech is very important. In order to convince listeners to agree with you, it is essential to give them a reason to trust you and to see you as a person who thinks as they do. You can do this by first discussing:

- Common goals (we all want the same basic things in life)
- Common problems (we are all concerned about this particular problem)
- Common experiences (we all know what it is like to . . .)

The openers below demonstrate how two speakers built on areas of agreement with their audience.

EXAMPLE A: "Highway Speed Limits Should be Reduced to Fifty Miles Per Hour"

Most of us know people who have had friends or family injured or killed in terrible car accidents on the highways. Certainly we've all read or heard about these tragedies in the news. We all want to live long, happy, healthy lives. No one wants to worry about whether they will arrive at their destination safely every time they get in a car.

EXAMPLE B: "Capital Punishment Should Be Legal"

I'm sure everyone here is concerned about crime in our community. Many of us know that it isn't always safe to go out alone at night or even to walk through a dark parking lot to get to our car. All of us want to feel safe in our homes, in our cars, and on the streets. We would all like to see the amount of crime reduced.

2. Clearly State Your Persuasive Claim

After showing your audience that you are a sensible person who shares their values and beliefs, you should clearly state your persuasive claim.

EXAMPLES:

- The maximum speed limit on U.S. highways should be fifty miles per hour.
- Capital punishment should be legal nationwide.

3. Prepare a Preview of Main Persuasive Points

After stating your specific persuasive claim, you should preview the main arguments you will present in the body of your speech. Study the sample previews that follow.

EXAMPLE A: "Donate Blood to a Hospital Blood Bank"

I hope to persuade you to donate blood to a hospital blood bank for several reasons.

I. Blood donations save lives.

II. Blood donation is perfectly safe and painless.

III. It is very convenient.

EXAMPLE B: "Casino Gambling Should Be Legal in Los Angeles"

There are three important reasons why we should support casino gambling in our city.

I. The creation of new jobs will reduce unemployment.

II. A proposed sales-tax increase will not be necessary.

III. The city will have more funds to improve public facilities.

4. Prepare the Body

You must present evidence that will convince listeners to agree with you. Your audience analysis will help you decide how to convince listeners who are indifferent or who disagree with your claim.

Persuading Indifferent Listeners Indifferent listeners do not see how a topic relates to them. In order to persuade listeners with this attitude, you must convince them that your topic is:

- interesting.
- important.
- relevant to them.

EXAMPLE A:

A student wanted to persuade the class to buy water-purification systems. According to this speaker's opinion survey, his classmates were indifferent to this topic because they had never given it any thought and didn't believe it was important. However, he found a newspaper story claiming that the quality of water in their community was the worst in the United States. In the article, doctors warned that drinking this water could increase the risk of getting cancer. This fact helped persuade the audience that the topic was relevant to them.

EXAMPLE B:

Another student gave a speech entitled "Casino Gambling Should Be Legal in Los Angeles." After doing her audience analysis, she found that her classmates were indifferent to her topic for several reasons. Some students said they didn't gamble, while some international students said they would live in Los Angeles for only a couple of years. The speaker explained that casino gambling would help the city's finances so that a proposed sales-tax increase would not be necessary. If the sales tax were not increased, prices in all stores and restaurants would be lower. Then everyone (gamblers and nongamblers, permanent residents and students on temporary visas) would benefit. In this way she was able to show how the topic was important and relevant to her listeners.

Persuading Hostile Listeners Hostile listeners are those who strongly disagree with your opinion or belief. In order to persuade such listeners, you need to learn their reasons for disagreeing with you and convince them that these reasons are not valid.

EXAMPLE A:

One student wanted to persuade the class to donate blood to a hospital blood bank. According to this student's audience analysis, there were two reasons why his classmates didn't want to be blood donors.

- They were afraid of catching a disease from a dirty hypodermic needle.
- They didn't have transportation to get to the hospital.

To refute the first reason, the student interviewed the nurse in charge of the hospital blood bank. She explained:

- An individually wrapped and sterilized needle is used for every blood donor.
- All needles are thrown away after each use. Therefore, it is impossible to catch a disease.

To refute the second reason, the speaker explained that it is very easy to get to the hospital because

- a bus goes from campus directly to the hospital every fifteen minutes; and
- the hospital offers a free transportation service to all blood donors.

EXAMPLE B:

One student gave a speech entitled "Capital Punishment Should Be Legal throughout the United States." This student's audience analysis showed that his classmates strongly disagreed with his claim for these reasons:

- Some believed that capital punishment does not reduce crime.
- Some audience members believed that murderers should be rehabilitated.

To refute the first reason, the student:

- presented evidence that fewer murders are committed in states with the death penalty than in states without it; and
- quoted a law enforcement expert who stated that criminals are less likely to commit murder if they fear the death penalty.

To refute the second reason, the speaker reported:

- results of studies showing the ineffectiveness of attempts to rehabilitate criminals; and
- specific studies showing that most lawbreakers released from jail after participating in rehabilitation programs continue to commit the same crimes.

5. Prepare a Summary

An effective persuasive speech includes a summary of the evidence presented. This will remind your audience of why they should agree with you. The examples below show how the summaries were outlined in two speeches.

EXAMPLE A: "Donate Blood to a Hospital Blood Bank"
I'm sure you now realize that you should donate blood.

I. It's rewarding and worthwhile.
    A. Think of a dying person whose life you might save.
    B. Think of the great personal satisfaction you'll have.
II. It's perfectly safe and painless.
    A. Donating blood doesn't hurt a bit.
    B. There is no chance of catching any kind of disease.
III. It's very convenient.
    A. It will only take a few minutes of your time.
    B. Free round-trip transportation to the hospital is available.

EXAMPLE B: "Casino Gambling Should Be Legal in Los Angeles"
As you can now see, legalizing casino gambling in Los Angeles would greatly benefit you and all residents of the city.

I. A proposed sales-tax increase will not be necessary.
    A. It will keep prices you pay in restaurants lower.
    B. It will keep prices you pay in retail stores lower.

II. Los Angeles's finances will improve.
   A. More money will be available to improve the roads you use.
   B. More money will be available to improve the public parks and beaches you enjoy.
   C. More money will be available for public schools.

6. Prepare Memorable Concluding Remarks

Your concluding remarks should reinforce why listeners should change a belief, an opinion, or a behavior. An effective way to do this is to make them think about the future and to remind them to take some type of action.

EXAMPLE A:

You might be healthy now, but think about your health in a few months or in several years. We all know that the water in this city is unhealthy. With a home purification system, you'll never worry about drinking polluted water again. For less than seventy-five dollars, you can turn your kitchen faucet into a reservoir of fresh water. It is in your best interest to install a purification system for your sink today.

EXAMPLE B:

Be the best you can be! Just think—in a few short weeks, a beautiful, slender, athletic body can be yours. Heads will turn as you walk down the street. [Speaker shows this photo.]

So go out and start an exercise program today!

7. Prepare Transitions

In a speech to persuade, transitions serve a unique purpose. They both acknowledge listeners' reasons for disagreeing with your claim and announce your intention to change the listeners' minds. In other words, your transition should restate the reason your classmates gave for disagreeing with your persuasive claim. Then it should announce the evidence you will use to prove their reason is not valid.

EXAMPLE A:

At least half of you in this audience stated you would not donate blood due to fears about being infected with a disease. I will now prove to you that donating blood is completely safe and this should not be a concern.

EXAMPLE B:

Many people are against capital punishment because they believe murderers should be rehabilitated. I'm about to present the results of many studies and expert testimony proving that rehabilitation programs simply don't work.

II. Presentation Preview

Your goal in this chapter is to present a persuasive speech on an issue about which you have a strong opinion.

ACTIVITY 1   Listen to a Model Presentation

Listen to Feng's model speech. Notice the following components:

• Opener building on areas of agreement
• Statement of persuasive claim
• Preview of main persuasive points
• Body
• Summary
• Memorable concluding remarks
• Transitions

Feng's Presentation: Acupuncture Is the Way to Go!

INTRODUCTION

Opener Building on Areas of Agreement
We all know someone who has been sick or in pain. Maybe you or someone you know has had painful surgery or suffers from depression. Often, prescription medicines have side effects and make the patient feel even worse. When we don't feel well, we'd all like to feel better as quickly as possible. Acupuncture might be the solution.

Statement of Persuasive Claim
So today, I would like to persuade you to consider acupuncture when you are sick or in pain.

Preview
There are many reasons you should consider acupuncture instead of traditional Western medicine.

First, acupuncture is a medically proven treatment.
Second, acupuncture is safe.
And third, acupuncture effectively treats many conditions.

Transition Many of you might be skeptical about acupuncture because you believe it is an unproven treatment. You will be amazed to learn that acupuncture has been used for thousands of years and is medically respected worldwide.

BODY According to the Encyclopedia Britannica, acupuncture is an ancient Chinese medical technique for relieving pain and curing disease. It has been used successfully in Asian cultures for more than 2,500 years.

Acupuncture is endorsed by American mainstream medicine as well as by international organizations. In 1997, a panel of scientists at the National Institutes of Health, also known as the NIH, determined that acupuncture had been clinically proven to be effective against a variety of medical problems and diseases. The World Health Organization—also called the WHO—has endorsed acupuncture as a medical therapy for over fifteen years.

Transition Another reason you might avoid acupuncture is that you worry it is not safe. You will be very pleased to learn that acupuncture is in fact very safe.

According to the *Medical Acupuncture Online Journal*, acupuncture is extremely safe with virtually no chances of side effects, unlike prescription medicines. Many patients become addicted to pain medicines. This won't happen with acupuncture. According to the book *Acupuncture for Everyone* by Dr. Ruth Kidsor, acupuncture is not addictive. Also, there is absolutely no risk of catching any type of communicable disease from acupuncture needles. This is because modern acupuncturists use only sterilized, individually packaged needles that they throw away when they're done with each treatment. Have a look at this photo of a calm, happy patient receiving acupuncture. She knows how safe it is!

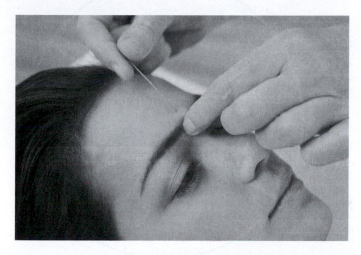

Transition Next, some of you might think that acupuncture is helpful for only a few minor problems. I'll now prove to you that acupuncture treats a wide variety of problems and diseases.

First, clinical studies have shown that acupuncture helps patients with chronic pain. The WHO and the NIH have determined that it is effective in reducing pain from migraines, arthritis, and surgery.

According to a 2003 WHO report, acupuncture has also been proven to help people with allergies, asthma, and heart problems. Both the WHO and NIH found that acupuncture reduces a patient's nausea from anesthesia and chemotherapy. Additionally, acupuncture helps people's immune systems to function better. This helps them to avoid colds, the flu, and other respiratory infections. Many people simply use acupuncture as an effective form of preventive medicine.

Acupuncture also effectively treats many emotional problems. It helps patients with anxiety disorders, and it alleviates stress. For example, in 1998 researchers at the University of Arizona found that acupuncture was effective in treating depression. In July 2011, a Massachusetts General Hospital study also demonstrated that acupuncture effectively treats clinical depression.

CONCLUSION **Summary**
So, I hope I have convinced you to consider acupuncture when you are sick or in pain. Remember: Acupuncture is a clinically proven and respected medical

(continued)

(continued)

treatment. It's perfectly safe; and finally, acupuncture treats a wide variety of physical and emotional problems.

Memorable Concluding Remarks
Now you can throw away those medicines that bother your stomach or make you sleepy. Remember, there is an alternative. The next time you aren't feeling well physically or emotionally, why not *kill two birds with one stone*. Acupuncture can help you with both!

* Solve two problems with one action

ACTIVITY 2 Model Presentation Discussion

Discuss these questions in small groups:

1. How did Feng build on areas of agreement? Was this effective? Why or why not?
2. How did Feng state his specific persuasive claim?
3. What were the persuasive points Feng included in his preview?
4. How did Feng phrase his transitions? Were they effective, in your opinion?
5. Was Feng's summary effective? Why or why not?
6. Will you remember Feng's concluding remarks? Why or why not?
7. Were you convinced that acupuncture is medically beneficial? Why or why not?
8. Were Feng's presentation aids persuasive? Why or why not?
9. How could Feng have been even more persuasive?

ACTIVITY 3 Outline Feng's Speech

1 Work with a partner. Using the model speech as a guide, complete the outline below.

Feng's Persuasive Speech Outline

Introduction

I. **Opener Building on Areas of Agreement**

We all know someone who has been sick or in pain. Maybe you or someone you know has had painful surgery or suffers from depression. Often, prescription medicines have side effects and make the patient feel even worse. When we don't feel well, we'd all like to recover as quickly as possible. Acupuncture might be the solution.

II. **Statement of Persuasive Claim**

So today, I would like to persuade you to consider acupuncture when you are sick or in pain.

III. **Preview**

There are many reasons to consider acupuncture instead of traditional Western medicine.

A. _____

B. _____

C. _____

Transition: Many of you might be skeptical about acupuncture because you believe it is a new and unproven treatment. You will be amazed to learn that acupuncture has been used for thousands of years and is medically respected worldwide.

Body

I. _____

A. Acupuncture is an ancient Chinese technique.

   1. Relieves pain

   2. _____

   3. _____

B. Acupuncture is endorsed by national and international health organizations.

   1. _____

   2. _____

Transition: Another reason you might avoid acupuncture is that you worry it is not safe. You will be very pleased to learn that acupuncture is in fact very safe.

II. _____

A. There are no side effects.

B. _____.

(continued)

(continued)

C. _____

    1. <u>Only sterilized, individually packaged needles are used.</u>

    2. _____

Transition: Next, some of you might think that acupuncture is helpful for only a few minor problems. I will now prove to you that acupuncture treats a wide variety of problems and diseases.

III. _____

  A. _____

    1. migraines

    2. _____

    3. _____

  B. Medical conditions

    1. _____

    2. _____

    3. _____

    4. _____

      a. _____

      b. chemotherapy

  C. Helps the immune system function better

    1. _____

    2. _____

  D. Emotional problems

    1. Anxiety disorders

    2. _____

    3. _____

Conclusion

I. I hope I have convinced you to consider acupuncture when you are sick or in pain.

  A. Acupuncture is a clinically proven and respected medical treatment.

  B. Acupuncture is perfectly safe.

  C. Acupuncture treats a wide variety of physical and emotional problems.

II. Now you can throw away those medicines that bother your stomach or make you sleepy. Remember, there is an alternative. The next time you aren't feeling well physically or emotionally, why not *kill two birds with one stone*. Acupuncture can help you with both!

2 **Work in small groups and compare your completed outlines.**

III. Pronunciation Practice: Stress within the Sentence

A. Normal Sentence Stress

Effective use of strong and weak stress in phrases and sentences is important to communication. Just as it's awkward to give all syllables in a word equal stress, it's unnatural to stress all the words in a sentence equally. Which words should you stress?

Content words (nouns, verbs, adjectives, adverbs, negatives, and question words) are words that convey meaning. These are the important words in a sentence, and they are normally stressed when spoken. *Function* words (articles, pronouns, conjunctions and prepositions) are less important to meaning; we usually do not stress them.

ACTIVITY Stress Content Words

Listen and repeat the expressions. Be sure to stress the boldfaced content words.

1. in a **moment**
2. to **tell** the **truth**
3. **Silence** is **golden.**
4. **Honesty** is the **best policy.**
5. A **penny saved** is a **penny earned.**
6. as **good** as **gold**
7. as **light** as a **feather**
8. It's **now** or **never.**
9. **luck** of the **draw**
10. as **dry** as a **bone**

B. Contrastive Stress

Speakers often use contrastive stress in a sentence to emphasize information or to convey a special meaning. Speakers can stress any word(s) they wish in a sentence. Even words that normally are not stressed can receive strong stress if the speaker wants to emphasize them.

EXAMPLE:

He is my speech teacher. (This emphasizes who the teacher is.)

He is **my** speech teacher. (This emphasizes that he is the speaker's teacher.)

He is my **speech** teacher. (This emphasizes what kind of teacher he is.)

ACTIVITY 1 Use Contrastive Stress

Listen and repeat the statements. Be sure to emphasize the information in boldface.

1. Our exam will be **Monday**. It won't be **Wednesday**.
2. I ordered a **diet** soda. I didn't order **regular** soda.
3. My **son** has a bad cold. My **daughter** is fine.
4. She wants to wear a **red** dress, not a **white** one.
5. The student studied for three **hours**. He needed to study for three **days**.

ACTIVITY 2 Use Stress for Emphasis

1 Listen and repeat the following sentences from the model speech. Stress the boldfaced words. Give extra emphasis to the capitalized words.

a. **Acupuncture** might be the **solution** for what is ailing **YOU.**
b. **Consider ACUPUNCTURE** when you are **sick** or in **pain.**
c. You'll be **AMAZED** to learn that **acupuncture** has been used for **thousands** of years.
d. **Acupuncture** is **EXTREMELY safe** and **painless.**
e. **Acupuncture** treats many **physical AND emotional** problems.

2 In small groups, discuss the following questions:

  a. Why did the speaker choose to emphasize the boldfaced words?

  b. Why did the speaker give extra emphasis to the capitalized words?

  c. Would you emphasize any other words? Which ones?

IV. Playing with Sayings: Sayings with Contrastive Stress

ACTIVITY 1 Learn the Meanings

1 Read the following sayings. Check the ones you heard in the Model Speech on page 192. Refer back to the model speech if necessary. Notice the contrastive stress.

_____ a. **Kill TWO birds with ONE stone:** Solve two problems with one action.
I can *kill two birds with one stone* by seeing some old friends when I visit my parents in New York.

_____ b. **HASTE makes WASTE:** Acting too quickly results in mistakes.
I left the house in a hurry and forgot my wallet. I had to turn around and drive back home to get it. Now I know that *haste makes waste.*

_____ c. **HALF a loaf is better than NONE:** Something is better than nothing.
The manager offered me part-time work even though I wanted a full-time job.
I accepted because I realized that *half a loaf is better than none.*

_____ d. **His BARK is worse than his BITE:** A person's actions are not as bad as their threats.
Don't let her words scare you. *Her bark is worse than her bite!*

_____ e. **You catch more flies with HONEY than VINEGAR:** You'll be more successful if you're nice than if you're mean.
The waiter ignored the couple making loud demands and served the polite couple first.
The nice couple knows that *you catch more flies with honey than vinegar.*

2 Work with a partner. Practice reading the sayings and examples. Use contrastive stress.

ACTIVITY 2 Use the Sayings

1 Work with a partner. Complete each sentence with the saying that best fits the context.

  a. Take your time and do it right the first time because _____.

  b. I can _____ by asking the repairman to fix my broken dishwasher and microwave during the same service call.

  c. My teacher threatens to fail students when they make mistakes or don't show up on time, but he never actually fails anyone. We don't worry about his threats because we know that
  _____.

  d. My dog wouldn't obey when I yelled at him to come, so I gave him a treat instead. I realized
  _____.

  e. My son wanted a new car. I was able to buy him a used one. It wasn't what he wanted, but he decided that _____.

2 Practice reading your sentences aloud in small groups.

V. Presentation Project: A Speech to Persuade

Choose a topic that is controversial and about which you feel strongly. Your project is to prepare and present a four- to five-minute speech to persuade. Your goal is to convince your audience to agree with your point of view.

STEP 1 | Formulate a Persuasive Claim

Review Choosing Your Topic on page 181 to refresh your memory on how to choose a topic and formulate a persuasive claim. You may choose any of the sample topics on page 182 or another one.

STEP 2 | Analyze Your Audience

A Review Analyzing Your Audience on page 185.

B Interview as many classmates as possible to learn how they feel about your specific persuasive claim. Use the opinion survey form below to record your findings. If they disagree or are indifferent, ask them why.

AUDIENCE ANALYSIS FORM

Persuasive Claim: _____

Record how each of your classmates feels about your topic by placing a checkmark in the appropriate column.

Disagree	Indifferent	Agree
✓ _____	✓ _____	✓ _____
_____	_____	_____
Total = _____	Total = _____	Total = _____

If your classmates are indifferent, it is because (check all reasons given):

_____ They don't think your topic affects them.

_____ They have never heard of your topic.

_____ They have never given your topic any thought.

_____ Other: _____

_____

If your classmates disagree with your opinion, it is because (write all reasons given):

1. _____

2. _____

3. _____

4. _____

5. _____

A Review your completed outline of Feng's persuasive speech on page 195. Pay attention to the parts of his speech.

B Read the guidelines for organizing your speech.

Introduction
1. Build on areas of agreement.
2. State your specific persuasive claim.
3. Preview your main persuasive arguments.

Body
1. Include three persuasive arguments to support your claim.
2. Provide evidence.
   - Cite sources.
   - Use examples.
   - Use presentation aids.
3. Include transitions stating the reasons why listeners disagree with your claim and your intention to disprove those reasons.

Conclusion
1. Repeat your persuasive claim in the opening summary sentence. Then summarize your main persuasive points.
2. Conclude with memorable remarks.

C Read the Useful Language you can use during your persuasive speech. Place a check mark ✓ next to the expressions you like best.

USEFUL LANGUAGE: BUILDING ON AREAS OF AGREEMENT
_____ I'm sure everyone here worries about . . .

_____ The majority of people would agree that . . .

_____ Most of us know someone who . . .

_____ We all love and care about our families and dear friends. Therefore we all hope that…

USEFUL LANGUAGE: TRANSITIONS
_____ Many of you disagree with [topic] because. . . . Let me assure you that . . .

_____ Some of you don't think [topic] is important. My evidence proves _____ is very important.

_____ Many of you were against [topic] because. . . . I have solid proof that shows . . . [the opposite]

D Complete the following outline for your speech.

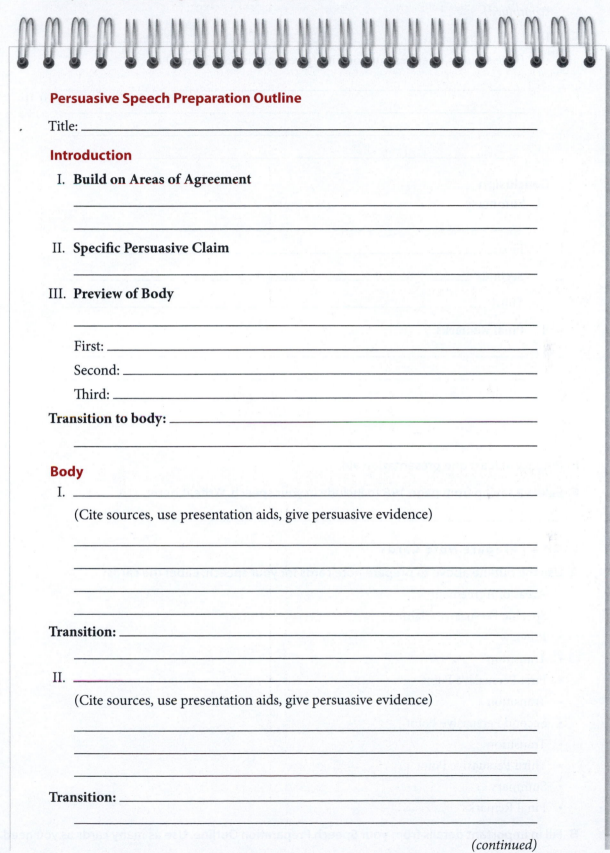

Persuasive Speech Preparation Outline

Title: _____

Introduction

I. **Build on Areas of Agreement**

_____

_____

II. **Specific Persuasive Claim**

_____

III. **Preview of Body**

_____

First: _____

Second: _____

Third: _____

Transition to body: _____

_____

Body

I. _____

(Cite sources, use presentation aids, give persuasive evidence)

_____

_____

_____

Transition: _____

_____

II. _____

(Cite sources, use presentation aids, give persuasive evidence)

_____

_____

_____

Transition: _____

_____

(continued)

(continued)

III. _____

(Cite sources, use presentation aids, give persuasive evidence)

_____

_____

_____

Conclusion

I. **Summary**

_____

First: _____

Second: _____

Third: _____

II. **Final Remarks**

_____

_____

E Prepare at least one presentation aid.

F Select a saying from page 198 to include in your speech. Write it here:

_____.

STEP 4 | Prepare Note Cards

A Use the outline above to prepare note cards for your speech. Label the cards:

- Areas of Agreement
- Specific Persuasive Claim
- Preview
- Transition
- First Persuasive Point
- Transition
- Second Persuasive Point
- Transition
- Third Persuasive Point
- Summary
- Final Remarks

B Fill in important details from your Speech Preparation Outline. Use as many cards as you need.

C Add Useful Language and a saying from 198 to your notes.

D Number your cards.

STEP 5 | Practice Your Speech

A Practice your speech with your note cards and presentation aid(s). Record it and listen to it at least once. Be sure it is between four and five minutes.

B Complete the speech checklist. Is there anything you want to change or improve before you present your speech in class?

Speech Checklist	YES	NO
1. In my introduction I built on areas of agreement.	☐	☐
2. I stated my specific persuasive claim and included a preview.	☐	☐
3. I included three persuasive arguments in support of my claim.	☐	☐
4. I included transitions.	☐	☐
5. I included a summary and final remarks.	☐	☐
6. I included a saying from the chapter.	☐	☐
7. I included a presentation aid.	☐	☐
8. My stress within sentences is effective.	☐	☐
9. My speech is between four and five minutes.	☐	☐

C Practice again with your note cards and presentation aid.

D Your teacher and/or your classmates may evaluate your speech. Study the form on page 239 so you know how you will be evaluated. You may use the items on the form to make final changes to your speech.

STEP 6 | Present Your Speech

A Relax, take a deep breath, and present your speech.

B Listen to your audience's applause.

CHAPTER 10

DARE TO DEBATE

A debate is an academic contest between two teams to see who can win an argument. In a debate, you present a controversial point of view about a topic just as you do in a persuasive speech. The difference is that you have an opponent who argues against you. You have to discredit your opponent's persuasive arguments, and your opponent tries to refute yours.

CHAPTER CHALLENGE This chapter will help you sharpen your skills as a debater. You will present well-thought-out persuasive arguments and defend them against attacks. You will learn to predict what your opponent will say and then plan ways to refute your opponent's information. When you complete this chapter, you will be able to:

- choose a topic and turn it into a proposition
- organize, plan, and participate in a debate about a proposition
- use the techniques of cross-examination and rebuttal

I. Propositions

Propositions suggest that a specific action or procedure should be adopted. For example:

- High school students should be required to wear uniforms.
- Capital punishment laws should be made by the federal, not state, governments.

In a formal debate, topics are always phrased as propositions. One team debates in support of the proposition; this team comprises the *affirmative* speakers. The other team speaks against the proposition; this team comprises the *negative* speakers.

At this time, it will help you to review page 182 in Chapter 9: Speaking to Persuade. Forming debate propositions is the same as forming specific persuasive claims.

ACTIVITY 1 Form Propositions from Topics

1 Work in small groups. Reword the following topics as propositions. The example shows how several propositions can be developed from the same topic.

EXAMPLE:

Topic: Insufficient parking spaces in the college parking lot

Proposition: The school should build a new parking garage.
Proposition: Reserved parking spots should be eliminated.
Proposition: Visitors should not be allowed to park in the parking lot.
Proposition: The school should convert the soccer field into a parking lot.

   a. Topic: Car thefts in the neighborhood

      Proposition: _____

   b. Topic: Traffic congestion in the city

      Proposition: _____

   c. Topic: Students buying research papers on the Internet

      Proposition: _____

   d. Topic: Motorcycle accidents

      Proposition: _____

   e. Topic: Overcrowded classrooms in public schools

      Proposition: _____

2 Share your propositions with the class.

ACTIVITY 2 Collaborate with a Classmate

1 Work with a partner. Choose a story in the news that describes a problem. Write a summary of the problem.

2 Form one or two propositions of policy to help solve that problem.

EXAMPLE:

News Story: A story in the newspaper reported that many government officials are dishonest. They hire family members and pay them inflated salaries. The family members don't even show up to work. The news story also said that these officials use public funds to take expensive vacations.

Proposition 1: A committee of private citizens should be formed to study government corruption.
Proposition 2: Government officials who hire family members should be forced to resign.
Proposition 3: Government workers caught using public funds for personal use should be jailed.

News Story: _____

_____

_____

_____

Proposition 1: _____

Proposition 2: _____

3 Share your news stories and propositions with the class.

II. Organization of a Debate

A formal debate includes three types of presentations, called "constructive speeches," "cross-examination," and "rebuttal." Most debates follow a similar organization, but time limits may vary. Notice the sequence and the time limits that will be followed in this debate.

1. Affirmative team's constructive speeches   4 minutes
2. Negative team's cross-examination   2 minutes
3. Negative team's constructive speeches   4 minutes
4. Affirmative team's cross-examination   2 minutes
5. Negative team's rebuttal speeches   3 minutes
6. Affirmative team's rebuttal speeches   3 minutes

III. Constructive Speeches

Constructive speeches present the debaters' basic arguments for or against the proposition being debated.

A. Affirmative Constructive Speeches

Affirmative constructive speeches present basic arguments in *favor* of the proposition. Affirmative constructive speakers perform these functions:

1. **State the proposition**
   EXAMPLE:
   Slot machines should be legal in hotels and restaurants in Florida.

2. **Explain the proposition**
   EXAMPLE:
   This means that Florida laws will permit any restaurant or hotel to have slot machines.

3. **Define terms**
   EXAMPLE:
   A slot machine is a gambling machine operated by inserting coins into the machine in the hopes of winning money.

4. **Explain a need for a change from the present situation**
   EXAMPLE:
   Florida needs the money that it would get from slot machines because it currently does not have enough money to meet the needs of its citizens.

5. **Present persuasive arguments (evidence, logic, source citations) to support the proposition**
   EXAMPLES:
   We will argue there are three reasons why slot machines should be legal in hotels and restaurants in Florida: 1) They will increase tourism. 2) They will create jobs. 3) They will help reduce organized crime.

   The governor of Florida is quoted in the October issue of *Time Magazine* as saying, "If slot machines were legal, Florida would be in a better financial position to meet the needs of its population."

6. **Summarize the affirmative arguments**
   EXAMPLE:
   In summary, legalizing slot machines in Florida will:

   1. increase tourism to the state;
   2. create jobs;
   3. reduce organized crime.

B. Negative Constructive Speeches

Negative constructive speeches present basic arguments *against* the proposition. Before the debate, negative constructive speakers try to predict the affirmative team's arguments. A good negative team:

- anticipates possible affirmative arguments;
- prepares persuasive points to discredit those arguments.

For example, suppose you are the negative team in a debate about capital punishment. In order to prepare your arguments against the death penalty, you must try to think like the affirmative team. First, make a list of arguments the team is likely to use in support of capital punishment. Second, think of arguments you need to prepare to "attack" or discredit each affirmative argument you predicted. Finally, locate evidence and prepare logical arguments to support your arguments.

During a debate, negative constructive speakers perform these functions:

1. **State their disagreement with what the affirmative speakers said**

    EXAMPLE:

    We disagree with the arguments our opponents just presented.

2. **Present persuasive arguments (evidence, logic, source citations) that refute the proposition**

    EXAMPLE:

    Legalizing slot machines will not reduce organized crime in Florida. In fact, according to a statement made by Juan Fernandez, the spokesperson for Citizens Against Legalizing Slot Machines, and quoted in The Miami Herald on January 18, it will increase crime.

3. **Demonstrate the harm(s) or disadvantage(s) that would result if the proposition were adopted**

    EXAMPLE:

    Legalizing slot machines would have a disadvantage that the affirmative team has ignored. By legitimizing gambling, legalization would contribute to the problem of gambling addiction.

4. **Summarize the negative arguments**

    EXAMPLE:

    In summary, legalizing slot machines in Florida is a terrible idea. It will:

    1. increase crime;

    2. cause gambling addictions;

    3. decrease tourism.

ACTIVITY Brainstorm Arguments *for* and *against* a Proposition

1 Work in small groups. Check ✓ one of the following propositions or select another one.

_____ Capital punishment should be abolished in the United States.

_____ Smoking should be outlawed in public places.

_____ Highway speed limits should be increased.

_____ Cell phones should be banned from schools.

_____ Physician-assisted suicide should be legal.

_____ All taxpayers should be required to have health insurance.

_____ Other: _____

2 Think of three compelling arguments in favor of the proposition and write them in the spaces below.

EXAMPLE:

Proposition: Junk-food vending machines should be banned from schools.

a. *Junk food contributes to obesity.*

b. *Junk food interferes with students' ability to learn.*

c. *Junk-food vending machines encourage unhealthy eating habits.*

Arguments in favor of your proposition:

a. _____

b. _____

c. _____

3 Now, think of three arguments *against* the same proposition and write them below.

EXAMPLE:

a. Students like the taste of fast food.

b. The ingredients in fast food help students stay awake in class.

c. Fast food is cheap. Some students can't afford to buy healthier, more expensive food.

Arguments against your proposition:

a. _____

b. _____

c. _____

4 Share your propositions and arguments with the class. Ask your classmates to think of additional arguments either for or against the proposition your group chose.

IV. Cross-Examination

After each constructive speech, the opposing team has two minutes to ask questions. This part of the debate is called "cross-examination." The purpose is to cast doubt upon the reliability of the opposing team's arguments. Cross-examination questions should relate to the opponent's:

- Sources
- Evidence
- Logic and reasoning

EXAMPLES:

- Where did you get your information that slot machines will reduce organized crime?
- Please clarify. I don't understand how slot machines decrease tourism.
- At the beginning of your speech you said . . . But later you said . . . Don't these statements contradict each other?

GUIDELINES FOR ASKING AND ANSWERING QUESTIONS DURING CROSS-EXAMINATION

Guidelines for Asking Questions	Guidelines for Answering Questions
• Keep questions brief and simple. • Do not argue with your opponent at this time. • Do not comment on weak responses (you will attack these at a later time.) • Ask follow-up questions if your opponent's answer is evasive or incomplete.	• Listen carefully to the question. Think before responding. • Answer truthfully, but do not "volunteer" information that can hurt your case. • Remember that your opponent will try to show weaknesses in your constructive speech. Try to avoid admitting that you have made a mistake.

ACTIVITY Analyze Cross-Examination Questions

1 Work with a partner. Read the following sample cross-examination questions and answers.

EXAMPLES:

Question: Where did you get your information that cell phones cause brain cancer?

Answer: A recent CNN news report on TV.

Question: Who provided the information and why is this person qualified to make such a statement?

Answer: I think it was a cancer researcher from a hospital.

2 Discuss the following questions:

    a. Were the sample questions effective? Explain.

    b. Were the responses weak or strong? Explain.

    c. How could the responses be improved?

    d. What additional cross-examination questions would you ask?

3 Read the scenario below. Then write three questions that you could ask during cross-examination. (Remember, you may question the source, evidence, or logic of the arguments.)

Scenario:

In a debate on the proposition "Junk-food vending machines should be banned from schools," the affirmative team offered two arguments:

    a. Junk food contributes to the inability of students to learn.

    b. Junk food causes many health problems.

    1. Question: _____

    2. Question: _____

    3. Question: _____

---

4 Share your questions with the class.

V.   Rebuttal Speeches

Following the constructive speeches and cross-examinations, formal debates include a rebuttal stage in which each team responds to the other team's presentation and restates its own best arguments. In a rebuttal speech, you should do the following:

1 Present additional research as needed to discredit the opposing team's arguments.

EXAMPLE:

The affirmative team misled you by stating that junk food interferes with students' ability to learn. Our research clearly proves the opposite. Leading experts like Dr. Elaine McCray at the National Nutrition Center state that sugar in junk food provides a quick energy boost that helps students focus their attention and learn.

2 Defend your arguments against your opponent's attacks.

EXAMPLE:

The negative team attacked our argument that legalizing slot machines would create jobs. However, the team offered no evidence to prove its position. The truth is it *will* create many new jobs. The mayor, the county commissioners, and even the governor have publicly stated that thousands of new jobs would be created if slot machines were legal.

3 Point out arguments that the opposing team "ignored" or did not respond to adequately.

EXAMPLE:

The affirmative team has failed to respond to our evidence from the National Nutrition Center that junk food helps students focus their attention and learn.

4 End the rebuttal with a strong final statement in which you restate your position and say that the other team failed to prove its case.

We win this debate because the affirmative team has clearly proven that junk food harms students' health and concentration. The negative team has not responded with any evidence that disproves our case. We urge you to agree with the affirmative team that junk food should be banned from school vending machines!

ACTIVITY Compose a Rebuttal

1 Work in small groups. Read the summary of a newspaper article about a controversial issue.

> A story in the news reported that a young man was suspended from high school for having a cell phone in his backpack. The principal believes that students who have cell phones in school should be suspended. When interviewed, the principal gave the following reasons for his position:
>
> - Cell phones interfere with teaching and learning.
> - Cell phones are unnecessary in school.
> - Principals have the right to set all school rules.

2 Read the following letter to the editor opposing the boy's suspension.

> Dear Editor,
>
> A recent story in the news reported that a high school principal suspended a student for having a cell phone in school. I completely disagree with the policy of suspending students for simply having cell phones in school. I offer the following arguments in opposition to this principal's policy:
>
> - Simply having cell phones in school is not disruptive or distracting in any way.
> - Students should be allowed to have cell phones in school to use in case of an emergency.
> - Suspending students simply for possessing cell phones is an unreasonable punishment.
>
> The principal should immediately stop the policy of suspending students who have cell phones in school.
>
> *Sincerely,*
> (Name)

3 Imagine that your group is the affirmative team in a debate. Form a rebuttal to the letter to the editor. Take the position of a person who agrees with the principal and disagrees with the letter writer.

a. Discuss your responses to the three arguments in the letter.

b. Make an outline of the points in your rebuttal.

c. Choose a member of your group to deliver a short rebuttal speech to the class.

EXAMPLE:

We disagree with the arguments made by the letter writer and support the principal's decision to suspend the boy who had a cell phone in school.

First, the letter writer said simply having cell phones in school is not distracting. That is inaccurate. Cell phones, even when not being used, can be very distracting. Students show one another their phones and discuss their different features. Some students become jealous because a classmate has a better cell phone. Students have trouble concentrating in class because they are thinking about checking their phones at the first possible opportunity.

Second, the letter writer stated that students should have cell phones to use in case of an emergency. In contrast, we believe this is not necessary. . . . Finally . . . In conclusion, we disagree with the letter writer because . . .

VI. Taking Notes during a Debate

You need to take notes during a debate in order to remember what your opponents say. A special type of outline called a "flow sheet" is the most efficient way to do this. On a flow sheet, you list your and the opposing team's arguments in the order they are presented. You use arrows and other symbols to show the "flow," or progression, of the arguments from the beginning of the debate to the end. Tip: If you use a fourteen-inch legal pad and turn it sideways you will have more room to take notes.

The following is a simple example of a debate flow sheet. The arrows show the direction and flow of the arguments. You can list your cross-examination questions at the bottom of your paper or on note cards.

Proposition: _____

Affirmative Constructive	Negative Constructive	Negative Rebuttal	Affirmative Rebuttal
1st Affirmative argument →	Negative counter-argument to affirmative argument 1 →	Restate / expand counter-argument to affirmative constructive argument 1 →	Refute negative rebuttal argument 1
2nd Affirmative argument →	Negative counter-argument to affirmative argument 2 →	Restate / expand counter-argument to affirmative constructive argument 2 →	Refute negative rebuttal argument 2
3rd Affirmative argument →	Negative counter-argument to affirmative argument 3 →	Restate / expand counter-argument to affirmative constructive argument 3 →	Refute negative rebuttal argument 3
	New negative constructive argument →	Restate / expands new negative constructive argument →	Refute new negative constructive arguments

Negative cross-examination questions (Questions to ask the affirmative team)	Affirmative cross-examination questions (Questions to ask the negative team)
1.	1.
2.	2.
3.	3.

A. How to Take Notes Using a Flow Sheet

Read the following guidelines for using a flow sheet to take notes during a debate.

1 Use two different-colored pens or pencils. Write the affirmative notes in one color, the negative notes in another. This is the best way for you to clearly see the flow of the arguments through the entire debate.

2 Divide your paper into four columns as shown in the model flow sheet on page 213.

3 If you are on the affirmative team:

- Outline your constructive arguments in the first column of your flow sheet. You should do this *before* the debate.

- As you listen to the negative constructive speeches, list their responses to your constructive arguments in column 2 directly opposite those arguments. List new negative arguments at the bottom of the column.

- During the negative team's rebuttal, write their rebuttal arguments and evidence in column 3.

- In column 4, quickly take notes to counter the negative team's rebuttal points and list the arguments you will use to conclude the debate.

4 If you are on the negative team:

- As you listen to the affirmative constructive arguments, outline them in column 1 of your flow sheet.

- At the same time, write the arguments you will make to refute the affirmative arguments in column 2. (This is not easy to do!)

- Just before your rebuttal, list the arguments that you plan to restate or expand upon in column 3.

- During the affirmative rebuttal, take notes on the affirmative team's responses to your rebuttal arguments and their final points in column 4.

5 Use abbreviations for common words. For example, in a debate about banning junk food in public schools, abbreviate "junk food" as *jf* or *j-fd.*

6 Use a system of symbols to show the flow of arguments during the debate and to highlight important attacks or points you want to remember. For example:

$\longrightarrow$	Draw an arrow from one team's point or argument to the other team's response. This allows you to trace an argument all the way through the debate.
$\longrightarrow$ X	Draw an arrow from one column to an "X" in the next column to show that your opponent did not respond to an argument. If this happens, point it out in your cross-examination or rebuttal.
✓	Place a check mark next to a point or argument to show that a speaker used evidence to support it. If an item does not have a check mark, you could ask a question about it in cross-examination or point out in your rebuttal that the opposing team failed to prove their point.
?	Place a question mark next to any point or argument to show that you would like to ask the other team a question about it in your cross-examination period.

ACTIVITY Complete the Sample Flow Sheet

1 Work with a partner. Examine the incomplete flow sheet on page 215 for a debate on the proposition "All students in public high schools should be required to wear uniforms."

2 Read the affirmative arguments in favor of the proposition. Then read the example negative cross-examination question. Write two more questions.

3 Complete the negative constructive speech with negative responses to the affirmative arguments. (Predict the affirmative team's answers to the cross-examination questions. Use this information to refute the affirmative arguments.)

4 Fill in additional disadvantages of uniforms that the negative team might argue in its constructive speech. (Hint: Read the points in the negative rebuttal on page 216.)

5 Fill in cross-examination questions that the affirmative team might ask the negative team. (An example is provided.)

Proposition: All students in public high schools should be required to wear uniforms.	
Affirmative Constructive	**Negative Constructive**
Argument 1: School uniforms enhance learning in public schools.	→ Response 1:
Argument 2: School uniforms reduce crime on campus.	→ Response 2:
Argument 3: Requiring uniforms will save students money.	→ Response 3:
	Disadvantages of Uniforms
	Argument 1:
	Argument 2:

Negative cross-examination questions (Questions to ask the affirmative team)	**Affirmative cross-examination questions** (Questions to ask the negative team)
1. School uniforms are expensive. How will requiring uniforms save students money?	1. Would you agree that clothing can distract students from learning?
2.	2.
3.	3.

6 Read the points in the negative rebuttal. Fill in one more point. (Hint: Point out affirmative constructive arguments that were ignored or not proved.)

7 Think of a response to each of the negative team's rebuttal points and fill in possible affirmative responses. (The first item is done as an example.)

Negative Rebuttal	Affirmative Rebuttal
1. School uniforms don't allow students to express their individuality.	→ Students can express individuality in other ways, e.g., hairstyles, extra curricular activities.
2. Many students can't afford school uniforms.	→
3.	→

8 Compare your sample flow sheets in small groups.

VII. Presentation Preview

Your goal is to participate in a debate on a controversial proposition. One team will argue the affirmative side of the proposition. The opposing team will argue the negative side.

ACTIVITY 1 Listen to a Model Debate

Listen to a Model Debate about abolishing the use of cash in the United States. The affirmative team consists of Luci and Rolando. The negative team consists of Rick and Lilliana.

Model Debate: The Federal Government Should Abolish the Use of Cash in the United States

Moderator: Good afternoon everyone. Our debate will begin now with the affirmative constructive speeches. Affirmative speakers, you have four minutes. Luci, please begin.

Affirmative Constructive Speeches

Luci: We are here to debate the proposition that the federal government should abolish the use of cash in the United States. Our plan is that the government should substitute electronic money cards for cash. We define *cash* as all coins and paper money that people use to pay for goods and services. *Abolish* means to stop the use of cash for all payments in the United States.

Rolando and I will argue that the use of cash harms the United States in three significant ways. First, the use of cash increases violent crime. Second, the use of cash causes overcrowding in our country's prisons. And third, the use of cash makes it easier for people to avoid paying taxes.

The affirmative team will now present arguments to show how abolishing cash will help us solve all three of these problems.

Our first argument is that abolishing cash would reduce violent crime. That's because it would eliminate cash robberies. The FBI reports that over 800 people are murdered every year in robberies for cash. If we abolish cash, we will eliminate an important reason why criminals rob people. We would save hundreds of lives each year.

And now I would like to share with you our second significant reason for abolishing cash, and that is that abolishing cash will

---

reduce overcrowding in our prison system and save taxpayers millions of dollars.

Eighty percent of the prisoners in our country's jails are there for a crime that involves cash. They either stole or killed someone for cash. By eliminating cash, we'll eliminate an important reason why people are put in prison, and our prisons will be less crowded.

And now my partner, Rolando, will explain one more important reason why cash should be abolished.

Rolando: Thank you, Luci. The third reason we believe cash should be abolished is that it will stop people from cheating on their taxes. There is a huge underground economy in this country. People often don't report the income they receive when they're paid in cash for goods or services they provide. If they don't report the income, they don't have to pay taxes on it. Tax cheaters cost the U.S. government more than 300 billion dollars a year. Using electronic money cards is the only way to stop income tax evasion.

Now please allow me to summarize our case in today's debate.

Luci and I have proven that there is a need for a change from the present system and that abolishing cash would provide three important advantages.

First, abolishing cash would reduce violent crime and save hundreds of lives each year.

Second, abolishing cash would save the government millions of dollars by reducing overcrowding in the prison system.

And third, abolishing cash would prevent tax evasion.

Moderator: Thank you, Luci and Rolando. The negative team will now begin their cross-examination. You have two minutes.

Negative Team Cross-Examination

Lilliana: OK. My first question is for Rolando. Where did you get your information that tax evasion costs the government 300 billion dollars a year?

Rolando: I have that right here. My information comes from David R. Warwick, an attorney and author of the book *Ending Cash: The Public Benefits of Federal Electronic Currency*. He says that abolishing cash would be an effective way to stop income tax evasion.

Lilliana: Thank you. My next question is, if the government abolishes cash and starts issuing electronic money cards, don't you think people will be concerned about their loss of privacy?

Rolando: Maybe, but I'm sure most people are more worried about being victims of a robbery than about loss of privacy.

Lilliana: Thank you for your opinion, Rolando. Next, don't you think people will find other ways to cheat on their taxes if cash is eliminated?

Rolando: Absolutely not. It would be impossible.

Lilliana: Why? People are clever. Isn't it possible that they would find ways to avoid using the money cards?

Rolando: I don't see how.

Lilliana: Thank you, Rolando. Now Rick has some questions for Luci.

Rick: That's right. Luci, you said 80 percent of prisoners are in jail for committing a crime involving cash. Where did you get that statistic?

Luci: On the Internet.

Moderator: Thank you for that exciting cross-examination. We will now hear negative constructive speeches. Negative team, you have four minutes. Rick, please begin.

(continued)

(continued)

Negative Team Constructive Speeches

Rick: We disagree with the arguments presented by the affirmative speakers. We feel that abolishing the use of cash in the United States is a bad idea!

Let's take the affirmative arguments one at a time and analyze why they are wrong.

The affirmative's first argument was that abolishing cash would save hundreds of lives a year. Well, if cash were abolished, it's true that criminals wouldn't rob people for money. But they would still rob or even kill people for things besides cash, such as jewelry, gold, art, cars, even expensive clothing. Yes, cash robberies would not happen, but criminals would still rob people and we would still have violent crime. The affirmative plan has no advantage over the present system.

The affirmative's second argument was that abolishing cash would reduce overcrowding in the prison system.

This is simply not true. Abolishing cash would not reduce prison overcrowding. As I just explained, thieves steal things besides cash. They would still steal expensive watches, jewelry, paintings, computers, and so on. They could try to trade these things for goods or services or sell them for cash overseas. There would be just as many crimes, and just as many people would get caught and sent to prison.

In addition, I would like to point out that the affirmative team has no real evidence that abolishing cash would reduce prison overcrowding. Luci stated that over 80 percent of prisoners are in jail for committing a crime involving cash. But when we asked her where she got this statistic, she said, "the Internet." This is not real evidence. The Internet is not a source—anyone can post any nonsense on the Internet. The affirmative team did not prove their argument. We maintain that abolishing cash will not reduce overcrowding in prison.

So far I have proven that there are two major flaws in the affirmative case. And now my partner, Lilliana, will tell you why abolishing cash will not stop people from cheating on their taxes.

Lilliana: That's right. Rolando told us in cross-examination that it would be impossible for people to cheat on their taxes if cash is eliminated, but that's not correct. As I said, people are clever. There are other ways for people to avoid paying taxes. Just like criminals, workers could trade their services for things they want instead of being paid in cash. A medical doctor might provide treatment for a lawyer in exchange for legal advice. They would never have to report any income or pay taxes to the government.

Therefore, abolishing cash would *not* stop people from cheating on their taxes. The tax cheaters would still *have the last laugh!*

In summary, Rick and I have proven that the affirmative speakers have serious flaws in their reasoning and in addition, they have failed to show that abolishing cash would have any advantage over the present system in reducing violent crime, overcrowding in our prisons, or tax evasion.

Rick and I maintain that the federal government should not abolish the use of cash in the United States.

Moderator: Now it's time for the affirmative team to conduct its cross-examination. Luci and Rolando, you have two minutes.

* Succeed when others were sure you would fail

Affirmative Team Cross-Examination

Rolando: Rick, you said that people are robbed for things other than cash. But isn't it true that most robberies involve cash?

Rick: I don't know if that's true. It's up to you to prove that.

Rolando: But don't you agree that if we eliminate cash, we would eliminate an important reason why robberies occur?

Rick: Yes, but like I said, robberies for cash would just be replaced by robberies for gold or other valuable things. Your proposition doesn't fix the problem.

Rolando: OK, let's move on. Luci has some questions for Lilliana.

Luci: Right. Lilliana, you said that abolishing cash wouldn't stop people from cheating on their taxes. They would just trade services instead of paying cash and avoid paying taxes that way. Do you have any evidence to prove that?

Lilliana: Well, you know, cash didn't always exist. For most of human history people have gotten the things they want by trading. It's nothing new.

Luci: But how would a system of trading work? Wouldn't it be very complicated and inconvenient?

Lilliana: I don't know how it would work, but I'm sure people would find a way.

Moderator: Time's up. The negative team will now present its rebuttal speeches. Lilliana and Rick, you have three minutes. Lilliana will begin.

Negative Rebuttal Speeches

Lilliana: Rick and I win this debate because the affirmative team has never proven that abolishing cash would solve the problems they talked about in their constructive speech. Let's review their arguments.

First, the affirmative team claimed that abolishing the use of cash would reduce violent crime in the United States. In our view they did not prove this. It's true that cash robberies could not happen anymore, but robberies would still take place. Other things like gold, art, and personal property would simply replace cash. We would still have people robbing people! We would still have violent crime! The affirmative loses this point.

Next, the affirmative team argued that abolishing cash would reduce prison overcrowding. They based all their evidence for this argument on an unnamed Internet source. Moreover, the argument makes no sense. We all know that if cash no longer exists, thieves will find other things to steal. They will steal expensive jewelry and electronics. They will steal your shiny new car. And then they will be caught and thrown in jail, just like they are today. Therefore we see that prison overcrowding will not be reduced. The affirmative loses this point as well.

Rick will now continue with our rebuttal.

Rick: The affirmative team's third argument was that abolishing cash would stop dishonest people from cheating on their taxes. But we argue that dishonest people will simply find other ways to cheat. For example, they could trade for the goods and services they want instead of using cash. There won't be any record of these transactions, so the government will not be able to tax them. The government will still lose billions of dollars every year, just like it does now.

Lilliana and I win this debate because the affirmative proposition will not solve any of the problems they talked about. In fact, it will create new problems like increasing the amount of computer fraud

(continued)

(continued)

and taking away people's privacy. Using electronic money cards instead of cash will allow the government to keep track of every single thing you buy and sell. The American people will never agree to this invasion of privacy. In summary, abolishing cash is a terrible idea. The negative team wins this debate!

Moderator: Thank you for your rebuttal, Lilliana and Rick. Now the affirmative team will present their rebuttal speeches. Luci and Rolando, you have three minutes. Rolando will begin.

Affirmative Rebuttal Speeches

Rolando: Luci and I should win this debate because we proved that abolishing the use of cash would, first, reduce cash robberies, second, reduce overcrowding in our prison system, and *last but not least*, stop people from cheating on their taxes.

We have presented evidence from the FBI that over 800 people are murdered every year in cash robberies. The negative team remained silent on this point. They could not prove otherwise. If cash were abolished, it is a fact that many lives could be saved each year.

Next, we proved that abolishing cash would help solve the problem of prison overcrowding. We pointed out that the majority of people in prison are there because they committed a crime involving cash. If we eliminate cash, the number of people in prison will go down.

Luci: Moreover, Rolando and I should win this debate because we proved that abolishing the use of cash would eliminate the underground economy. With electronic money cards, there would be a record of all transactions, and this would force people to pay taxes on the goods and services they buy and sell. This would save our government billions of dollars every year and bring benefits to all the residents of this country.

The negative team said that if cash were abolished, people would still avoid paying taxes. They would simply trade for things instead of using cash. But they couldn't explain how this trading system would work. We think it would be incredibly inconvenient and complicated. The affirmative team wins this point as well.

The negative team tried to scare you by saying that government-issued money cards would take away your privacy. First of all, they did not use evidence to support this argument. Second, their arguments are illogical. We think people are more concerned about crime than they are about privacy.

In conclusion, the affirmative team has proven the following three points in this debate:

First, abolishing cash would reduce violent crime.

Second, abolishing cash would reduce overcrowding in the prison system.

And third, abolishing cash would stop people from cheating on their taxes.

I urge you to agree with the affirmative team that the federal government should abolish the use of cash in the United States.

* Last in a sequence but as important as other things

ACTIVITY 2 Complete a Flow Sheet for the Model Debate

1 Listen to the model debate again and complete the flow sheet on pages 222–223 as you listen. Use different colors for affirmative and negative arguments. Some information has been filled in for you.

2 Compare your completed flow sheets in small groups.

ACTIVITY 3 Model Debate Discussion

1 Use your flow sheet from the Model Debate to discuss the following questions:

a. What were the three affirmative arguments in favor of the proposition? What evidence did Luci and Rolando use to support each argument? Was this enough evidence? Was the evidence strong?

b. How did the negative team respond to the affirmative arguments? What evidence did Rick and Lilliana use? Was this sufficient?

c. What additional arguments against the proposition did the negative team propose?

d. Which arguments were addressed or restated in every part of the debate? Which arguments were ignored?

e. Were each team's cross-examination questions effective? Why or why not?

f. Were each team's responses to the cross-examination questions effective? Why or why not?

g. Which team had stronger rebuttal speeches? Why?

h. Which additional arguments could have been used in favor of the proposition?

i. Which additional arguments could have been used against the proposition?

j. In your opinion, which team won the debate? Why?

VIII. Pronunciation Practice: [l] and [r]

A common error is to confuse the sounds [l] and [r]. If you confuse them, *rice* sounds like *lice* and *berry* sounds like *belly!*

Pronounce [l] by placing the tip of your tongue against the gum ridge just behind your upper front teeth. Pronounce [r] by curling your tongue upward but not letting it touch the roof of your mouth.

ACTIVITY 1 Word and Sentence Contrast Practice

Listen and repeat the following pairs of words and sentences. Concentrate on pronouncing [l] and [r] correctly.

[l]	[r]
1. late	rate
2. led	red
3. elect	erect
4. list	wrist
5. tile	tire
6. Do you feel it?	Do you fear it?
7. It was long.	It was wrong.
8. We will play at once.	We will pray at once.
9. Don't collect the papers.	Don't correct the papers.
10. Move to the light.	Move to the right.

Proposition: The Federal Government Should Abolish the Use of Cash in the United States

Affirmative Constructive	Negative Constructive
1. Abolishing cash would reduce violent crime →	Abolishing cash would not reduce violent crime.
—FBI: 800 people a yr murdered in robbs. for cash →	
—Abolish cash = eliminate reason for robbs, save 100s of lives →	Criminals would still rob for jewelry, gold, art, etc. Still have violent crime.
2. Abolishing cash would reduce prison overcrowding, save taxpayer money →	
—80% of prisoners in jail = crime involving cash →	
—Eliminate cash = elim. reason why people are in jail so jails less crowded →	
3. Abolishing cash would stop people from cheating on taxes →	People will find new ways to avoid paying taxes.
—Many people don't report cash income to gov., don't pay taxes, costs gov > $300 billion a yr. →	
—Electronic money cards will prevent tax evasion →	

Negative Cross-Examination

1. Where did you get info that tax evasion costs gov $300 billion?
2. If cash is replaced by money cards, won't people worry about loss of privacy?
3. _____
4. _____

Negative Rebuttal	Affirmative Rebuttal
Thieves will still steal, get caught, go to jail.	
Unnamed Internet source = their only evidence.	
Dishonest people will find other ways to cheat, e.g., trade, no record, gov. can't tax, will lose billions of $	Money cards = record of transacts., force people to pay tax, save gov. money —Neg team could not explain trading system
	Abolish cash = eliminate tax evasion
New prob 1: Increase comp fraud	
New prob 2: Take away people's privacy—citizens will not agree	No evidence —People more worried about crime than privacy

Affirmative Cross-Examination

1. True that most robbs involve cash?
2. If we elim cash, don't we elim important reason for robbs?
3. _____
4. How would trading work? Would be inconvenient, complicated?

Listen and repeat the following sentences from the model debate. Be sure to pronounce the [l] and [r] words carefully.

1. Abolishing cash would reduce violent crime.
2. Abolishing cash will reduce overcrowding in our prison system.
3. Tax cheaters cost the U.S. government more than 300 billion dollars a year.
4. Allow me to summarize our case.
5. Let's take the affirmative arguments one at a time and analyze why they are wrong.
6. There are two major flaws in the affirmative case.
7. Just like criminals, workers could trade their services for things they want.
8. A medical doctor might provide treatment for a lawyer.
9. The tax cheaters would still have the last laugh.

ACTIVITY 3 Speech Practice

1 The Model Debate on pages 216–220 has many words pronounced with [l] and [r]. Circle twenty words pronounced with [l] and underline twenty words with [r].

2 Work with a partner. Take turns pronouncing the words you circled and underlined.

3 Practice the Model Debate in a small group. Pay attention to your pronunciation of [l] and [r].

IX. Playing with Sayings: Sayings with [l] and [r]

ACTIVITY 1 Learn the Meanings

Read the following sayings. Check the ones you heard in the Model Debate.

_____ 1. **Let sleeping dogs lie:** Leave something alone if it might cause trouble.
Don't bring up the subject of his traffic ticket; *let sleeping dogs lie.*

_____ 2. **Rob Peter to pay Paul:** To try to solve one problem and in the process create a different problem.
If you borrow money to pay your credit card bill, you're just *robbing Peter to pay Paul.*

_____ 3. **Have the last laugh:** To succeed in the end when others expected you to fail or when they were sure they would defeat you.
Mark played a trick on me. I played a better one on him and *had the last laugh.*

_____ 4. **Rub (someone) the wrong way:** To annoy someone.
For some reason, the sound of her voice always *rubs me the wrong way.*

_____ 5. **Last but not least:** When something or someone is last in a sequence but as important as the items before it.
The first two witnesses have testified, and now, *last but not least,* the third has been called.

ACTIVITY 2 Use the Sayings

1 **Work in small groups. Complete each sentence with a context that fits the saying.**

EXAMPLE:

Everyone said the candidate would lose the election, but in the end he *had the last laugh* because <u>he beat everyone else by thousands of votes.</u>

a. Don't _____. *Let sleeping dogs lie.*

b. His sister *rubs him the wrong way* when she _____.

c. It's foolish to *rob Peter to pay Paul* by _____.

d. The announcer said *last but not least* when he _____.

2 **Share your sentences with the class. Be sure to pronounce [l] and [r] correctly.**

X. Presentation Project: Debate a Proposition

Your goal is to be part of a two-member team that will debate a proposition of policy against another two-member team.

STEP 1 | Choose a Topic

Work in groups of four. You may choose one of the following propositions or select your own.

Elementary schools should ban junk-food sales.	High school students should not be allowed to carry cell phones on campus.
The legal driving age should be 18.	Beauty pageants should be illegal.
The United States should ban the death penalty.	The use of plastic and paper shopping bags should be forbidden.
Zoos should be abolished.	High school classrooms should have closed-circuit cameras.
There should be year-round schooling for students through high school.	All young people should be required to do a year of national service after high school.
Teachers should be allowed to spank children who misbehave.	The legal drinking age should be lowered to 18 years old.
Physician-assisted suicide should be legalized.	Foreign-born citizens should be allowed to serve as president of the United States.
All new drugs should be tested on animals before they are tested on humans.	All forms of cigarette advertising should be banned.

STEP 2 | Choose Sides

Decide which two-person team will take the affirmative position and which team will take the negative.

STEP 3 | Plan Your Debate

A Review the Model Debate starting on page 216.

I. Before the Debate

A. Affirmative team: Prepare affirmative constructive speeches.
   1. State the proposition.
   2. Explain the proposition and define terms.
   3. Present persuasive arguments to support the proposition. Include:
      • Evidence
      • Logic
      • Examples
      • Expert quotes
   4. Summarize the affirmative arguments.

B. Negative team: Prepare negative constructive speeches.
   1. Anticipate possible affirmative arguments.
   2. Prepare persuasive points to discredit those arguments.
   3. Prepare additional harms or disadvantages that would result if the proposition were adopted.

II. During the Debate

A. Affirmative team:
   1. Deliver your prepared constructive speech.
   2. Listen to the negative constructive speeches and take notes on your flow sheet.
   3. Formulate cross-examination questions.
   4. Respond to negative cross-examination questions.
   5. Deliver rebuttal speeches.
      • Use your research to discredit your opponent's constructive speech arguments.
      • Defend your arguments against your opponent's attacks.

B. Negative team:
   1. Listen to the affirmative constructive speeches and take notes on your flow sheet.
   2. Formulate cross-examination questions.
   3. Deliver your constructive speeches.
      • State your disagreement with what the affirmative speakers said.
      • Present persuasive arguments (evidence, logic, source citations) that refute the proposition.
      • Demonstrate the harm(s) or disadvantage(s) that would result if the proposition were adopted.
      • Summarize the negative arguments.
   4. Respond to the affirmative cross-examination questions.
   5. Deliver rebuttal speeches.
      • Use your research to discredit your opponent's constructive speech arguments.
      • Defend your arguments against your opponent's attacks.

C Read the Useful Language you can use when disagreeing with your opponents. Place a check mark ✓ next to the expressions you like best.

> ### USEFUL LANGUAGE: DISAGREEING WITH YOUR OPPONENTS
>
> _____ We disagree with the (affirmative/negative) team's position that . . .
>
> _____ The (affirmative/negative) team misled you by stating . . .
>
> _____ Our opponents are completely incorrect about . . .
>
> _____ The (affirmative/negative) team has no valid evidence that . . .
>
> _____ The opposing team is not giving you all of the facts concerning this issue . . .

D Select a saying from page 224 to include during the debate. Write it here:

_____

STEP 4 | Prepare Note Cards

A Note cards for the affirmative team

1. Prepare at least one note card for each step in the debate. Label the cards:
   - Proposition
   - Explanation of Proposition
   - Definition of terms
   - Need for a change from the present situation
   - 1st Argument
   - 2nd Argument
   - 3rd Argument, 4th Argument, etc.
   - Summary of Arguments
2. Add important details from your research.
3. Number your cards.

B Note cards for negative team

1. Prepare the following note cards
   - Disagreement with Affirmative Speakers
   - Response to First Argument (based on your prediction of affirmative team's possible arguments)
   - Response to Second Argument
   - Response to Third Argument, etc.
   - Disadvantages if proposition is adopted
   - Summary of Arguments
2. Add important details.
3. Number your cards.

STEP 5 | Practice Your Speeches

A Practice your speeches at least three times with your partner if you are on the affirmative side of the debate. Record them and listen to them at least once. Teams on the negative side of a proposition should anticipate key arguments and practice answering and defending possible affirmative arguments.

B Complete the speech checklist. Is there anything you want to improve before your scheduled debate in class?

Speech Checklist: Affirmative Team	YES	NO
1. We stated the proposition.	☐	☐
2. We explained the proposition.	☐	☐
3. We defined terms.	☐	☐
4. We explained the need for a change from the correct situation.	☐	☐
5. We presented arguments to support the proposition.	☐	☐
6. We asked and answered cross-examination questions effectively.	☐	☐
7. We summarized our arguments.	☐	☐
8. We included a saying from the chapter.	☐	☐
9. We have at least one note card for each step in the debate.	☐	☐
10. Our constructive speeches are four minutes maximum.	☐	☐
11. Our pronunciation of [l] and [r] is correct.	☐	☐

Speech Checklist: Negative Team (Revised)	YES	NO
1. We have at least one note card for each step in the debate.	☐	☐
2. We anticipated affirmative arguments and practiced disagreeing with them.	☐	☐
3. We planned and practiced negative constructive arguments.	☐	☐
4. We anticipated affirmative cross-examination questions and practiced answering them.	☐	☐
5. We practiced summarizing our arguments for the rebuttal speeches.	☐	☐
6. We selected a saying from the chapter to use during the dabate.	☐	☐
7. Our pronunciation of [l] and [r] is correct.	☐	☐

C Your teacher and/or your classmates may evaluate your debate performance. Study the forms on pages 240–243 so you know how you will be evaluated. You may use the items on the form to make final changes to your notes.

STEP 6 | Present Your Debate

A Relax, take a deep breath, and present your debate.

B Listen to your audience's applause.

SPEAKER: _____   DATE: _____

EVALUATOR: _____

DELIVERY	RATING					COMMENTS
POSTURE	1	2	3	4	5	_____
EYE CONTACT	1	2	3	4	5	_____
VOLUME OF VOICE	1	2	3	4	5	_____
RATE OF SPEECH	1	2	3	4	5	_____
ENTHUSIASM	1	2	3	4	5	_____
ADHERENCE TO TIME LIMIT	1	2	3	4	5	_____

CONTENT	RATING					COMMENTS
INTRODUCTION	1	2	3	4	5	_____
BACKGROUND/EARLY CHILDHOOD	1	2	3	4	5	_____
INFORMATION ABOUT FAMILY	1	2	3	4	5	_____
PRESENT INVOLVEMENTS	1	2	3	4	5	_____
HOBBIES/SPECIAL INTERESTS	1	2	3	4	5	_____
FUTURE PLANS/DREAMS	1	2	3	4	5	_____
CONCLUSION	1	2	3	4	5	_____
SAYING FROM CHAPTER	1	2	3	4	5	_____
USEFUL LANGUAGE	1	2	3	4	5	_____
PICTURES	1	2	3	4	5	_____

ADDITIONAL COMMENTS

_____
_____
_____
_____
_____
_____
_____

RATING KEY

1 = POOR   2 = FAIR   3 = ACCEPTABLE   4 = GOOD   5 = EXCELLENT

The "Old Bag" Speech (Page 11)

SPEAKER: _____   DATE: _____

EVALUATOR: _____

DELIVERY	RATING					COMMENTS
POSTURE	1	2	3	4	5	_____
EYE CONTACT	1	2	3	4	5	_____
VOLUME OF VOICE	1	2	3	4	5	_____
RATE OF SPEECH	1	2	3	4	5	_____
ENTHUSIASM	1	2	3	4	5	_____
ADHERENCE TO TIME LIMIT	1	2	3	4	5	_____

CONTENT	RATING					COMMENTS
OPENING GREETING	1	2	3	4	5	_____
"BAG" ANALYSIS	1	2	3	4	5	_____
ITEM 1: (PAST)	1	2	3	4	5	_____
ITEM 2: (PRESENT)	1	2	3	4	5	_____
ITEM 3: (FUTURE)	1	2	3	4	5	_____
SUMMARY SENTENCE	1	2	3	4	5	_____
THANKED THE AUDIENCE	1	2	3	4	5	_____
SAYING FROM CHAPTER	1	2	3	4	5	_____
USEFUL LANGUAGE	1	2	3	4	5	_____

ADDITIONAL COMMENTS

_____

_____

_____

_____

_____

_____

_____

_____

RATING KEY

1 = POOR   2 = FAIR   3 = ACCEPTABLE   4 = GOOD   5 = EXCELLENT

Exceptional Experience Speech (Page 34)

SPEAKER: _____   EXPERIENCE: _____

EVALUATOR: _____   DATE: _____

DELIVERY	RATING					COMMENTS
POSTURE/BODY LANGUAGE	1	2	3	4	5	_____
EYE CONTACT	1	2	3	4	5	_____
VOLUME OF VOICE	1	2	3	4	5	_____
RATE OF SPEECH	1	2	3	4	5	_____
ENTHUSIASM	1	2	3	4	5	_____
ADHERENCE TO TIME LIMIT	1	2	3	4	5	_____

CONTENT	RATING					COMMENTS
CHOICE OF EXPERIENCE	1	2	3	4	5	_____
INTRODUCTION	1	2	3	4	5	_____
SUPPORTING DETAILS	1	2	3	4	5	_____
CLEAR ORGANIZATION	1	2	3	4	5	_____
CONCLUSION	1	2	3	4	5	_____
PRESENTATION AIDS	1	2	3	4	5	_____
SAYING FROM CHAPTER	1	2	3	4	5	_____
USEFUL LANGUAGE	1	2	3	4	5	_____

ADDITIONAL COMMENTS

_____

_____

_____

_____

_____

_____

_____

_____

_____

RATING KEY

1 = POOR   2 = FAIR   3 = ACCEPTABLE   4 = GOOD   5 = EXCELLENT

Point of View Speech (Page 53)

SPEAKER: _____   TOPIC: _____

EVALUATOR: _____   DATE: _____

DELIVERY	RATING					COMMENTS
POSTURE	1	2	3	4	5	_____
EYE CONTACT	1	2	3	4	5	_____
VOLUME OF VOICE	1	2	3	4	5	_____
RATE OF SPEECH	1	2	3	4	5	_____
ENTHUSIASM	1	2	3	4	5	_____
ADHERENCE TO TIME LIMIT	1	2	3	4	5	_____

CONTENT	RATING					COMMENTS
CHOICE OF TOPIC	1	2	3	4	5	_____
INTRODUCTION	1	2	3	4	5	_____
STATEMENT OF OPINION	1	2	3	4	5	_____
PREVIEW	1	2	3	4	5	_____
REASON #1	1	2	3	4	5	_____
REASON #2	1	2	3	4	5	_____
REASON #3	1	2	3	4	5	_____
SUMMARY	1	2	3	4	5	_____
FINAL REMARKS	1	2	3	4	5	_____
PRESENTATION AIDS	1	2	3	4	5	_____
SAYING FROM CHAPTER	1	2	3	4	5	_____
USEFUL LANGUAGE	1	2	3	4	5	_____

ADDITIONAL COMMENTS

_____

_____

_____

_____

_____

RATING KEY

1 = POOR   2 = FAIR   3 = ACCEPTABLE   4 = GOOD   5 = EXCELLENT

Poster Presentation/PowerPoint® Speech (Page 79)

SPEAKER: _____   TOPIC: _____

EVALUATOR: _____   DATE: _____

DELIVERY	RATING					COMMENTS
POSTURE	1	2	3	4	5	_____
EYE CONTACT	1	2	3	4	5	_____
VOLUME OF VOICE	1	2	3	4	5	_____
RATE OF SPEECH	1	2	3	4	5	_____
ENTHUSIASM	1	2	3	4	5	_____
ADHERENCE TO TIME LIMIT	1	2	3	4	5	_____

CONTENT	RATING					COMMENTS
GREETING	1	2	3	4	5	_____
PREVIEW OF CONCEPTS	1	2	3	4	5	_____
EXPLANATION OF CONCEPTS	1	2	3	4	5	_____
EXAMPLES FROM CHAPTER	1	2	3	4	5	_____
AUDIENCE INVOLVEMENT	1	2	3	4	5	_____
APPLICATION TO REAL LIFE	1	2	3	4	5	_____
SUMMARY	1	2	3	4	5	_____
CONCLUSION	1	2	3	4	5	_____
QUESTION/ANSWER SESSION	1	2	3	4	5	_____
VISUAL APPEAL OF POSTER/ POWERPOINT® SLIDES	1	2	3	4	5	_____
SAYING FROM CHAPTER	1	2	3	4	5	_____
USEFUL LANGUAGE	1	2	3	4	5	_____

ADDITIONAL COMMENTS

_____
_____
_____
_____
_____

RATING KEY

1 = POOR   2 = FAIR   3 = ACCEPTABLE   4 = GOOD   5 = EXCELLENT

Speech to Inform (Page 107)

SPEAKER: _____ TOPIC: _____

EVALUATOR: _____ DATE: _____

DELIVERY	RATING					COMMENTS
POSTURE	1	2	3	4	5	_____
EYE CONTACT	1	2	3	4	5	_____
VOLUME OF VOICE	1	2	3	4	5	_____
RATE OF SPEECH	1	2	3	4	5	_____
ENTHUSIASM	1	2	3	4	5	_____
ADHERENCE TO TIME LIMIT	1	2	3	4	5	_____

CONTENT	RATING					COMMENTS
CHOICE OF TOPIC	1	2	3	4	5	_____
ATTENTION GETTER	1	2	3	4	5	_____
PREVIEW	1	2	3	4	5	_____
MAIN SECTION 1	1	2	3	4	5	_____
MAIN SECTION 2	1	2	3	4	5	_____
MAIN SECTION 3	1	2	3	4	5	_____
CLEAR ORGANIZATION	1	2	3	4	5	_____
TRANSITIONS	1	2	3	4	5	_____
SUPPORTING DETAILS	1	2	3	4	5	_____
SUMMARY	1	2	3	4	5	_____
FINAL REMARKS	1	2	3	4	5	_____
PRESENTATION AIDS	1	2	3	4	5	_____
SAYING FROM CHAPTER	1	2	3	4	5	_____
USEFUL LANGUAGE	1	2	3	4	5	_____

ADDITIONAL COMMENTS

_____
_____
_____
_____
_____

RATING KEY

1 = POOR   2 = FAIR   3 = ACCEPTABLE   4 = GOOD   5 = EXCELLENT

Job Interview Role Play (Page 131)

JOB APPLICANT: _____ POSITION: _____

EVALUATOR: _____ DATE: _____

APPEARANCE/DELIVERY	RATING	COMMENTS
POSTURE	1 2 3 4 5	_____
EYE CONTACT	1 2 3 4 5	_____
VOLUME OF VOICE	1 2 3 4 5	_____
RATE OF SPEECH	1 2 3 4 5	_____
ENTHUSIASM	1 2 3 4 5	_____
APPROPRIATE ATTIRE	1 2 3 4 5	_____
ADHERENCE TO TIME LIMIT	1 2 3 4 5	_____

CONTENT	RATING	COMMENTS
GREETING	1 2 3 4 5	_____
SMALL TALK	1 2 3 4 5	_____
RESPONSES TO QUESTIONS	1 2 3 4 5	_____
APPLICANT QUESTIONS	1 2 3 4 5	_____
CLOSING CONVERSATION	1 2 3 4 5	_____
SAYING FROM CHAPTER	1 2 3 4 5 N/A	_____
USEFUL LANGUAGE	1 2 3 4 5 N/A	_____

ADDITIONAL COMMENTS

_____
_____
_____
_____
_____
_____
_____
_____

RATING KEY

1 = POOR   2 = FAIR   3 = ACCEPTABLE   4 = GOOD   5 = EXCELLENT   N/A = NOT APPLICABLE

Impromptu Speech (Page 154)

SPEAKER: _____   TOPIC: _____

EVALUATOR: _____   DATE: _____

DELIVERY	RATING					COMMENTS
POSTURE	1	2	3	4	5	_____
EYE CONTACT	1	2	3	4	5	_____
VOLUME OF VOICE	1	2	3	4	5	_____
RATE OF SPEECH	1	2	3	4	5	_____
ENTHUSIASM	1	2	3	4	5	_____
ADHERENCE TO TIME LIMIT	1	2	3	4	5	_____

CONTENT	RATING					COMMENTS
ATTENTION-GETTING OPENER	1	2	3	4	5	_____
STATEMENT OF TOPIC	1	2	3	4	5	_____
PREVIEW OF ORGANIZATIONAL PATTERN	1	2	3	4	5	_____
SUPPORTING DETAILS	1	2	3	4	5	_____
CLEAR ORGANIZATION	1	2	3	4	5	_____
MEMORABLE CONCLUSION	1	2	3	4	5	_____
SAYING FROM CHAPTER	1	2	3	4	5	_____
USEFUL LANGUAGE	1	2	3	4	5	_____

ADDITIONAL COMMENTS

_____
_____
_____
_____
_____
_____
_____
_____

RATING KEY

1 = POOR   2 = FAIR   3 = ACCEPTABLE   4 = GOOD   5 = EXCELLENT

Problem-Solving Group Discussion
Individual Participant Evaluation (Page 174)

SPEAKER: _____   TOPIC: _____

EVALUATOR: _____   DATE: _____

PREPARATION	RATING					COMMENTS
EVIDENCE OF PLANNING	1	2	3	4	5	_____
EVIDENCE OF RESEARCH	1	2	3	4	5	_____

PARTICIPATION	RATING					COMMENTS
STAYED ON TRACK	1	2	3	4	5	_____
MADE SUFFICIENT CONTRIBUTIONS	1	2	3	4	5	_____
DEMONSTRATED ENTHUSIASM	1	2	3	4	5	_____

VALUE OF CONTRIBUTIONS	RATING						COMMENTS
PROOF PROBLEM EXISTS	1	2	3	4	5		_____
CONSEQUENCES OF THE PROBLEM	1	2	3	4	5		_____
CAUSES OF THE PROBLEM	1	2	3	4	5		_____
POSSIBLE SOLUTIONS TO THE PROBLEM	1	2	3	4	5		_____
EVALUATION OF SOLUTIONS	1	2	3	4	5		_____
SOURCES CITED	1	2	3	4	5		_____
PRESENTATION AIDS	1	2	3	4	5		_____
SAYING FROM CHAPTER	1	2	3	4	5	N/A	_____
USEFUL LANGUAGE	1	2	3	4	5	N/A	_____

ADDITIONAL COMMENTS

_____

_____

_____

_____

_____

_____

RATING KEY

1 = POOR   2 = FAIR   3 = ACCEPTABLE   4 = GOOD   5 = EXCELLENT   N/A = NOT APPLICABLE

Problem-Solving Group Discussion
Group Leader Evaluation (Page 174)

LEADER: _____   TOPIC: _____

EVALUATOR: _____   DATE: _____

EFFECTIVENESS	RATING						COMMENTS
INTRODUCTION OF PARTICIPANTS	1	2	3	4	5		_____
INTRODUCTION OF PROBLEM	1	2	3	4	5		_____
ABILITY TO KEEP GROUP ORGANIZED	1	2	3	4	5		_____
KNOWLEDGE OF TOPIC	1	2	3	4	5		_____
ENCOURAGED PARTICIPATION	1	2	3	4	5		_____
TRANSITIONS BETWEEN STEPS	1	2	3	4	5		_____
GRACEFUL CONCLUSION	1	2	3	4	5		_____
THANKED PARTICIPANTS	1	2	3	4	5		_____
SAYING FROM CHAPTER	1	2	3	4	5	N/A	_____
USEFUL LANGUAGE	1	2	3	4	5	N/A	_____

ADDITIONAL COMMENTS

_____

_____

_____

_____

_____

_____

_____

_____

_____

_____

_____

_____

_____

_____

RATING KEY

1 = POOR   2 = FAIR   3 = ACCEPTABLE   4 = GOOD   5 = EXCELLENT   N/A = NOT APPLICABLE

Speech to Persuade (Page 179)

SPEAKER: _____ TOPIC: _____

EVALUATOR: _____ DATE: _____

DELIVERY	RATING					COMMENTS
POSTURE	1	2	3	4	5	_____
EYE CONTACT	1	2	3	4	5	_____
VOLUME OF VOICE	1	2	3	4	5	_____
RATE OF SPEECH	1	2	3	4	5	_____
ENTHUSIASM	1	2	3	4	5	_____
ADHERENCE TO TIME LIMIT	1	2	3	4	5	_____

CONTENT	RATING					COMMENTS
AREAS OF AGREEMENT	1	2	3	4	5	_____
SPECIFIC PERSUASIVE CLAIM	1	2	3	4	5	_____
PREVIEW	1	2	3	4	5	_____
MAIN POINT 1	1	2	3	4	5	_____
MAIN POINT 2	1	2	3	4	5	_____
MAIN POINT 3	1	2	3	4	5	_____
CLEAR ORGANIZATION	1	2	3	4	5	_____
TRANSITIONS	1	2	3	4	5	_____
PERSUASIVE SUPPORT	1	2	3	4	5	_____
SUMMARY	1	2	3	4	5	_____
FINAL REMARKS	1	2	3	4	5	_____
PRESENTATION AIDS	1	2	3	4	5	_____
SAYING FROM CHAPTER	1	2	3	4	5	_____
USEFUL LANGUAGE	1	2	3	4	5	_____

ADDITIONAL COMMENTS

_____
_____
_____

RATING KEY

1 = POOR   2 = FAIR   3 = ACCEPTABLE   4 = GOOD   5 = EXCELLENT

Debate a Proposition (Page 199)
First Affirmative Speaker

DEBATER: _____   PROPOSITION: _____

EVALUATOR: _____   DATE: _____

DELIVERY	RATING					COMMENTS
POSTURE	1	2	3	4	5	_____
EYE CONTACT	1	2	3	4	5	_____
VOLUME	1	2	3	4	5	_____
RATE OF SPEECH	1	2	3	4	5	_____
ENTHUSIASM	1	2	3	4	5	_____
ADHERENCE TO TIME LIMITS	1	2	3	4	5	_____

CONSTRUCTIVE SPEECH	RATING					COMMENTS
STATEMENT OF PROPOSITION	1	2	3	4	5	_____
EXPLANATION OF PROPOSITION	1	2	3	4	5	_____
EXPLANATION OF NEED FOR CHANGE	1	2	3	4	5	_____
ARGUMENTS	1	2	3	4	5	_____
SUPPORTING EVIDENCE	1	2	3	4	5	_____

CROSS EXAMINATION	RATING					COMMENTS
QUESTIONS	1	2	3	4	5	_____
RESPONSES	1	2	3	4	5	_____

REBUTTAL SPEECH	RATING					COMMENTS
ARGUMENTS	1	2	3	4	5	_____
SUPPORTING EVIDENCE	1	2	3	4	5	_____
SAYING FROM CHAPTER	1	2	3	4	5	_____
USEFUL LANGUAGE	1	2	3	4	5	_____

ADDITIONAL COMMENTS

_____

_____

RATING KEY

1 = POOR   2 = FAIR   3 = ACCEPTABLE   4 = GOOD   5 = EXCELLENT

Debate a Proposition (Page 225)
Second Affirmative Speaker

DEBATER: _____   PROPOSITION: _____

EVALUATOR: _____   DATE: _____

DELIVERY	RATING					COMMENTS
POSTURE	1	2	3	4	5	_____
EYE CONTACT	1	2	3	4	5	_____
VOLUME	1	2	3	4	5	_____
RATE OF SPEECH	1	2	3	4	5	_____
ENTHUSIASM	1	2	3	4	5	_____
ADHERENCE TO TIME LIMITS	1	2	3	4	5	_____

CONSTRUCTIVE SPEECH	RATING					COMMENTS
ARGUMENTS	1	2	3	4	5	_____
SUPPORTING EVIDENCE	1	2	3	4	5	_____
SUMMARY OF ARGUMENTS	1	2	3	4	5	_____

CROSS-EXAMINATION	RATING					COMMENTS
QUESTIONS	1	2	3	4	5	_____
RESPONSES	1	2	3	4	5	_____

REBUTTAL SPEECH	RATING					COMMENTS
ARGUMENTS	1	2	3	4	5	_____
SUPPORTING EVIDENCE	1	2	3	4	5	_____
SUMMARY OF ARGUMENTS	1	2	3	4	5	_____
RESTATEMENT OF PROPOSITION	1	2	3	4	5	_____
SAYING FROM CHAPTER	1	2	3	4	5	_____
USEFUL LANGUAGE	1	2	3	4	5	_____

ADDITIONAL COMMENTS

_____

_____

_____

_____

RATING KEY

1 = POOR   2 = FAIR   3 = ACCEPTABLE   4 = GOOD   5 = EXCELLENT

Debate a Proposition (Page 225)
First Negative Speaker

DEBATER: _____   PROPOSITION: _____

EVALUATOR: _____   DATE: _____

DELIVERY	RATING					COMMENTS
POSTURE	1	2	3	4	5	_____
EYE CONTACT	1	2	3	4	5	_____
VOLUME	1	2	3	4	5	_____
RATE OF SPEECH	1	2	3	4	5	_____
ENTHUSIASM	1	2	3	4	5	_____
ADHERENCE TO TIME LIMITS	1	2	3	4	5	_____

CONSTRUCTIVE SPEECH	RATING					COMMENTS
ARGUMENTS	1	2	3	4	5	_____
SUPPORTING EVIDENCE	1	2	3	4	5	_____

CROSS EXAMINATION	RATING					COMMENTS
QUESTIONS	1	2	3	4	5	_____
RESPONSES	1	2	3	4	5	_____

REBUTTAL SPEECH	RATING					COMMENTS
ARGUMENTS	1	2	3	4	5	_____
SUPPORTING EVIDENCE	1	2	3	4	5	_____
SAYING FROM CHAPTER	1	2	3	4	5	_____
USEFUL LANGUAGE	1	2	3	4	5	_____

ADDITIONAL COMMENTS

_____

_____

_____

_____

_____

_____

RATING KEY

1 = POOR   2 = FAIR   3 = ACCEPTABLE   4 = GOOD   5 = EXCELLENT

Debate a Proposition (Page 225)
Second Negative Speaker

DEBATER: _____   PROPOSITION: _____

EVALUATOR: _____   DATE: _____

DELIVERY	RATING					COMMENTS
POSTURE	1	2	3	4	5	_____
EYE CONTACT	1	2	3	4	5	_____
VOLUME	1	2	3	4	5	_____
RATE OF SPEECH	1	2	3	4	5	_____
ENTHUSIASM	1	2	3	4	5	_____
ADHERENCE TO TIME LIMITS	1	2	3	4	5	_____

CONSTRUCTIVE SPEECH	RATING					COMMENTS
ARGUMENTS	1	2	3	4	5	_____
SUPPORTING EVIDENCE	1	2	3	4	5	_____
SUMMARY OF ARGUMENTS	1	2	3	4	5	_____

CROSS-EXAMINATION	RATING					COMMENTS
QUESTIONS	1	2	3	4	5	_____
RESPONSES	1	2	3	4	5	_____

REBUTTAL SPEECH	RATING					
SUMMARY OF ARGUMENTS	1	2	3	4	5	_____
SUPPORTING EVIDENCE	1	2	3	4	5	_____
RESTATEMENT OF NEGATIVE POSITION	1	2	3	4	5	_____
SAYING FROM CHAPTER	1	2	3	4	5	_____
USEFUL LANGUAGE	1	2	3	4	5	_____

ADDITIONAL COMMENTS

_____

_____

_____

RATING KEY

1 = POOR   2 = FAIR   3 = ACCEPTABLE   4 = GOOD   5 = EXCELLENT